Expatriate Compensation & Benefits

Expatriate Compensation & Benefits

An Employer's Handbook

John Rayman and Bill Twinn

First published in Great Britain in
1983 by Kogan Page Ltd,
120 Pentonville Road, London N1 9JN

British Library Cataloguing in Publication Data
Rayman, John
Expatriate compensation and benefits.
1. Alien labor, British 2. Employers rights –
Great Britain
I. Title II. Twinn, Bill
341.7′63 HF5549.5.A43
ISBN 0-85038-613-6

Printed in Great Britain by Anchor Press and bound
by William Brendon and Son, both of
Tiptree, Essex

Contents

Preface

The material in this book is based on the authors' practical experience, gained over a number of years, in the field of overseas employment. The aim of the book is to provide a review of the basic philosophy of overseas employment conditions and the problems most often encountered by a company trying to provide an adequate compensation and benefits package for its employees. The book also serves as a practical guide to the establishment of systems, necessary to ensure the effective management of compensation and benefits packages when operating in a multitude of overseas environments.

Naturally, there are always choices of approach and technique – some extremely complicated and others simplistic, perhaps to the point of being crude. The book attempts a range of possible solutions to the most common problems and, where feasible, a straightforward approach is used, governed by the assumption that no two international companies are exactly alike.

The contents of the book are laid out in logical steps in order to simplify what becomes a very complex subject. Thus, Chapter 2 summarizes the different types of expatriation and the types of contract of employment that would normally apply. Chapter 3 deals with the problems of initial expatriation and subsequent overseas transfers.

The second part of the book covers the subject of the expatriate compensation and benefits package. Starting with a guide to undertaking a salary survey (Chapter 4), compensation is then broken down into base salaries (Chapter 5) and various types of overseas premiums (Chapter 6). Chapter 7 details the possible benefit packages that may be applied to expatriates. After reviewing the tax implications of the expatriate employment package (Chapter 8), Chapter 9 describes the various ways in which the whole package is integrated into the company's overall compensation policy.

Chapter 10 describes what may be termed the 'half way' stage to expatriate employment – the 'rotator' who lives in his home country but travels overseas on a regular work pattern.

Chapters 11 and 12 deal with the type of pension and insurance benefits normally associated with expatriate employment. Chapter 13 deals with the problems of repatriation.

Chapter 14 looks at the problem of controlling employment policies on an international scale and Chapter 15 proposes some guidelines for the expatriate manager when trying to manage his own local employees. Finally, Chapter 16 provides a selective bibliography.

This book should be particularly relevant to the company about to start overseas operations. It should also provide a framework through which established multi-national companies can review their present policies. Lastly, the consultant or student of international personnel management should find the book of some assistance. While there are many consultancies that offer specially prepared information on overseas employment (to be discussed later) very little has been written on the overall logic of expatriate compensation and benefits. Equally, international personnel management has not, as yet, become a well-established subject in management and professional personnel training.

The use of expatriates is expensive – a total annual cost of $100,000 per expatriate is typical of many organizations; and the figure is very much higher for senior expatriate positions. This cost, which should be considered as much as an investment as an expense, has to be managed effectively and professionally.

The book is intended to provide the manager with an overall conceptional framework of expatriate compensation and benefits, to help him avoid the obvious pitfalls and to create consistent and effective expatriate personnel policies.

1. Introduction

The phenomenon of overseas employment is almost as old as employment itself. Commercial organizations set up manufacturing and trading centres overseas soon after they became established in their home country or, in some unusual cases, developed overseas without ever having established a home base at all. In the majority of cases the home country company began its overseas operations in two ways: by sending out key members of staff to organize, at least initially, the overseas base, and later by recruiting staff locally.

The purpose of this book is very straightforward: to provide those concerned with the employment of expatriates with a clear and concise guide to the key compensation and benefits issues they will need to address – and resolve. The book also outlines the necessary considerations involved in managing the compensation and benefits package of local employees in an overseas country.

DEVELOPMENT OF OVERSEAS EMPLOYMENT

The scale of overseas employment is hard to quantify. Since the end of the last war the pattern has moved away from commercial organizations reflecting colonial or neo-colonial interests, such as UK companies in Nigeria, or French companies in Gabon, to companies based in many of the developed industrial nations (and some less developed ones) operating on a genuinely global basis. There are three identifiable categories:

- manufacturing industry expanding in order to meet new market demands for their products, or, simply because of government employment policy – for example, the call for the overseas manufacturing of Japanese products including the call for the establishment of Japanese automobile assembly plants in Europe;
- service industries which have to operate in foreign locations ie where the business is to be found (hire cars, oil companies, hotels, telecommunication);
- technical expertise being 'bought' by an overseas country, either on a turnkey basis – where a factory or power station is handed over as a going concern, or a continuous supply of particular skilled personnel – eg the supply of doctors to Saudi Arabia.

Whichever category the activity falls into, the result has been a formidable growth of MNCs (multi-national corporations) ranging from small specialist firms to multi-billion dollar enterprises. Furthermore, the accepted concept that such corporations are invariably the result of western and Japanese capitalism is now being challenged. New multi-nationals are now appearing from other sources:

- state corporations operating in the key industrial areas of mining, steel production, automobile manufacturing and the oil and petro-chemical industries are increasingly becoming more multi-national in outlook. As a result many state corporations have established works in overseas countries and employ home country nationals, local people and third country nationals;
- the Soviet Union has expanded its multi-national activity, a recent US Government report compiling a list of 84 Russian multi-nationals. These activities usually promote products manufactured in the USSR but employ personnel from the host country. Apart from trading and banking interests the Russians have made great advances in their transport and merchant marine sectors;
- multi-nationals from the developing countries. A number of Third World countries have created multi-national enterprises. For example, India's Hindustan Machine Tool Company has factories in Iran, Yugoslavia, Algeria and Libya. South Korea, Hong Kong, the Philippines, Brazil and Taiwan also have expanding multi-national companies. In Fortune's recent survey of 500 overseas companies, 34 had their headquarters in developing countries (albeit some are familiar household names taking advantage of tax havens).

In all these examples the common driving force has been a need for economic expansion that cannot be satisfied within the confines of one country. With the recession in world trade during the early 1980s (which has caused some companies to become more cautious concerning their overseas interests) the expansion of multi-national business continues.

Expatriation and overseas compensation and benefits will be a concern of more and more organizations as they grow through acquisition or expansion into overseas markets. Increasingly the successful executive will need to be multi-lingual, with experience of managing in different cultural environments. Even a company with very few expatriates has to concern itself with precisely the same compensation and benefits problems as those faced by multi-national corporations employing several thousand expatriates.

IMPORTANCE OF COMPENSATION AND BENEFITS

Compensation and benefits represent a crucial element in the overall personnel management policies in any organization. While research has clearly demonstrated that compensation and benefits programmes cannot effectively motivate individuals, it has also shown that such programmes, poorly designed, implemented or communicated, can be among the most powerful demotivators. While there are many basic concepts of compensation and benefits that are of general application, every organization is different and needs to tailor its policies to fit its particular industry, size, maturity, culture, structure, and so forth. In particular, compensation and benefits policies must be consistent with and reinforce the other personnel policies of the organization.

PROBLEMS WITH OVERSEAS PERSONNEL

The effective manager of expatriate personnel will need to be able to master a range of skills more demanding than those required in a domestic environment and be able to respond to such common problems as:

- the expatriate employee who has performed perfectly adequately at home, but who cannot cope with the stresses of overseas employment;
- how to establish a market position, internal relativities and merit criteria in an overseas salary structure which might have to cope with many nationalities working in several countries;
- how to effectively integrate benefits packages within home and host country systems and the treatment of third country nationals (TCNs);
- inexperience in the management of foreign locals combined with little knowledge of the cultural, legal and fiscal environment of the host country;
- inadequate planning and control systems to monitor the use of personnel resources overseas.

Even those employers who have established excellent personnel procedures at home are frequently overwhelmed by such problems overseas.

Some companies employing expatriates have developed excellent procedures, but our experience indicates that large numbers of overseas operators have, surprisingly, not come to grips with the complexities that undoubtedly exist.

TYPES OF EXPATRIATES

When discussing expatriates it is important to remember that they are not an amorphous group; an understanding of their motivation is certainly important.

The reasons why people expatriate themselves from their predictable and familiar domestic environments to an alien location overseas are as varied as the people themselves. This book looks at the expatriation of highly skilled, educated people – from developed or developing countries for whom expatriation represents a choice of lifestyle. (We do not cover the many millions of unskilled or semi-skilled people who expatriate themselves because of sheer economic necessity and who are normally treated as locals in the country in which they work.) The motivation may be the opportunity to travel, to experience different lifestyles, to have responsibility at an earlier age than in their home country or the challenge of a tough environment, but it will also be financial. Any expatriate will expect not only to earn but also to save substantially more money than he would have been able to do at home and his compensation and benefits package needs to reflect this. He will also anticipate, in many foreign assignments, a significantly better material standard of living than in his home country. It can be difficult for a personnel manager without direct expatriate experience to appreciate the compensation needs of an expatriate employee.

When people are expatriated they are inevitably put in a position of dependence on their employer. Typically, they will no longer benefit from their home country social security umbrella. Therefore, once working abroad, even if a social security system does exist and even if they are eligible to benefit from it, they are unlikely to have the least understanding of its workings. In every respect – housing, children's education, medical facilities, insurance and repatriation – their employer is wholly and directly involved. This necessitates the provision of a comprehensive range of short-term benefits, plans and clearly written policies so that the expatriate is aware of exactly how he stands. Long-term benefits also need to reflect the particular needs of those who opt for an expatriate life and not disadvantage people who transfer frequently from one country to another during their career in the organization.

SELECTION OF EXPATRIATE PERSONNEL

The selection process for an overseas assignment requires the same skills as selection for an important home country based job. A first criterion for successful selection for an overseas job must always be the personnel manager's knowledge of the job, the environment and the specific problems that are likely to be encountered. At the same time an expatriate assignment has an added dimension. Because of greater isolation and lack of support, the candidate must be expected to possess maturity, self-sufficiency, and interest in, and tolerance of, other cultures. A sense of humour is invaluable, as is the ability to train and be patient with the frustrations and communication failures that will be encountered. For married employees the same considerations apply; flexibility, confidence to use limited language skills to sort out everyday problems and sufficient resilience to cope with a different and strange environment.

Although selection criteria and the necessary training and preparation to equip the expatriate for his assignment are important, this book does not cover the subject in detail. Selection, after all, is unique to each industry, company and individual job description. Although certain broad characteristics are desirable we do not subscribe to elaborate psychological tests for expatriation, and it is interesting to note that one survey indicates that there has been a steady decline in the use of such techniques (1981 ORC Survey *Personnel Practices and Compensation for Expatriate Personnel*). The host countries too are as varied as the prospective candidates – the 'ideal' profile is as hard to define as the ideal husband – and many different profiles can be equally successful. While the employer must do his best with recruitment, he can maximize his chances of success with careful, well-thought-out policies covering the period of expatriation.

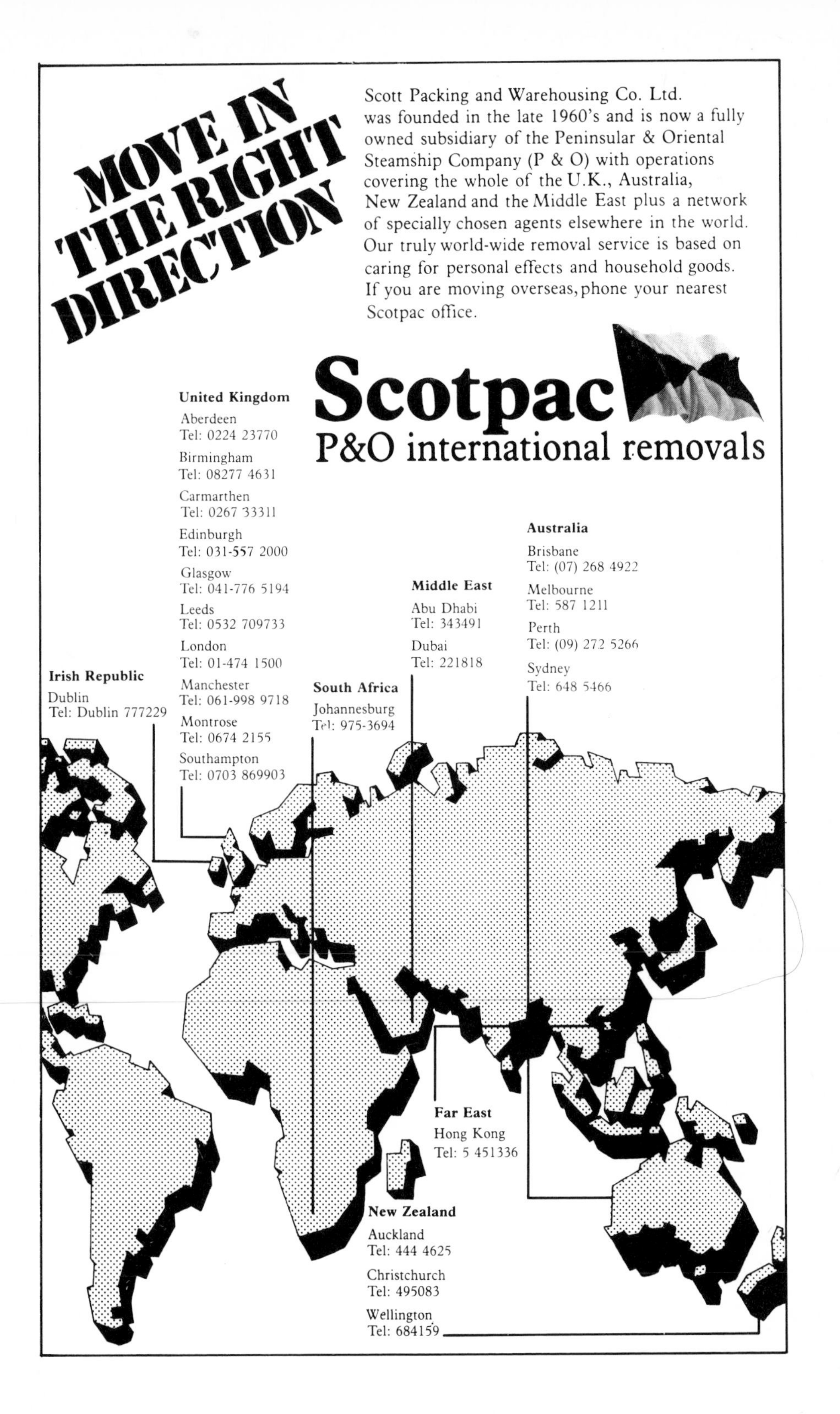
MOVE IN THE RIGHT DIRECTION
Scott Packing and Warehousing Co. Ltd. was founded in the late 1960's and is now a fully owned subsidiary of the Peninsular & Oriental Steamship Company (P & O) with operations covering the whole of the U.K., Australia, New Zealand and the Middle East plus a network of specially chosen agents elsewhere in the world. Our truly world-wide removal service is based on caring for personal effects and household goods. If you are moving overseas, phone your nearest Scotpac office.
Scotpac
P&O international removals
United Kingdom
Aberdeen Tel: 0224 23770
Birmingham Tel: 08277 4631
Carmarthen Tel: 0267 33311
Edinburgh Tel: 031-557 2000
Glasgow Tel: 041-776 5194
Leeds Tel: 0532 709733
London Tel: 01-474 1500
Manchester Tel: 061-998 9718
Montrose Tel: 0674 2155
Southampton Tel: 0703 869903
Irish Republic
Dublin Tel: Dublin 777229
South Africa
Johannesburg Tel: 975-3694
Middle East
Abu Dhabi Tel: 343491
Dubai Tel: 221818
Australia
Brisbane Tel: (07) 268 4922
Melbourne Tel: 587 1211
Perth Tel: (09) 272 5266
Sydney Tel: 648 5466
Far East
Hong Kong Tel: 5 451336
New Zealand
Auckland Tel: 444 4625
Christchurch Tel: 495083
Wellington Tel: 684159

2. Expatriate contracts of employment and the law

INTRODUCTION

This chapter examines the practicalities of setting up an expatriate contract of employment and the ways in which the compensation and benefits package can interact with the legal environment within which the company operates. The different kinds of expatriation are described, together with the key elements that need to be covered in the contract of employment for each type.

Many, if not most, countries have a mass of employment legislation. This legislation governs the relationship between employees and employers to a greater or lesser extent. It frequently deals with employment contracts (minimum wages, hours of work, holidays), with job security (wrongful dismissal, unfair dismissal, etc), collective bargaining, other industrial relations issues and with employees' individual rights. In general, legislation acts in two ways: it provides protection for the employee against arbitrary or unreasonable actions by the employer and it regulates relationships between employers and employees. In many countries the system is a comprehensive one which has developed over many years into a major part of the judicial system. In addition, legislation on the law of contracts, social security legislation and legislation on employers and public liability can all play an important part in employment.

Clearly, in home country employment, there are two major implications in the legal system. The employer needs to be fully aware of the legislative requirements of the country and that the company's employment practices meet these requirements. The employee for his part, whether he is aware of it or not (and most employees are not), has a certain protection afforded to him which limits the freedom of action of the employer. Whether the protection afforded is substantial or not, whether the role of the legal system is appropriate or otherwise, are not issues to be discussed here. The legal situation for international employment is extremely complex; the international employer will have to have the same understanding of legal structures in several countries as the domestic employer has of a single country. At the same time, the expatriate employee, little as he may understand his legal position in his home country, is even less likely to have such an understanding overseas and thus may be, or consider himself to be, in a vulnerable position with respect to his employer.

Litigation or the threat of litigation seldom occurs in practice between an expatriate (especially at the executive level) and an employer and, indeed, it must be a major objective of any company to avoid such action in the way in which it handles its people. However, it is obvious that the legal implications of employment should be solved by the company before they occur, rather than afterwards. This necessitates expatriate contracts being structured in a way that takes into account the requirements of the legal system within which the company operates.

WHICH LEGAL SYSTEM?

Imagine a typical expatriate employment. A French company recruits an American employee to work for it in Nigeria. Which country's legal system would apply if there were a dispute between the employee and the employer? Would it be the USA, since the employee is an American citizen and was hired and perhaps signed the contract of employment in the USA? Would it be France, since that is where the company has its head office and files its accounts? Would it be Nigeria since that is where the employee is working? Unfortunately for the multi-national company, the answer could be 'yes' to all three questions depending on the particular circumstances.

An international company will very often give its employees a contract of employment which contains a statement to the effect that 'this contract of employment is agreed by both parties to be determined subject to the legal system of country X.' This may provide clarity to the employer who will probably choose X for sound reasons. In practice it is likely to mean nothing at all to the employee who will know little about the labour laws in country X and, should a dispute arise, will probably have no practical recourse to any legal system in country X.

Whatever is specified in the contract of employment, an employee – or more likely an ex-employee – can take his case to the legal system of whatever country he sees fit. An employer can and, of course, will file that the court has no jurisdiction, but such a claim frequently fails – to the surprise of the employer. In most countries where employment tribunals or labour courts exist, there is a strong predisposition to find in favour of the individual (ex-) employee and this applies equally to the court's deciding on its competence to examine the case. The process is, of course, a much longer and more complex one than can be described here, but the international company must recognize that it cannot, unilaterally, decide under what country's legal system it will operate. The following example highlights this point:

> An Englishman was recruited by a Panamanian company. He worked for four months in a training centre in the UK and, as a trainee, also in the UK. He was transferred by the company to Norway where he was put on the payroll of the Norwegian branch. Some 18 months later he was dismissed, still in Norway. He returned to the UK and took his case to the Industrial Tribunal claiming unfair dismissal under the prevailing legislation. The Tribunal found in his favour, even though he did not work for a UK company or in the UK and the maximum award (then £5000) was made.

THE EMPLOYEE'S 'RIGHTS'

In practice, an expatriate employee is unlikely to have any conception of which legal systems might govern his employment. A company which expatriates an employee to some extent puts him into a kind of limbo where the normal protection afforded by legal systems, social security systems, etc, does not apply. The employer, therefore, has to fill the gap created by the absence of the social protection the employee would have expected in his home country. It is no less important that an employer of expatriates does not take advantage of the employee's ignorance of and lack of obvious access to the legal systems in the more difficult aspects of employment (such as termination, repatriation and disciplinary procedures). Moral reasons apart, handling employee procedures with the recognition that the entire issue might be discussed in a court or a tribunal can have an extremely beneficial effect on the amount of thought and application of responsible management practice, with a consequent improvement in the quality of employer/employee relations.

Some expatriate employment contracts state that the employee may be dismissed at any time without notice – irrespective of performance. This is common practice among MNCs and is based on the assumption that their ex-employees will have neither theoretical nor practical access to any court. Application of such a contract would almost certainly be unenforceable in any court in which it was tested by the ex-employee. A more serious issue is the reaction of other employees and the probable management style of a company that treats its employees in this way. Where this type of contract exists, it is in practice infrequently applied – in other words, notice is given and 'customary' rules about disciplinary and dismissal procedures are followed on an informal basis by management, irrespective of the formal contract itself.

Employment laws are designed to redress the balance between the power of the employer and that of the employee. It is important in the way it treats expatriates that the company recognizes that it cannot afford to have them feel that they are subject to arbitrary management. Greater material rewards in the form of higher salaries and benefits are seldom accepted by employees as adequate compensation for a lack of job security.

THE INTERNATIONAL CONTRACT

Standard letters of employment cover the basic and essential terms and conditions of employment and usually refer to a staff manual which provides greater details. Further details are often provided by specific booklets on pensions, sickness, etc. Finally, specific agreements on, for example, the confidentiality of information are often maintained as separate documents.

Companies must try to give the employee a clear and comprehensive statement of terms and conditions of employment in a way he can understand. While contracts of employment have to be legally sound, they must be written in language ordinary enough to be understood and should, therefore, be written by personnel managers using legal advice rather than by corporate lawyers.

To understand a contract of employment, like any contract, the intention behind it needs to be examined. An employment contract is a regulation of what is expected of one party by the other – in the context of expatriate employment, it is possible to distinguish between a number of different types of expatriation, each requiring a quite different approach.

The other determinant of the contract structure will be the company philosophy (eg one single contract for all expatriates or local contracts in each assignment) and the corporate legal structure, ie which of the companies in the group is the employer. Most large MNCs have an extremely complex corporate structure and it is frequently a matter of great importance to identify the correct legal entity for the particular employment. Mistakes in this area can obviously lead to major fiscal and legal problems.

Finally, it should be remembered that most countries do not permit individuals to 'sign away their rights' in their legal system. Thus any contract signed by the individual in some way restricting his legal rights in that country, for whatever reason, would not necessarily afford the employer any certain protection in the event of legal action. Let us look at the different kinds of expatriation.

Home country employee – expatriated for one overseas assignment

This is perhaps the most common form of expatriation and the one found most frequently in MNCs. The high-potential employee is expatriated for a fixed period (typically two to three years) for development in an overseas operation and then on completion of the assignment returns to his home country. The expatriate's terms and conditions of employment tend to be based upon those which would have existed in the home country with whatever additions and benefits are deemed necessary. The individual employee expects to further his career as a result of the assignment, have an interesting job while overseas, save substantially more (and live better) than he would have done at home and make a successful re-entry to his home country. The employer expects to get the overseas job done, motivate the employee (by the interest, status and rewards of a foreign assignment) and develop the management, technical or professional skills of a long-term employee.

As a result, the expatriate's contract of employment would usually look very much like one operating in the domestic environment. Although some companies in this situation would apply a host country employment contract, this is relatively rare (although local legal regulations may require that a formal local contract of employment exists). It would be probable that any disputes arising out of the overseas employment would be resolved in the context of the legal system of the home country.

Apart from the general contents of any expatriate contract of employment a number of specific issues will be dealt with separately. For example:

Re-entry
The anticipated duration (if known) of the assignment and the terms under which the expatriate will return to his home country employment (job, location, salary grade) should be specified in clear terms.

Disciplinary and grievance procedure
Does the employee normally expect to be dealt with under home or host country procedures?

Termination of employment
Does the home or host country termination policy apply?

Contract employee

A frequent type of overseas employment is the fixed term contract. In this case, an expatriate is engaged for a predetermined period – usually from two to three years – to provide specific skills for the company. This is the normal approach for companies whose only operations are in developing countries, eg hospital staff in Libya, airline staff in Saudi Arabia or oil industry staff in Abu Dhabi. At the end of the contract period, a bonus or gratuity is paid. In many cases, the contract can be renewed.

The contract employee tends to have more of a mercenary and calculative relationship with his employer than the long-term career-orientated employee. Clearly, the employee will expect to develop professionally, have an interesting job, be treated 'reasonably' and have a good standard of expatriate life. However, the expectation of the employee is of short-term material rewards, related to the job performed (and the location it is performed in), together with an improved marketability for the next contract. As far as the employer is concerned, a contract employee represents a quick way of acquiring cheaply (without expensive training) relevant experience with no long-term commitment to pensions or responsibility created by re-entry. Next to the previous type of expatriate, contract overseas employment represents the largest group.

The contract of employment may be defined in relation to the law of the country in which the employee is to be working (the most usual), in which case the company needs to have a very good understanding of the relevant legislation, eg an American hired to work on a contract in Saudi Arabia by a Swiss company should normally have a contract of employment subject to Saudi Arabian labour law. Less often, the contract is defined in terms of the law of the country in which the company is based. From the employer's viewpoint, it is probably wise to avoid having an employment contract subject to the employee's home country legal system rather than one chosen by the employer. Such employment contracts are usually better signed overseas, since in some countries merely signing a contract there can result in the law of that country applying to it.

The employment contract must specify which country's employment legislation will apply and, in addition to the 'standard' contents of any expatriate contract, should cover:

- terms and procedures for renewal of the contract;
- contract bonus and circumstances in which it might be forfeited;
- procedures in the event of non-fulfilment of contract ie resignation by the employee or dismissal by the company.

Long-term mobile expatriates

This group of expatriates, frequently TCNs, will follow all or most of their careers within the organization but outside their home country; indeed, there may be no company operation in their home country. Typically, they may change assignments every two or three years.

During their careers, the contracts of employment of these individuals could be subject to the legal systems of their countries of assignment and of the company's home base as well as that of their own home country. In many cases they will be employed by different entities within the company corporate structure depending upon their assignment.

For a group such as this, it seems reasonable that a company should endeavour to create an employment contract that, as far as possible, is the same for each individual, no matter what his nationality, where he works or by which of the corporate group companies he is employed. All other things being equal, for example, the period of notice to which an expatriate employee is entitled in the event of dismissal should not depend on the country where the employee is working at that time.

A worldwide contract of employment for an MNC with such a group of expatriates should, therefore, as far as possible, meet the legal requirements of the countries in which the employee works, from where he is recruited and where the employer is based. The contract should also be written to ensure that it applies no matter in which of the entities in a corporate set-up the employee is situated. Such a contract covers the basic corporate employment philosophy and employment rules.

This group of employees tends to be characterized by an independence of spirit. Company loyalty seems to extend only so far as the employer can meet short- to medium-term goals (financial, promotion, assignments in 'nice' places). They will have a higher mobility between organizations than equivalent domestic employees. In many ways, this group avoids contact with legal and administrative structures. (They do not pay tax in their home country, they do not believe much in social security and feel they are competent to handle their own business without state or institutional assistance.)

In setting up the employment contract, the employer needs to try to avoid the cynicism that leads him to conclude that this kind of employee will never test the contract in a court, so that it does not matter whether or not it is a valid contract.

Finally, as we mentioned before, there is frequently a requirement to create a contract of employment in the country of assignment to conform with local legislation – often as a prerequisite to obtaining a residence visa or work permit. These kinds of contract, usually regarded by the company as nominal, which represent a visible statement of the employee's terms and conditions of employment, so far as the host country is concerned, need to be structured carefully to cover only what is required by local labour law. The level of salary and benefits that are mentioned must be appropriate to the particular country. Such contracts will be in the local language which the expatriate may or may not be able to understand.

The fact that the signed contract exists implies that its contents and wording need to be carefully studied by the employer since, although they may regard it as an administrative device, an employee has recourse to the local legal process, at least potentially.

Single country expatriate

Another type of expatriate is the individual who is assigned for a long, perhaps indefinite, period of time to the host country, eg an American managing his company's branch in Egypt for a period of 20 years. The home company will probably want to ensure that the employment contract and conditions resemble that of the country to which the expatriate is assigned. The only additional elements that would need to be covered would be:

Repatriation
Under what conditions and to what extent the company will repatriate the employee upon termination of employment.

Vacations
Whether, and how frequently, a vacation trip is provided to the point of origin.

It seems that this is a rarer form of expatriation in the developing world as local nationals are asked to take up these positions. However, in developed countries, there are still many examples of this type of long-term expatriation, where individuals are fully integrated into the host country.

Rotation employees

This is where an individual is based in his home country and works in another on a regular work schedule, for instance, on a four weeks on/four weeks off basis. The kind of contract of employment he has will depend upon the factors already discussed. Where companies have both permanently resident expatriates and rotation employees, they usually find it convenient to have the same contract of employment for all.

The principal difference between this group and previous ones is that this group is likely not only to have recourse to, but actually to be dealt with by, the legal processes in the home country, even though employment is completely overseas. However tenuous the threads, courts and tribunals tend to take a very wide view of the scope of their influence. This is especially true where the employee is employed as an expatriate by a company related in some way to a company operating in the domestic environment.

These, then, are the various types of expatriation that a company might have. (See also Chapter 5 where compensation implications are analysed in detail.)

CONTENTS OF EXPATRIATE EMPLOYMENT CONTRACTS

In the documents which together add up to a complete contract of employment, what areas ought to be covered? The following is a list of the key elements which should be included in an expatriate compensation and benefits package:

General

- Name of employing company and address
- Job title and location
- Statement of geographical mobility required in the job
- Statement of willingness to accept geographical transfer

Compensation

- Base salary
- Overseas incentive premium
- Overseas cost of living adjustments
- Tax and social security equalization programme
- Currency and location of payment
- Bonuses
- Deductions – housing, pensions, etc
- Transfer allowances

Benefits

- Hours of work
- Vacations and vacation travel
- Rest and recreation (R & R)
- Housing
- Transport
- Children's education
- Sick pay
- Medical expenses
- Dental expenses
- Life and accident insurance
- Pension plans
- Deferred benefits and savings plan
- Severance indemnity

Conditions of employment

- ○ Discipline procedure
- ○ Grievance procedure
- ○ Notice entitlement
- ○ Repatriation entitlement
- ○ Confidentiality agreements
- ○ Non competition agreement
- ○ Collective bargaining rights
- ○ Conflict of interests
- ○ Reimbursement of expenses

Clarity of definition

The expatriate contract of employment and compensation and benefits package are more complex than the domestic equivalent. A wide variety of employment circumstances is encountered and more aspects of the employee's life are covered in the relationship with the employer than his domestic counterpart. Policies must be clearly defined and some of the terms used need much more careful elaboration than might be imagined at first glance. The more important areas of definition are:

Point of origin
Where is the employee to be repatriated in the event of termination of employment? Imagine an Australian from Sydney who studies in a university in the USA, is hired in London and is married to a French girl. His point of origin is not obvious. A usual practice is to fix this at the time of hire as his last 'permanent' address and not to change it subsequently.

Nationality
In the expatriate world, there are many people of a truly international background, carrying passports of more than one country; born in one country, resident of a second, and citizen of a third. Commonly, nationality is fixed as that of the passport on which the employee customarily travels at the time of hiring and not subsequently changed.

Family status
Many expatriate benefits relate to family status, ie wives and children. In defining 'wife' it is essential to establish an acceptable way, in company terms, of treating common-law wives, as opposed to girlfriends, separated wives, divorced ex-wives for whom an alimony award has been made by a court, and wives of employees from ethnic groups, who may be polygamous.

Dependants
The definition of 'child' needs to cover age (which might differ according to the particular benefit provided); whether the child is living with the employee and the status of children not in the custody of, but legally required to be

supported by, the ex-husband.

An example of these considerations is shown in the following extract from a personnel manual:

Family status

1. For the purposes of this manual the terms single status, married status and dependent children are used in connection with policies regarding housing, transportation, medical, education and insurance plans. The definition of these terms is shown below and is not subject to any other interpretation.

Single status

2. Single status means either a bachelor, or a married employee, when the spouse and family are not living in the employee's place of assignment. Trainees are always on single status until their promotion.

Married status

3. Married status means the employee is legally married and the spouse and family live in the place of assignment.

Dependent children

4. The definition of a dependent child is as follows:
   (a) an unmarried child or a child in legal custody of the employee under 19 years of age.
   (b) this status is extended to the academic year in which the child reaches 21 for medical and vacation travel purposes only, if the child is enrolled in post-secondary or university level education.
   (c) documentary evidence is necessary for reimbursement of any expense, including birth certificates and, where appropriate, legal custody agreements.

Impact of local laws

In all of these areas, there is not only a need for a very clear definition of precisely what the company's policies are, but there may be a major impact from the local legislative system. Consider the situation for a company with a significant number of expatriates in a number of different countries, all with the same employment contract.

GENERAL

Employing company

A local employment contract in the local language may be required. This contract may contain many provisions, relating to legally imposed regulations governing a specific industry in which the company is classified or where collective contracts have been signed between unions and employers' organizations for the particular industry concerned. This is very common in France, Italy and Spain and terms and conditions of employment may be laid down which, if not excluded specifically from the expatriate's package, could lead to major difficulties.

Job title

In some countries special rules apply to the employment of people with particular job titles (such as Italy for people called 'directors', France for 'presidents'). In Germany, for example, there is a strict definition of the word 'engineer'.

Mobility to accept transfers

Many contracts specify that the employee must accept a transfer at any time, depending on the company's needs; refusal to accept a transfer may be considered as resignation on the part of the employee. This may well be regarded by a court in the country of assignment as being unacceptable as a reason for dismissal.

Changes in the contract

Many countries have the concept of an acquired benefit to which the employee is entitled and which cannot be withdrawn by the employer. Thus, a monthly allowance which ceased after a period of time or a fringe benefit, which was for one reason or another withdrawn, could fall under this kind of legislation.

Compensation

Few countries have not applied at some time some form of wages control policy whether in the form of a 'freeze' or a ceiling on wage increases. That such policies seldom, if ever, work has not dissuaded governments from using them as tools in their attempts to control inflation. Such wages policies are normally policed by the honesty and respect for the law of the companies themselves and generally contain loopholes which management is able to exploit. There are many examples, particularly in western Europe in the past two decades, of different formulas and a wide range of management response to them. It is even more common in the developing world for governments to impose rigid wages policies.

If the company wants to treat all its expatriates in the different countries in which it operates in the same way, problems arise in countries with salary restraints when general or merit increases are due or when the cost of living allowance is about to be raised. Difficulties could also arise if the local currency devalues against the currency in which the expatriate's salary is denominated. (This happens infrequently and will only apply if the entire salary is converted into and paid in the local currency.)

Ways in which the problem is solved have included:

- doing nothing, ie following the wages policy requirements;
- making a retrospective payment at a later date;
- making whatever adjustments are necessary on the portion paid outside the country (in the event of a split salary being paid);
- ignoring the wages policy requirements altogether (risking legal sanctions).

A number of other problems are created when local regulations require that more of the employee's salary is paid in the host country than he is able to spend there. Exchange controls, or non-convertibility of currency (or very poor exchange rates), may make it impossible for him to export any excess. In these cases, companies will need to make appropriate administrative arrangements to allow employees to 'recycle' excess local currency.

Working patterns

Legislation on numbers of hours worked tends to apply only to manual-type occupations and thus affects relatively few of the types of expatriation covered by this book. There are a few important exceptions, however, such as Norwegian legislation on working on offshore oil and gas rigs in the North Sea, and legislation on the number of hours that can be worked by certain specific occupations such as airline pilots.

However, it is frequently the case that legislation on minimum amounts of vacation affects the expatriate. In European countries, for example in France where a minimum five weeks' vacation is legally required, a US multi-national company with a typically North American vacation entitlement of two to three weeks per year will have problems.

In many Middle Eastern countries, a five and a half day week – finishing midday Thursday and with Friday off – is common, which might be in marked contrast to the working pattern in the expatriate's home country.

TERMINATION OF EMPLOYMENT OVERSEAS

It is at the time of termination of employment that the legal implications become of prime importance. Not only is this frequently the aspect of employer/employee relations most often dealt with by the legal system but, the relationship of employer/employee having broken down, recourse to the legal system carries no additional 'risk' for the ex-, or about to be ex-, employee. Although there are a few exceptions, it is rare for a legal system to have reinstatement as an enforceable option for a court to impose in the event of dismissal. Whereas conciliation and reinstatement by agreement with the employer are frequently the result in dismissal cases, it would be a brave judge (and employee) who would enforce a reinstatement without prejudice against an unwilling employer – any more than a judge would contemplate resolving a divorce case by requiring the two parties to cohabit against their expressed wishes.

The most common problem facing the employer is the amount of compensation which should be paid to the employee. Just how much is due to an employee from the employer on dismissal? In this context, there seem to be three different elements: deferred benefits or separation benefits that an employee is deemed to accrue during employment; the notice of termination of employment to which he may be entitled; and the award that may be made by a court or tribunal in the event of a dismissal being judged 'unfair', 'wrongful' or 'unreasonable' (the vocabulary depending on the country concerned).

Separation indemnities

Some countries, notably South American countries, but also Italy or Spain, stipulate that an employee who resigns or is dismissed is entitled to a separation payment. This payment is usually expressed as so many months of final salary, per year of continuous seniority; seniority with affiliated companies in other countries may also be included.

Notice periods

An enormous variety of notice periods is specified in different legal systems. Frequently, this period of notice of termination of employment is stipulated for the employer (in dismissal) and is nominal for the employee (upon resignation). Both the seniority of the employee and the level of his position in the organization have a major influence on the length of notice which must be given. Whatever is said in the expatriate's employment contract, he is likely to be entitled to, at least, an amount stipulated in local law. In most circumstances an employer is able to pay cash in lieu of notice. The terminating employee can hardly be compelled to complete his notice period nor would most employers want him to.

'Unfair', 'wrongful' or 'unreasonable' dismissal

Most countries' legal systems spell out to a greater or lesser extent the circumstances and the manner in which employees may be dismissed. Obviously, the company needs to have fully understood the labour law provisions in the particular country (which is more difficult than it appears given the problem of language and great differences in legal codes). In any event, many of the legal provisions represent what is merely 'good management' (such as having defined grievance and disciplinary procedures, performance appraisal systems, and so forth). An employee who believes that his dismissal falls into this category usually has recourse to an employment tribunal which will attempt a resolution by conciliation. The normal result of an action brought successfully by the ex-employee would be a money award, based either on a fixed scale or in relation to actual financial loss and/or with an element of punitive damages. Such an award would be made by a court, but in practice many employers anticipate what could be awarded and make a cash settlement with the employee.

Many companies will have termination benefit packages which pay lump sums on termination. In some circumstances, this lump sum benefit may be offset against whatever money is required to be paid by application of the local labour laws, depending largely on the wording of the rules of the termination benefit package (be it provident fund, end of contract bonus, pension plan, or whatever) and the particular country concerned. Thus, if the benefit plan is qualified under the IRS and ERISA legislation in the USA, it is most unlikely to be forfeitable in the case where a company wants to offset locally required payments against it.

It follows, therefore, that when setting up plans which have a pay-out at termination, careful consideration should be given to the way the plan is structured to maximize the degree to which they can offset local payments (if the objective is to treat all expatriates in the same way, wherever they are working when terminated). When termination of employment is necessary, a full appraisal of all the legal implications must be carried out and an estimate of local liability obtained. (The fact that an employee resigns, rather than is dismissed, does not itself change a great deal – the concept of constructive dismissal is widespread.)

Repatriation

When employment is terminated, there remains the question of the provision of transportation and baggage shipment for the repatriation of the expatriate and his family. In many countries the terms of the work permit clearly require the employer to return the employee to his point of origin. Thus the company will be liable even if the employee resigns voluntarily. Where there is no such legal requirement, the terms of the contract of employment will normally hold. These terms need to be defined – what the company will pay for and the circumstances in which such payment is withheld.

The contract of employment often states that the cost of repatriation will not be met if the employee is summarily dismissed (ie immediately) for such major misdemeanours as fraud, theft of company property, fighting, and so forth. Equally, many contracts specify that the employee who resigns without completing a given (large) proportion of a tour of duty will not have his costs of repatriation reimbursed. This might well be in conflict with local legislation which insists that no matter what the circumstances an employer must repatriate the ex-employee.

In practice, most companies normally bear the cost of repatriating dismissed employees in all except the most unusual circumstances. It is obviously very good practice to accrue the cost of repatriating expatriates as part of personnel costs, since every expatriate will return home eventually and the costs are substantial.

Some companies deduct from the first few months' salary of their expatriate employees the cost of their return ticket – money which is refunded if the employee successfully completes the required proportion of the tour of duty. This kind of policy does not help to foster good employer/employee relations and should be avoided.

Other legal aspects

Inevitably, there are many other areas where legislation affects in some way the employment of expatriate personnel. Such legal considerations are not dealt with in this book. Should the reader require more detailed information, the authors suggest that appropriate professional advice for the particular country concerned, be obtained.

Once established in an overseas country, particularly in the Third World, the expatriate is very much, if not totally, dependent on the company in his relationship with the legal system, even if actions which lead to legal problems bear no relation to the work environment. The expatriate employer must be prepared for anything. For example, an employee may find himself in prison (standard practice in Middle Eastern countries following a serious road accident). The employer must ensure that his employees have proper documentation (eg driving licences), adequate insurance, that they follow local regulations and know local customs (eg when employing domestic staff). Such eventualities must be adequately prepared for beforehand no matter how unusual they may appear to be.

Conclusion

The impact of legal systems on the employment, compensation and benefits of expatriates is wide ranging and extremely complex. The brief outline given in this chapter can only attempt to address the major issues and outline the key principles. In specific cases, expert professional advice must be sought by the personnel manager, rather than merely relying on common sense alone.

Our experience suggests that even though an MNC will usually have a highly competent corporate legal staff and many external legal advisors, the personnel manager needs to avoid constructing policies and procedures *a priori* on legal criteria. He should decide what personnel policies his organization want to pursue and then, in discussion with the legal *function*, examine the legal implications. There will always be a conflict between legal exactitude and complexity on the one hand and simplicity and consistency on the other.

3. Expatriation and foreign transfers

INTRODUCTION

The actual transfer of an employee and his family from one country to another represents a major potential source of stress for the individual and expense for the company. If the transfer itself is not smooth and effective, as far as the employee is concerned, the assignment following may be doomed to failure. As continually emphasized in the book the results of failure in an overseas environment are likely to be far more severe, in business and personal terms, than in the home country. A company must have clear, appropriate and effective transfer policies – even if the particular company has relatively few international transfers and the minimum of *ad hoc* special arrangements.

The transferee or his family will frequently not have the opportunity to examine the location of their future assignment, prior to transfer. Companies need to maintain good documentation in a standard format, regularly updated, about their various locations. For an example see Figure 3.1.

Many commercial publications, from guide books to specific information sources, are readily available. The direct experience of (trusted) colleagues who have worked or work in the particular assignment is of course extremely valuable and a company may find it worthwhile to include this kind of data in a reference bank. Again, the personnel manager with whom the transferee discusses his move ought to have had exposure to the location in question. The potential transferee should be given a clear idea of what he should expect; particularly the extent to which there are differences in the compensation and benefits package in the new assignment by comparison with the present package. This is crucial where an employee moves overseas for the first time.

A company must decide its overall philosophy in relation to transfers and ensure that all allowances and administrative arrangements set up conform to this policy.

The key questions that need to be asked are:

- How long will the overseas assignment be?
- Will the overseas assignment be a one-off followed by repatriation to the home country or will the employee expect to be re-assigned to another overseas location?
- How quickly will the employee be expected to move once a decision to relocate him has been taken?

○ How much will the expatriate employee be expected to use his house for work-related entertainment?

Figure 3.1 *Example of a company brief to expatriates about to take up employment in Gabon*

WELCOME XYZ COMPANY IN: GABON:

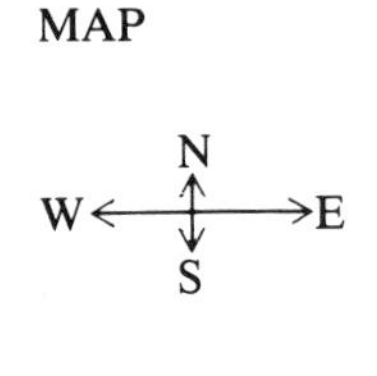

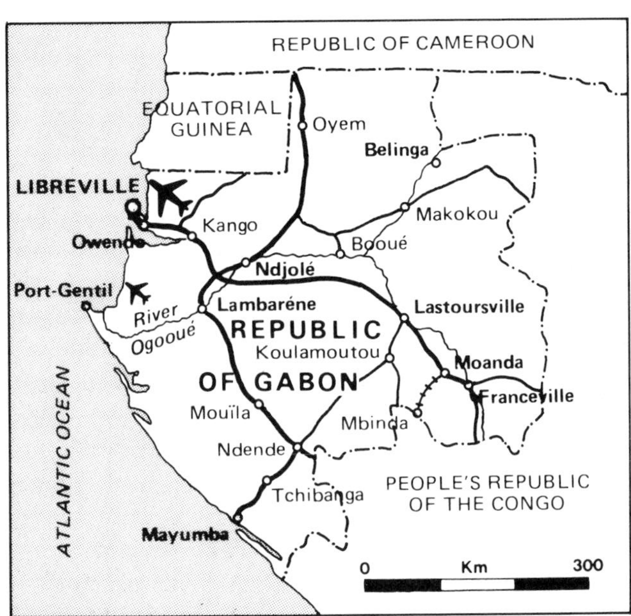

GABON is situated in West Africa, it has a population of 1 million inhabitants, its climate is EQUATORIAL, the local currency is CFA franc and equals 225 to 1 $US, the business hours are 07:00 to 18:00 Monday to Friday, the official language is French but other languages such as ______ / ______ , ______ , ______ are also spoken and understood.

The following public services are available ________ , ________ , telephone and mail services are MAIL: OK. TELEPHONE: Long-distance calls from Port-Gentil are very hard to obtain.

The electricity system is 50 cycles, or 220 volts.

Credit cards are not accepted, it is better to open a bank account at Port-Gentil.

You will arrive with a tourist visa which may have to be exchanged locally. For this you should bring the following documents: diploma, school certificate, etc.

The necessary vaccinations are: smallpox, yellow fever; do not forget to have a medical check-up regularly. (Cholera, sometimes required.)

- ○ To what extent will the expatriate be able to integrate within the host country?
- ○ What are the legal or practical problems involved in moving people and possessions from one country to another?

The cost of transferring people from one country to another is high (one company with over 1400 expatriates estimates $25,000 as the cost to the company for a move of a typical employee and his family from one country to another). This implies a very careful planning of personnel moves to minimize unnecessary transfers or excessive chains of moves, and to ensure that, as far as possible, the risk of any employee failing in a new expatriate assignment is carefully evaluated and minimized.

The company must bear the full cost of such a transfer and needs to structure its transfer policies in such a way that the individual is at least no worse off as a result of making the physical transfer than if he had not moved.

A transfer of any sort, particularly on an international basis, represents a period of considerable stress for the employee – this should not be compounded by his entering into negotiation with his employer. Thus a company should have a set of clearly written, coherent and well-communicated international transfer policies.

EXPATRIATION FROM HOME COUNTRY

This is potentially the most difficult type of international transfer since, for most people, it is the first move out of the domestic environment in which they have established themselves. In many international companies, with executives hardened to expatriation and mobility, the stress and shock associated with this kind of move are frequently under-estimated. Careful counselling of the employee (and his family), once the expatriation decision is taken, by managers with appropriate experience is essential from both a company viewpoint (success of move, rapid acclimatization) and from the viewpoint of the individual (adaptation, financial situation).

The key areas in an initial expatriation, as far as compensation and benefits are concerned, are:

- ○ Information about compensation and benefits package;
- ○ Disposal of house in home country;
- ○ Storage or shipping of furniture and personal effects;
- ○ Long-term home country benefits;
- ○ Personal finance;
- ○ Disturbance allowance;
- ○ Settling into the new assignment;
- ○ Miscellaneous issues, eg accommodation on arrival in assignment.

Information about compensation and benefits package

When an employee moves overseas for the first time, his compensation and benefits package in the new assignment should be fully explained to him. A member of the personnel department must work through the compensation package with the employee. This is particularly important when viewed in the context of complex expatriate compensation packages, where employees may be responsible for their own income tax during assignments, such a communication process is indispensable. Above all the expatriate must be fully briefed before beginning an overseas assignment.

Disposal of house in the home country

A normal objective of a company's expatriation reimbursement policy is to try to ensure that the individual does not lose out because of actions he may take as a consequence of his transfer and that the transfer takes place as quickly as required. Ideally companies want employees to be able to divest themselves of housing responsibilities in their home country quickly but need to ensure, as far as possible, that employees make the correct decision on whether to sell, rent or keep their homes empty.

When houses are sold on transfer, companies normally reimburse:

- estate agent's (realtor's) fees;
- contract completion (legal) fees;
- house sale programme costs (where the company acquires the house or an organization – which will, for a fee, buy the house for immediate cash) – particularly where the employee may have difficulty in disposing of the property rapidly and may be needed quickly in his new assignment.

An example of the relocation assistance programme for an American company is shown below:

Relocation assistance programme

Many people move to new locations every year as a result of an overseas assignment. The relocation assistance programme is designed to assist you and your family in your move from your present home to a new one with as little inconvenience as possible.

Basically, if you wish to sell your property, you have three choices:

- selling the house yourself;
- engaging an estate agent to be your agent for the sale;
- selling to a home-buying company whose services have been engaged free of charge for company employees.

The home-buying company's offer will be the average of three appraisals of your property providing none vary by more than 5 per cent from the average of the three.

The amount offered and the offer to buy are both guaranteed for 60 days from the date that you receive the purchase offer. During this time you may, if you wish, try to find a buyer other than the home-buying company. However, once you have accepted the offer, you may no longer attempt to market the home yourself.

If you have a clear house title, the sale can be closed quickly in most cases, and you will receive your equity cheque through the post. You will not be charged for any of the normal closing costs.

If the home-buying company subsequently sells your home for a price in excess of the average appraised value within 90 days after closing, it will remit any net gain to you upon completion of the sale.

Where houses are not owned but leased, it is normal for companies to pay the costs associated with the cancellation of the lease (legal fees and rent penalty to be paid), while not involving themselves in such areas as lost deposits, compensation for excessive wear and tear, and so on.

When a decision is taken to retain the house (empty or rented) in the home country, there are a number of areas a company may want to consider:

- providing general financial and legal counselling facilities;
- setting up a management contract for renting, recommending a reputable firm of estate agents/realtors and perhaps reimbursing some or all of the cost of the service;
- providing the facility for the regular payment of service bills.

Although employees should take sole responsibility for their own property when they rent it out, it is clearly difficult for them to do this from the other side of the world. Furthermore this should not occupy a substantial amount of time overseas. To solve this problem some companies reimburse the cost of a home maintenance contract while employees are working abroad.

Furniture and personal possessions

Most companies apply different policies for furnished or unfurnished accommodation.

If the overseas accommodation is fully furnished, the company might consider paying for the storage of the employee's own furniture while he is overseas (the cost of replacing a house full of furniture is substantial and it is almost always foolish for an employee to sell personal possessions prior to transfer). This storage could have a time or weight/volume limit.

Where overseas accommodation is not fully furnished, most companies reimburse the costs of packing, shipping and insurance up to certain limits on weight and/or volume. For example:

Furnished housing

If you are going to rent a house or an apartment that is furnished, the company will pay to ship personal effects by surface transportation to your work country location up to the following limitations:

- 1000 pounds if you are unmarried.
- 1500 pounds for you and your spouse.
- 200 pounds for each additional dependant.

When you return home, the company will pay to ship personal effects home up to the following limitations:

- 1200 pounds if you are unmarried.
- 1800 pounds for you and your spouse.
- 240 pounds for each additional dependant.

Air shipment may be authorized based on cost considerations.

Unfurnished housing

When you accept a long-term assignment, you may want to live in an unfurnished house or apartment. If authorized, you will be permitted to ship personal effects and household goods which will provide for a reasonably comfortable mode of living. You should realise that an assignment is a temporary one and that not all of your possessions may be required or desirable. We expect you to give careful consideration to the exposure to loss or damage to goods shipped and the need for certain items when living under different circumstances, such as an apartment versus a house or a significantly different climate.

In addition, the company will pay:

- to store your household goods not shipped;
- to ship your belongings back to your home country when your assignment is completed. However, you cannot ship back more than 10 per cent (or more than 360 pounds per person) over the gross weight that you first shipped;
- if you have been authorized to ship your furniture, you will receive a salary based on unfurnished housing at the work location.

The furniture – and indeed any personal possessions – must be fully insured, especially when the assignments are in remote areas. To be sure this is done, companies themselves may want to take out a corporate policy to cover such shipments – many reputable insurance companies are willing to do this at a reasonable price.

A company will normally want to define a certain amount of excess baggage that will be reimbursed for possessions taken with the employee on the transfer trip.

Reimbursements depend to a large extent on the company's overall philosophy on international careers. If the employee is expected to be highly mobile, moving every year or so (common in the oil industry), then a company may want him to 'travel light' and provide for all his needs in overseas accommodation – down to cutlery, crockery and linen. Other companies prefer that individuals 'personalise' their home (which obviously appeals more to wives and families). In the event of a longer term assignment, companies would normally expect an employee to take most of his possessions with him.

It is clear that the more possessions an individual takes with him, the more likely he is to have them stolen or damaged – especially in remote areas – with consequent effects on his (and his family's) morale. For this reason, many companies try to minimize the amount of shipment of employees' personal effects.

As an employee achieves more seniority, many companies increase the amount of additional reimbursement applied.

Disturbance allowance

A frequent practice is to pay a 'disturbance' allowance to cover general additional transfer costs. There are many forms this allowance might take; they usually depend on what else is reimbursed as part of the transfer package. Typical examples are:

- one and a half month's salary (with or without a ceiling);
- fixed monetary amounts, eg $1000 per adult and $500 per child.

There are many costs associated with international transfers that the employee will incur which will not be obvious in a domestic environment. Such costs are typically:

- the sale and re-purchase of items, such as stereos, which cannot be imported into some overseas countries, motor cars whose shipment is impracticable, and television systems which will not work in the next assignment (this area becomes more important the less the company provides in the way of furniture and fittings);
- the inevitable loss (by breakage, misdirection or pilferage) of items not fully reimbursed by insurance;
- a multitude of minor costs, for example:
  - replacement of electrical plugs where systems differ
  - purchase of transformers to ensure equipment works in the next assignment
  - early cancellation of rental or maintenance contracts
  - impact of the cost of buying warm clothes for people moving from a hot climate or vice versa (often this is taken care of with a separate allowance).

Personal finance and tax advice

This is not a book about personal finance and tax advice for expatriates – there are as many on the market as there are advisers providing professional taxation and finance services. The employer, while in no way giving financial advice to employees, must stress the need for employees transferring overseas to seek expert advice and tell the employee where he can obtain it. Indeed, many companies will reimburse the costs of such consultation. It is easy for an employee leaving for his first expatriate assignment to make financial 'mistakes' (eg selling his house prior to a period of high inflation) which will have enormous repercussions on his long-term financial position (on repatriation at a later date).

International transfers

Once an individual is working as an expatriate, subsequent international moves are much easier to effect than initial expatriation. Most of the issues already discussed apply equally to international transfers; there are a number of specific policy areas that need to be discussed. For example:

- Transfer via home country for vacation;
- Luggage allowances;
- Shipments home;
- Disturbance allowance;
- Local benefits accrued in present assignment.

Often, the better an employee performs and the more potential he shows, the more frequently he is moved. A company needs to set policies which not only ensure the reimbursement of reasonable transfer expenses and the substantial intangible costs of transfer, but are also well defined and therefore controllable and facilitate the transfer itself. Policies need to be clear and comprehensive and be seen to err, if at all, on the generous side. Simple policies with reasonable disturbance allowances to cover the multitude of loose ends are preferable to a host of complicated rules.

Transfer to next assignment

The actual move may be direct to the new assignment or via the home country allowing the expatriate to take a vacation. (Figure 3.2 shows some of the policy areas that need attention in these cases.)

Figure 3.2

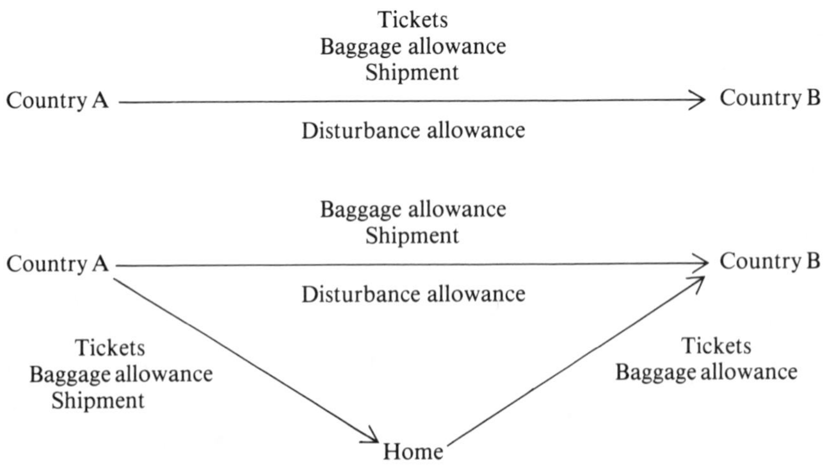

It is common policy for companies to time international moves at the end of the school year and for vacations to be taken at the time of transfer. This is most likely to facilitate the transfer, and policies are normally built around this kind of movement. In any event, after a year in a difficult location, a vacation may be essential.

Class of travel

Defining policies in this area is frequently difficult and is further complicated by attitudes towards 'luxury' (of first class travel) and the very great difference in cost between first class and economy air fares.

Where policies have been defined by companies, they normally:

- differentiate between vacations, business trips and transfers;
- define eligibility for economy, business or first class ticket as a function of the duration of the flight and the status of the individual employee;
- reimburse actual expenditure only (to avoid abuses; for example, claiming first class fare and travelling economy).

Shipments home

Some companies reimburse the cost of a shipment home every few years (with a clearly defined policy on how often and what weight/volume limits) to allow people to continue collecting possessions overseas – without becoming excessively over-burdened with them.

CONCLUSION

An expatriate employer, aware that expatriation and international transfer represent events of considerable emotional and financial stress for the employee and his family, needs to pay considerable attention to transfer policies. While trying to avoid an excessively bureaucratic approach, the employee needs to be given a clear, consistent and coherent package which meets his perceived needs and, while sufficiently flexible to apply in a wide range of cases, does not lead to an individually negoiated policy in each case. These policies should be seen by employees to be generous rather than unnecessarily restrictive – the economy involved in saving $1000 on a transfer cost may result in a much greater loss of money if it contributes to the failure of the overseas assignment.

These policies are most effectively communicated to employees by collecting them together in a concise but readable manual or booklet which can be given to the employee and his family at the time of transfer. It is also very good practice to nominate a member of the personnel department to explain company policy to the employee and to provide the necessary counselling for him and his family.

4. Conducting an international salary survey

INTRODUCTION

Salary surveys require a considerable amount of time and painstaking attention to detail. Such difficulties are magnified when undertaking an international compensation study. It is therefore necessary to ask at the outset – why do it? Is it really worth the effort? To answer this question the following considerations should be examined:

- An international salary survey may be necessary to obtain a global view of compensation in the particular industry concerned. Regardless of whether the company intends to use a home base structure for its expatriates it will need to know what the market rate is at any particular time. In other words, what is the salary market for the people the company recruits in their home country and in the overseas locations where they will work?
- When operating in an overseas environment the company must obtain a reasonable idea of what other companies consider normal for expatriation and hardship premiums in that location. Certainly the company must make the final decision itself, having taken into account its own circumstances, but not to have examined other companies' treatment of expatriates in a location results in a very exposed position.
- A precise knowledge of comparative net salaries is important. The company will often be presented with conflicting information on rates, basic pay and allowances – all of which are very difficult to discuss unless they can be fitted into the whole compensation package. Thus, the personnel manager must examine other companies' salary administration policies to see whether expatriates should meet the costs of housing, tax equalization and other deductions before arriving at an accurate net salary figure.
- A thorough understanding of the whole benefits package is essential. The expatriate usually expects a much more comprehensive package than his home country counterpart. The benefits of housing, car, medical scheme, vacations, education assistance and transport allowances are as important as direct questions of salary.
- Where a company no longer offers satisfactory remuneration to its employees specific problems may occur. Companies must offer

compensation and benefits packages at least comparable to those of their chief competitors.

Where all of the above are concerned, only detailed research will provide the information required. Most expatriate compensation and benefit policies are subject to central control – usually the company's head office. This is necessary to prevent all sorts of anomalies entering into employment conditions, making it impossible to transfer an expatriate from one location to another. At the same time, without a detailed knowledge of the market in each location, the head office is blind and incapable of taking action. For this reason alone there exists pressure to obtain as much accurate information as possible.

WHO UNDERTAKES THE SURVEY?

As with domestic salary surveys, a variety of approaches can be adopted for obtaining information. At its simplest level one individual in the organization can make the necessary contacts, undertake the interviews and compile the results. This can, with an international survey, result in a considerable amount of travel being undertaken by the individual and may therefore take a great deal of time.

Alternatively, a questionnaire approach may be adopted, with questionnaires being sent to all the participants. The problem here is one of definition – being able to define exactly what is required so that the data returned is genuinely valid for salary purposes. The advantage of this type of approach is that the questionnaire can be filled in over a period of time – thus avoiding a difficult schedule of interviews. Over the past ten years there has been a considerable growth of international salary clubs which exchange salary and benefit data on a regular basis. A standardized format is usually designed and administrated by a secretariat, institute or outside consultant. The advantage of such an arrangement is that the company, if it chooses its consultants correctly, can rely on a background of expertise and professionalism. However, other participating companies often prefer the neutrality and discretion the outside consultant should bring to the study. The disadvantage is that the use of consultants almost certainly makes this the most costly approach – paying the air fare, hotel bills and day rates of a consultant travelling to six or more multi-nationals will quickly produce a bill of many tens of thousands of dollars. Furthermore, the professionalism of the consultant may prove not to be a satisfactory alternative for detailed knowledge of the industry concerned. Where complicated job comparisons are required the consultant may have to spend an inordinate amount of time sorting out the relevant data, which somebody in the industry might find a much easier task.

The last category of salary survey, the commercial survey, is probably the least satisfactory. In many countries and some regions (particularly Europe) regular commercial surveys are published giving details of compensation and benefits for a wide spectrum of jobs. These surveys usually concentrate on senior positions – managing director, marketing manager, finance director, production manager, personnel manager together with an indication of the size of the company. While such surveys may give a reasonable indication of the market within one country they are of limited use in giving an accurate picture of remuneration packages because of their generality.

The selection of the appropriate method depends on a number of factors:

- Time – how much time has the company to undertake the survey?
- Expertise – can this be found inside the company or should the company go outside?
- Cost – can the company afford a consultancy to undertake the survey for them?
- Trust – will the other participants be happy with an 'in company' approach?
- Complexity – can a complex survey be satisfactorily undertaken by a questionnaire or by consultants?

Once these questions have been properly resolved the survey can be designed. This chapter discusses the general design of salary surveys and illustrates the approach with two detailed case studies: we focus on salaries and current benefits – housing, school fees, medical benefits, etc. Long-term benefits are considered separately in a later chapter.

DESIGNING A SALARY SURVEY

The design of the international salary survey depends to a large degree on the specific problems which the company is investigating. However, in broad terms the following considerations should apply to a wide ranging international survey.

Selection of participants

The participating companies could be in the same industry or in different industries in the same geographical locations. They could be in any industry which is a direct competitor for people at the recruiting stage (eg graduate engineers). Ideally the participating companies should have a similar geographical spread so that the logic of the expatriate compensation package can be reviewed on a comparative basis. Within the participating companies similar jobs and working patterns obviously help comparison. The perfect comparison is unlikely to exist and therefore a company has to compromise. The nature of the compromise depends on the problem being investigated. The participants need to be selected with the objective of getting a reasonable market sample – in other words, sufficient participants for statistical validity (enough jobs, enough people, enough locations) and, if possible, at different places in the salary market.

When comparing different overseas areas, the physical location of the employees must be taken into account. For example, are participants living in a town or in a work camp and what is the quality of their housing? These factors greatly influence the level of premiums paid.

Selection of jobs

As far as possible the jobs compared must be similar. No matter how accurate the collection and analysis of data may be, a salary survey is worthless if the jobs being compared are not, in fact, equivalent.

A great deal of time needs to be spent in forming accurate job comparisons. The procedure for this is very similar to that used in job evaluation: writing accurate job descriptions, obtaining organization charts and detailed comparisons of jobs using common factors. (In many companies the application of the HAY job evaluation method helps this kind of comparison.) It is usually easier to compare jobs in line rather than staff functions and at the top and bottom of an organization rather than in the middle.

A series of benchmark jobs should be chosen. These ought to be well defined jobs at different levels in the organization, to which the other jobs can easily be related (since a direct comparison of all jobs is impossible). These jobs should be performed in a reasonably large number of different geographical locations.

An alternative approach often used with professional staff is the comparison of salary trends for people with a given qualification as a function of their experience, almost regardless of the job they do. This is particularly relevant where French companies are concerned.

Statistics

Few companies are prepared to release confidential salary data on individual employees. The data collected in a salary survey is normally as follows: *salary ranges* (actual job tables or bracket) ie minimum, maximum and median or mid-point of a gross salary; *overseas net salary* after all deductions have been made (including tax and housing) ie the cash in the expatriate's hand.

THE COMMERCIAL SURVEY

Each year a number of organizations, including some listed in Chapter 16, produce surveys of personnel practice and compensation for expatriate employees. A typical survey samples some 300 organizations by distributing questionnaires. The surveys summarize items such as staffing patterns, recruitment and selection, orientation and language training, compensation for hardship, housing policies, income tax adjustments and benefit plans. The 1982 ORC Survey surveyed companies with a workforce of some 60,000 expatriates and 2,100,000 local national employees in a cross-section of industries ranging from non-profit organizations to banks, hotels and oil companies.

Such surveys, by their very nature, do not provide precise salary information on any particular industry or location. They do, however, give an extremely useful insight into expatriate employment practices as a whole. For a general analysis of hardship allowances, housing policies and benefits plans the survey indicates distinct shifts in policy amongst a significant proportion of companies employing expatriates. The survey covered:

Staffing patterns
Length of assignment
composition of nationalities
expatriate families.

Recruiting
Psychological testing
orientation training
language training
contracts of employment

Conditions of employment
Automobiles including driver
club memberships
medical plans
base salary structure
incentive bonuses
hardship allowances
housing costs
moving assistance
income tax adjustments
currency of salary payment
benefit plans.

Each question is accompanied by an indication of the statistical response (for an example see Figure 4.1).

Figure 4.1 *Example of the statistical representation of responses to a company practice questionnaire*

Group

1	2	3	4	5	6	7	8	9	10	11	12	13	14	Total
1	3	7	6	3	1	5	3	1	18	9	20	10	6	53
				1	4			2		1	2			10
	2	2	7	1	2	3	2	6	8	4	3	4		44
	1		1	2	1	1	3	1	3			2		15
	3	1			2	1	6	8	4	1	1	2	2	34
			3		1			1		1	1	2		9
			1	3	5	1		4	5	4	1	4		28
				1							1			2
1	2	6	11	6	4	6	3	2	4	7	6	3	5	65

Which of the following best describes your company's practice with respect to payment of compensation (including base salary, premiums, allowance, adjustments, etc) for US expatriates?

1. Paid entirely in US dollars
2. Paid entirely in local currency
3. Paid partly in US dollars and partly in local currency at the discretion of the employee
4. An amount approximating the pay of a comparable host country national employee is paid in local currency; the balance is paid in US dollars
5. An amount equivalent to the employee's spendable income for commodities and services plus domestic shelter, plus post and shelter differentials and

paid in the local currency; balance is paid in US dollars
6. Post and shelter differentials are paid in local currency; balance is paid in US dollars
7. Paid partly in local currency and partly in US dollars as determined by management on basis on factors other than 4, 5, or 6 above
8. None of the foregoing
0. Other

Numbers 1 to 14 inclusive indicate the industry of the participating company and correspond to the number of participants applying each policy.

Such surveys do not attempt to identify categories of jobs and give detailed salary ranges. They are therefore only useful to identify general trends rather than establish a precise fix on the market.

Some commercial surveys do attempt to identify salaries on a regional level. Top Management Remuneration (Management Centre Europe) issues an annual European survey which examines salary levels for senior positions in a number of countries. The presentation of this type of analysis is shown below.

Top Management Remuneration (Management Centre Europe)

The positions covered in this survey are chief executive, divisional director and senior and second position in marketing, sales, manufacturing, research, finance, personnel, purchasing and EDP. The survey covers all the major European countries and the United States.

A simple use of the linear regression techniques allows a correlation to be made between company size (in revenue or employee numbers) and salary. Salaries are presented with or without bonuses and both statistical dispersion and average measures are given (see Figure 4.2).

In all industrialized countries similar commercial surveys are produced on a national basis.

The problem when dealing with expatriates is that this sort of information is of limited value. It provides broad average figures for each national market but often the company will be using its home market or an international reference on which to build the base salary structure. The only meaningful salary figure for expatriates is the net, taking into account allowances, benefits and tax equalization systems; this will be discussed in more detail in Chapter 9.

Circulated questionnaire approach

By its very nature the circulated questionnaire for an international salary survey needs to be exhaustive to obtain all the relevant information. Such a questionnaire can be divided into two parts – compensation and benefits. Whether this questionnaire is sent by post to participants or is used by the personnel manager as his checklist when he personally visits the participating companies, the analytical framework should be of this form.

Figure 4.2 *Gross annual remuneration – all companies*

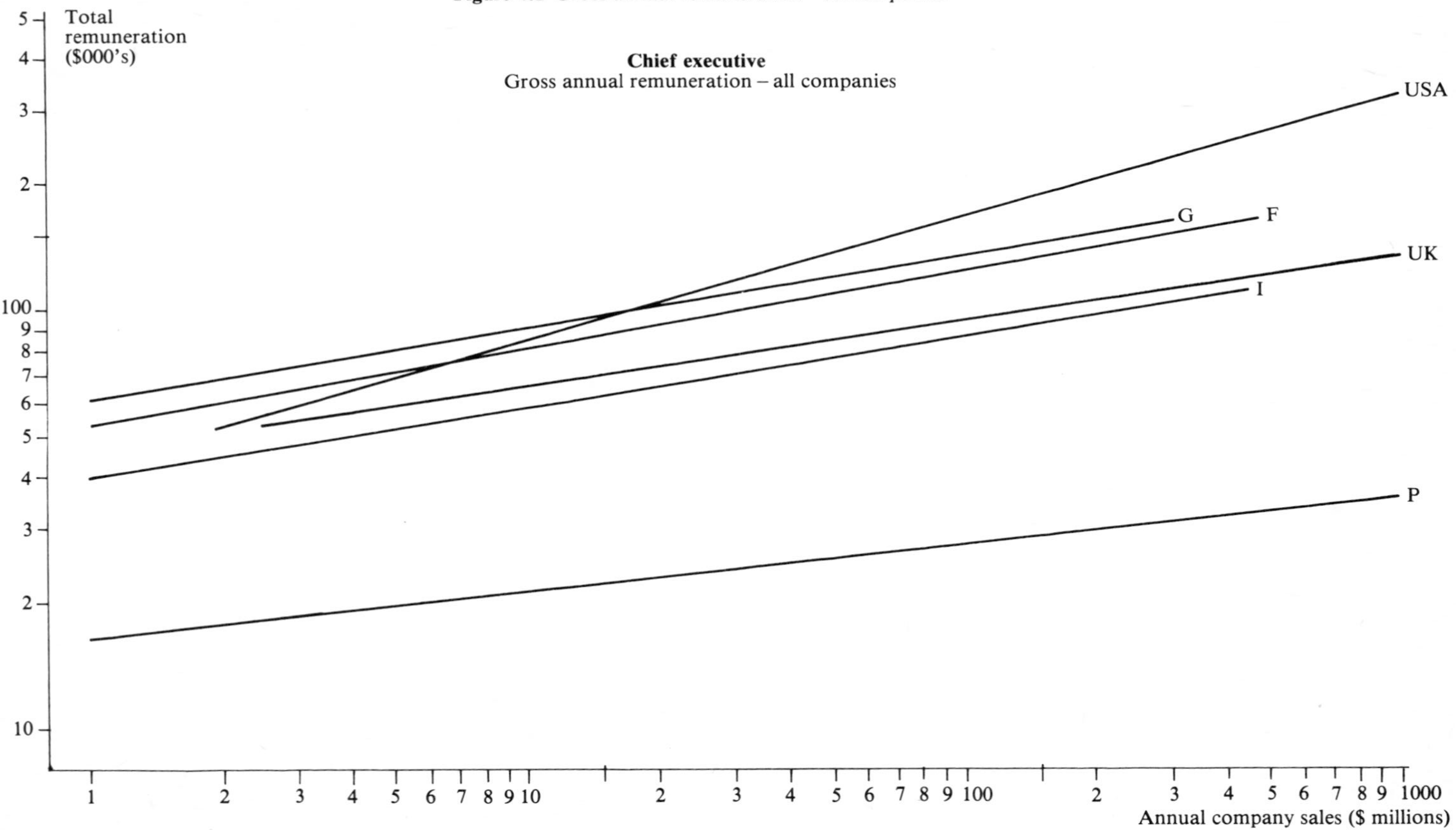

Compensation

To obtain an accurate picture of compensation, comparable jobs need to be identified in the participating organizations. Naturally, it would be unusual always to find a consistent 'fit' as companies are organized in different ways and with different geographical spreads. An effective way to obtain a near perfect fit is to provide a composite organization chart of the jobs being surveyed together with appropriate job descriptions. They should also identify the exact location of their expatriates, the number of expatriates in that location and the number of people doing the jobs being compared. Each company can then complete salary details according to a compensation checklist. An example of this procedure is shown in Figure 4.2.

Figure 4.3 *Compensation checklist questionnaire*

Monthly salary	*Assignment, country and location (sample of 6. to 8.)*
1. Base salary	
2. Theoretical deductions (if any)	
3. 1. minus 2.	
4. Foreign service premium Hardship allowance Other payment	
5. Housing Actual expense less home country housing deduction	
6. Housing allowance	
Cost of housing provided	
Cost of living allowance (a) Index	
(b) Spendable income	
Allowance (a) multiplied by (b)	
7. Other deductions or payments	
8. Total net monthly payment	
9. Exchange rate $US	

Benefits

Questionnaires on benefits can only give partial information on all companies' policies – details lie in manuals and in interpretation by senior personnel and operations executives. As will be discussed at length in Chapter 7 benefits can form a very important and complex part of the complete expatriate package. Such questionnaires look for general patterns and are usually divided into distinct areas. The examples shown are obviously not exhaustive but illustrate the approach used to collect data on housing, relocation and school fee reimbursement.

Figure 4.4 *Housing and housing allowances questionnaire*

If company housing is provided in the location, what 'rental' must the employee pay?

1. None
2. Flat amount applicable in all locations $__________
3. Varying rental amount, depending on circumstances: explain
4. Percentage of base pay, ________ per cent
5. Home country deduction; normally used in determining excess costs
6. Other (please describe) ____________________

If a housing allowance is provided in the location, how is the amount determined?

1. Flat amount from table. Please state source ____________
2. 100 per cent of the difference between overseas and home country housing cost
3. Less than 100 per cent of the difference between overseas and home country housing, what percentage? ________________ per cent
4. Other (please describe) ____________________

How is home country housing cost determined?

1. Actual home country cost $
2. Table from outside source. Please state source
3. Flat percentage of base pay. Please state percentage ______ per cent
4. Formula based on base pay. Please state formula and show graph
5. Other (please describe) ____________________

What items are included in housing cost reimbursed by the company?

1. Rent
2. Local taxes
3. Electricity
4. Gas
5. Water
6. Telephone
7. Other (please describe) ____________________

If company provide housing, what furnishing is provided?

1. None – in which case how much furniture is shipped by the employee and what, if any, lump sums are paid?
2. Hard furnishing only, ie chairs, tables, beds and cupboards, essential large appliances, ie washing machine, fridge, cooker, diswasher, freezer, air conditioning
3. Fully furnished
4. Other (please describe)

Figure 4.5 *Employee relocation questionnaire*

1. Is an exploratory trip provided prior to relocation?
2. What class of air transportation do you reimburse and under what circumstances?
3. How is shipment of expatriates' household goods handled (assuming large/ expensive items are excluded) and by what means of transport?
   (a) all reasonable shipping costs paid, no specific limit
   (b) all reasonable shipping costs paid, up to certain weight or volume limits. Limit
   (c) all reasonable shipping costs paid up to a specified maximum cost. Maximum cost
   (d) household goods are not shipped
   (e) other
4. What alternatives to shipment of household goods are provided?
   (a) storage
   (b) lump sum payment (disposal allowance). Basis
   (c) replacement of certain large household items (eg appliances) not shipped
   (d) compensation for 'forced sale' loss on specified items
   (e) furniture provided by company
   (f) other (please describe)
   (g) none
5. If you pay for storage costs in the home country, what is your normal practice?
   (a) storage costs paid without time or weight limits
   (b) storage costs paid for a limited period. Limit
   (c) storage costs paid up to a specified weight or volume. Limit
   (d) storage costs not paid
   (e) other (please describe)

Figure 4.6 *Home leave questionnaire*

1. How frequently is home leave provided?
2. What is the length of the home leave period?
   (a) specific duration. Amount
   (b) accrual based on length of stay. Accrual rate
   (c) home country vacation period
   (d) host country vacation period
   (e) greater than home or host country vacation period
   (f) other (please describe)
3. What travel expenses are reimbursed for home leave travel?
   (a) class of air travel (please specify)
   (b) excess baggage allowance (please specify)
   (c) do you allow expatriates to take these expenses in cash or is a return ticket to the point of origin provided?
   (d) other (please describe)

Figure 4.7 *Education costs for expatriates questionnaire*

1. Is reimbursement of primary and secondary education expenses provided?
   – minimum age
   – maximum age
2. Which of the following education expenses for primary and secondary schools are covered?
   (a) books
   (b) tuition
   (c) other *required* school fees
   (d) supplementary teaching in certain subjects
   (e) home study courses
   (f) special language instruction
   (g) room and board (if school is away from home)
   (h) student transportation expenses
   (i) parent travel expenses to nearest suitable school
   (j) other (please describe)
3. If the nearest school is away from home, what travel expenses for home visits will you pay for a student (primary and secondary level)?
   (a) none
   (b) one round trip per year
   (c) two round trips per year
   (d) three round trips per year
   (e) whenever the school's room and board facilities are closed
   (f) other (please describe)
4. If the expatriate elects to send a child to a school in his home country or another school other than the 'nearest suitable' school, what expenses are covered?
   (a) all expenses
   (b) all expenses up to the amounts that would be covered if incurred at the nearest suitable school
   (c) all expenses up to a maximum. Amount
   (d) other (please describe)
5. What is the level of educational expense reimbursement in the location?
   (a) 100 per cent of all expenses, please specify any maximum which applies
   (b) less than 100 per cent of all expenses. Please state percentage.
   (c) other (please describe)
6. Are costs of normal home country university education for an expatriate's child reimbursed?
7. What travel expenses for home visits do you pay for university students?
   (a) none
   (b) one round trip per year
   (c) two round trips per year
   (d) more than two round trips per year
   (e) other (please describe)

SALARY SURVEY – CASE STUDY A

The most effective means of collecting salary survey data is the questionnaire approach followed by individual discussion by the person doing the survey with each participant.

The data collected needs to be analysed into a meaningful format. The following example shows median actual salaries for four benchmark jobs surveyed within seven international companies. The salaries need to be converted to a common currency and currency fluctuations must also be taken into account, so two sets of exchange rates are shown in this case. The data may also be presented graphically as shown.

Company A pays in $US and is compared with six other companies in its field. Two pay in FF, one in DM, one in DFL and two in $US. It is clear that the rate of exchange against the $US has a very great effect on the competitiveness of the salaries paid by company A – imagine the results at, for example, $1 = 4.25FF.

Figures 4.9 to 4.11 illustrate base salary comparisons – indexed with company A = 100 and the net salaries for the same jobs in one overseas location – in this case Jakarta. The graph shows how the relative competitiveness of the salaries of company A vary in the organization (and also indicate that the comparison for base manager in company C is false). Finally, the company can compare the premium it provides for working in Jakarta with the market. The same analysis would be carried out for each geographical location studied. It is always useful to repeat salary surveys on a regular basis (annually or bi-annually) and comparison between surveys can show clearly whether the company's salary strategy is effective.

The date at which the participating companies' salaries were last increased and the anticipated amount and date of the next increases are key factors in arriving at a decision from the survey.

Results – current benefit survey

In this context it is difficult to make a quantitative comparison between companies. The normal procedure is to make a tabulation as shown for housing, the location and education. Obviously other comparisons can be made but they depend on specific company requirements.

FINDING A NET SALARY—CASE STUDY B

This is an example of a specialist study to identify and solve one particular problem – in nature micro rather than macro. The market consisted of a small number of companies employing specialist drilling engineers with a high market demand.

The employees of one company considered that for a given job the two competitors were paying more money. The problem was that each of the three companies had a different pay system philosophy as far as base salary, overseas premiums, tax deduction and daily bonus payment were concerned. Thus, although base salaries of company A were by far the highest, overseas premiums for company C were the highest of the three and guaranteed payment of company B together with no tax deduction produced an extremely complex pattern.

The following table shows the calculation necessary to arrive at the monthly net salary for drilling engineers in $US in five locations. The graph shows how the net salary arrived at varies in relation to the amount of time spent on the drilling rig. Significant is the fact that the net salaries are very similar, despite the variety of packages offered as remuneration for the same job.

Figure 4.8 *Annual base salaries (Jakarta) – case study A*

Company	Currency	Trainee engineer	Index	Base manager	Index	District manager	Index	Division manager	Index
A	$	27,540	100	36,000	100	66,000	100	87,240	100
B	FF	130,799		169,411		265,451		292,499	
	$ (1)	26,160	95	33,882	94	53,090	80	58,500	67
	$ (2)	23,357	85	30,252	84	47,402	72	52,232	60
C	FF	127,272		175,440		252,198		302,160	
	$ (1)	25,454	92	35,088	97	50,440	76	60,432	69
	$ (2)	22,727	82	31,328	87	45,035	68	53,957	62
D	DM	49,010		83,590		131,170		177,190	
	$ (1)	23,338	84	39,805	110	62,462	95	84,376	97
	$ (2)	20,767	75	35,419	98	55,580	84	75,080	86
E	DFL	41,550		64,950		99,300		155,800	
	$ (1)	17,910	65	28,000	78	42,802	65	67,155	77
	$ (2)	15,980	58	24,980	69	38,192	58	59,923	69
F	$	27,120	98	36,060	100	53,400	81	76,740	88
G	$	24,780	90	35,280	98	61,740	94	82,620	95

Figure 4.9 *Annual net salaries (Jakarta) – case study A*

Company	Currency	Trainee engineer	Index	Base manager	Index	District manager	Index	Division manager	Index
A	$	36,077	100	47,160	100	72,600	100	82,878	100
B	FF	204,351		264,615		407,026		448,117	
	$ (1)	40,870	113	52,923	112	81,405	112	89,623	108
	$ (2)	36,491	101	47,253	100	72,683	100	80,020	97
C	FF	190,416		281,616		387,360		443,808	
	$ (1)	38,083	106	56,323	119	77,472	107	88,762	107
	$ (2)	34,003	94	50,288	107	69,171	95	79,251	96
D	DM	61,090		106,336		156,307		201,624	
	$ (1)	29,090	81	50,636	107	74,432	103	96,011	116
	$ (2)	25,885	72	45,058	96	66,232	91	85,434	103
E	DFL	64,709		89,981		124,444		170,604	
	$ (1)	27,892	77	38,785	82	53,640	74	73,536	89
	$ (2)	24,888	69	34,608	73	47,863	66	65,617	79
F	$	36,924	102	47,544	101	64,968	89	79,404	96
G	$	31,872	88	43,680	93	68,124	94	80,424	97

Figure 4.10 *Graph showing salaries for various grades of personnel – case study A*

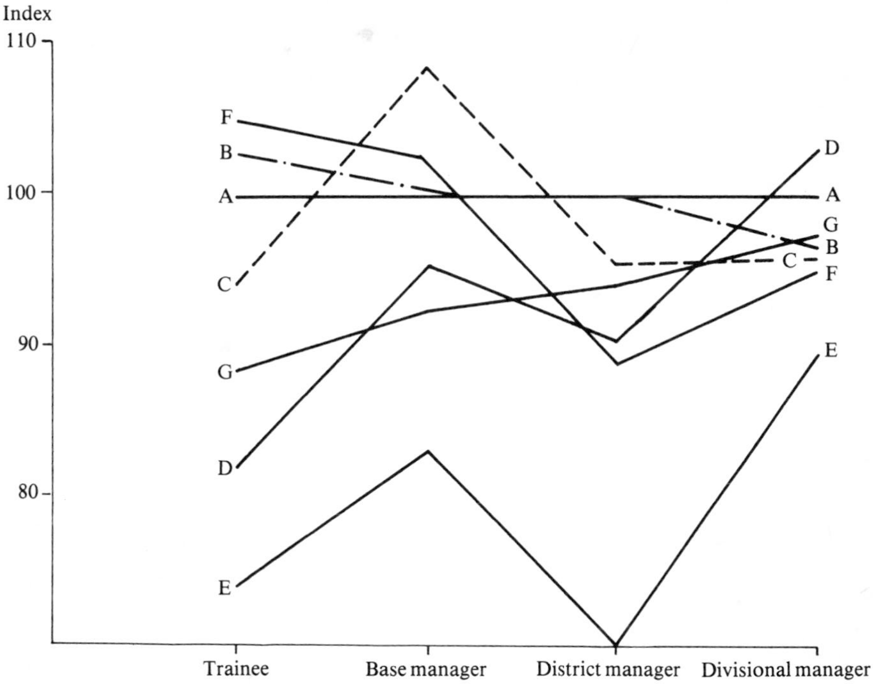

Figure 4.11 *Examples of company housing policies – case study A*

Company	Housing provided	Services	Employee housing deduction
A	Free furnished housing	Paid – but local limits on telephone expenses	No
B	Free furnished housing	Paid – if not taken into account in cost of living allowance	No
C	Free furnished housing	Paid	$150 per month flat deduction
D	Unfurnished housing, shipment of all necessary personal effects	Paid except telephone	US housing equivalent deduction (tables)
E	Housing allowance as a function of family size and grade of employee	Paid	US housing equivalent deduction with maximum
F	Free furnished housing	Paid (not for all categories of personnel)	No
G	Free housing with hard furnishing only	Paid except telephone	No

Figure 4.12 *Examples of company transfer policies – case study A*

Company	Air fares	Luggage	Insurance of personal effects paid by employer	Hotel expenses on arrival
A	Economy class	60kg adult 40kg child 10kg person for vacation	No	Up to one month's base salary
B	Economy class except Grade A and above	First assignment 25kg after 30kg round trip/adult + 20kg per child	Paid	Actual expenses paid
C	Economy class	25kg for the expatriate + 20kg/ family member + shipment up to 50kg	Paid	Hotel costs plus daily allowance up to four weeks (can be extended to eight weeks maximum)
D	First class	1001lbs/person	Paid $75,000 max (married) $37,000 max (single)	Fully reimbursed or moving expenses max 90 day period
E	First class trip + five hours otherwise tourist	33lbs excess/person	Paid	Settling allowance. One month's base salary up to $5000
F	Economy class	Assignment 15kg expatriate Assignment 15kg family Vacation: 10kg expatriate + wife 5kg per child	Paid	N/A
G	Economy class	150kg single + 100kg married + 100kg per child	Paid 5000F/100kg transported	Settling allowance 0.5 base salary plus flat amount depending on family status

Figure 4.13 *Examples of company child education policies – case study A*

Company	Age	Expenses reimbursed at place of assignment	Expenses reimbursed outside place of assignment	Number of trips paid
A	15 to 18	100%	100% of tuition/registration and books 50% of indirect school expenses up to $3500	2 trips
B	British 5 to 18 Dutch 6 to 19	100%	British: 85% of expenses up to £1105/term Dutch: 85% of expenses up to DFL 13721/term	2 trips plus one discretionary trip
C	5 to 20	100%	75% up to DM 9000/year	2 trips
D	5 to 25		All costs met with annual deductible of $150/1 child $250/2 children plus $30 for any additional child	2 trips
E	K to Grade 12		100% up to $5300	
F	5 to 25	100%	Minimum 5000F/year upon presentation of bills up to a ceiling of 18,800F/year Primary school 1150F/term	2 trips plus one trip if parents cannot take vacation between 15/7 and 1/9
G	5 to 25	100%	Secondary school 1400F 16 years old 1740F 16 years old University 1740 to 3520 max	2 trips

Figure 4.14 *Monthly net salaries for drilling engineers ($US) working 16 days per month on a rig*

Location	A		B		C	
Holland	Base	3000	Base	1850	Base	2370
	Allowance 20%	600	Foreign service	200	Expatriate allowance	592
	Bonus	3200	premium		Cost of living	308
	Deduction	(360)	Allowance	400	Bonus	4000
	Net	6440	Bonus	4000	Deduction	876
			Deductions	—	Net	6394
			Net	6450		
Brunei	Base	3000	Base	1850	Base	2370
	Allowance 45%	1350	Foreign service	200	Expatriate allowance	592
	Bonus	3200	premium		Cost of living	829
	Deduction	(435)	Allowance	600	Bonus	4000
	Net	7115	Bonus	4000	Deduction	(876)
			Deduction	—	Net	6915
			Net	6650		
UAE	Base	3000	Base	1850	Base	2370
	Allowance 35%	1050	Foreign service	200	Expatriate allowance	700
	Bonus	3200	premium		Cost of living	829
	Deduction	(405)	Allowance	500	Bonus	4000
	Net	6845	Bonus	4000	Deduction	(876)
			Deduction	—	Net	7033
			Net	6550		
Brazil	Base	3000	Base	1850	Base	2370
	Allowance 30%	900	Foreign service	200	Expatriate allowance	592
	Bonus	3200	premium		Cost of living	379
	Deduction	(390)	Allowance	500	Bonus	4000
	Net	6710	Bonus	4000	Deduction	(876)
			Deduction	—	Net	6465
			Net	6550		
Egypt	Base	3000	Base	1850	Base	2370
	Allowance 45%	1350	Foreign service	200	Expatriate allowance	592
	Bonus	3200	premium		Cost of living	—
	Deduction	(435)	Allowance	500	Bonus	4000
	Net	7115	Bonus	4000	Deduction	(876)
			Deduction	—	Net	6086
			Net	6550		

Pitfalls to avoid

As with any salary survey there are a number of key areas on which to focus in order to avoid typical pitfalls:

- jobs must be comparable (the variety of overseas jobs may make comparisons more complex than in domestic surveys);
- information must be correct (often the head office personnel manager may be unaware of special payments and some companies are unwilling

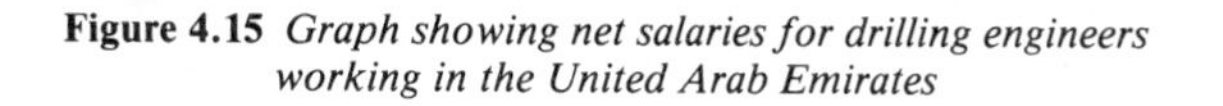

Figure 4.15 *Graph showing net salaries for drilling engineers working in the United Arab Emirates*

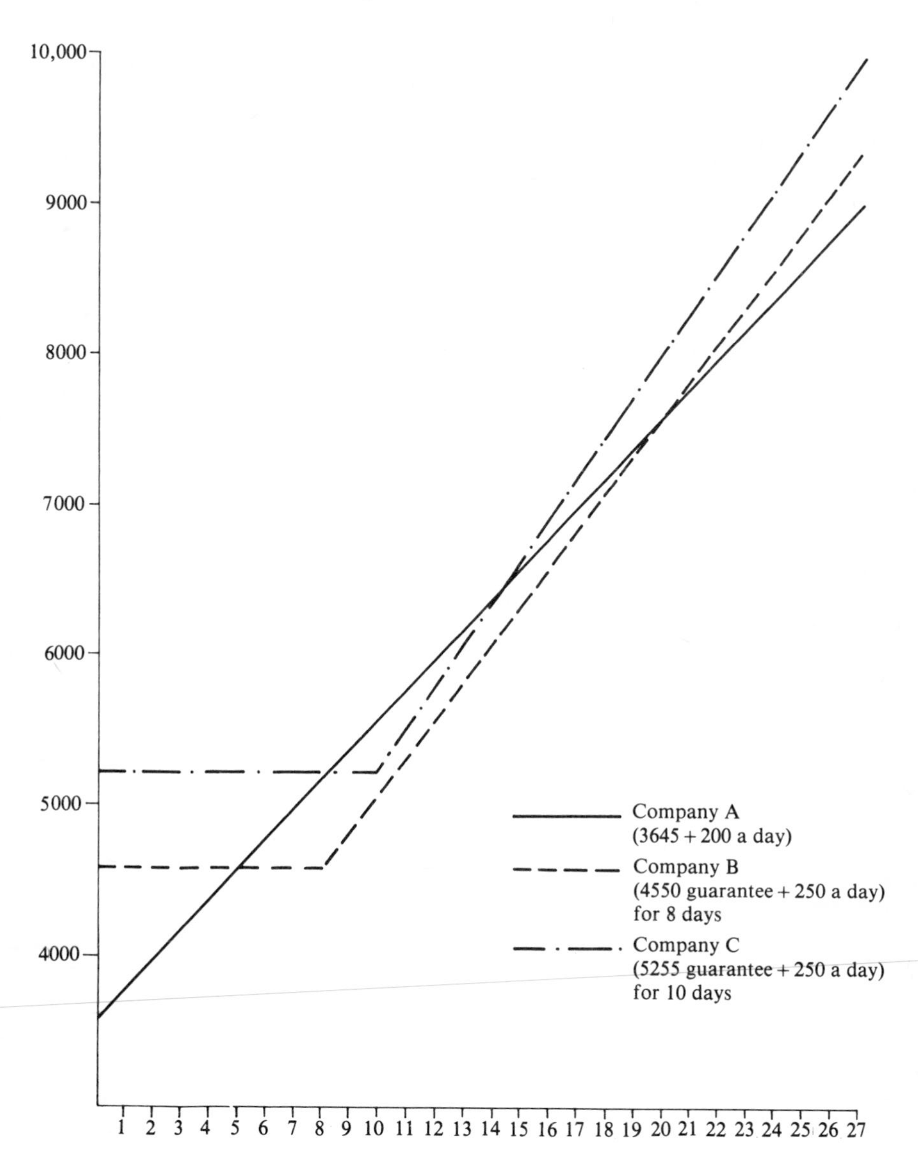

to divulge accurate information on senior salaries. In some overseas countries the low level of disclosure of salary levels to local authorities may hinder the collection of data);

- information must take account of fluctuating exchange rates and be presented in a way which allows the impact of changes in the exchange rate to be examined. Cost of living additions must be compared at the same time during the month since they will show frequent variation;

- the true net salary must be arrived at by taking account of all deductions and additions and comparing the same expatriate benefits (eg is company housing provided?);
- locations must be comparable – similar housing compounds, same town in the same country;
- statistical analysis needs to be objective and sound
  - enough participants
  - enough jobs and job holders
  - enough different locations
  - average procedures need to be valid.

CONCLUSION

We have not attempted to describe in great detail the basic methodology of salary surveys – this is amply covered in the compensation and benefits bibliography given in Chapter 16.

When undertaking an international salary survey, although the basic principles are the same as in a domestic context, there are additional areas of concern. It is important that a company is not only fully aware of its position in the salary market but sets a target of where it would like to be. This requires a good understanding by the compensation and benefits manager, not only of the net salaries paid by other companies but also of the way in which they are constructed and provided. In the following five chapters the various components of the package are analysed in detail.

5. International base salary structure

INTRODUCTION

The last chapter examined the way in which information is collected to enable a company to arrive at an overall compensation package for its expatriate employees. This chapter reviews the role of base salary within the compensation package, how the base salary is arrived at, managed and used and the managerial, social and economic issues involved.

In most domestic employment the basic salary is also the gross salary and represents the key element in the compensation package of any individual. What is done to this salary is the clearest indication to the employee of the way in which the company regards him. On the basis of salary, not only are living standards determined and thus his direct social status, self-esteem and so forth, but most of the other benefits offered by the employer are a function of salary. Pensions and risk benefits, for example, usually bear a direct relationship to the salary. Thus, conventionally, a very large amount of personnel management effort is concerned with the evaluation of jobs, the setting up and maintenance of associated grade structures and related salaries and the whole business of general salary increases, merit increases and promotion increases.

In an expatriate compensation and benefits package, the base salary is only one element of the total provision. An expatriate, more than any other kind of employee, really needs to look at his total net salary, not only after tax and social security have been deducted, but also after basic expenses such as housing, transport and other living costs have been met. In the same way, the personnel manager needs to be aware of, and to manage, relative expatriate net salaries. He needs to be able to compare overseas employees with those at home, expatriates at the same level in a multitude of overseas environments and those at different levels within the same expatriate environment.

One obvious problem is the expatriate's perception of the value of the compensation package agreed, compared to others on the market. In the domestic environment most executives have an idea of how their salary level compares with the market; after all they can pick up a Sunday newspaper and immediately acquire some quite useful data. Given the complexity of expatriate compensation it is seldom if ever possible for the expatriate to have a clear idea of where he stands, which may create a credibility gap for the personnel function.

Thus, within an expatriate compensation context, the base salary represents only one of the factors with which the company must be concerned. However, the base salary is of considerable importance and a company must pay very great attention to it in order to ensure a coherent and professional management of base salary policies. Whatever the company might wish, the expatriate employee usually considers the base salary to be a key reference point and may react strongly to any attempt at alteration.

Employees tend to look at the level of their own salaries in comparison with other people's, both within and outside their own organization. The most crucial comparisons tend to be with those within the organization, in particular with peers and direct subordinates. A company must have a logical base salary policy which gives a clear explanation of how their salaries are arrived at in relation to those of their peers. Differentials need to be acceptable in relation to the levels of responsibility involved, quite apart from whatever allowances and premiums are paid in an overseas assignment.

There are two fundamental reasons for the importance of a base salary structure:

- establishing internal relativities within an organization; and
- as a starting point for most, long-term and risk benefit structures.

INTERNAL RELATIVITIES

This book does not discuss job evaluation techniques in general, nor the way in which internal salary relativities may be established since there is a wealth of excellent literature on these subjects. However, there are a number of aspects of job evaluation, in an international context, which differ from those the personnel manager might foresee in a domestic setting. For example:

- Relative ranking of jobs in the salary hierarchy. Not only do differentials between jobs show a wide variation, depending on the country concerned, but there may not be a consistent hierarchy of jobs which are valid in any one country. For example, a newly recruited UK graduate engineer expects to earn a little less than a secretary, but in Germany or France, he can expect to earn more than twice as much. In some countries, finance positions are typically valued more than, say, engineering positions, in others the reverse is true. Some account has to be taken of the cultural values different nationalities bring to the multinational employer. Both the employee's nationality and the country of assignment have an effect on the company's employment policy.
- The need to ensure that when evaluating a job the process is sophisticated enough not only to separate out those factors (eg cost and hardship) which are separately compensated for in the expatriate package, but also to recognize the local elements which have an effect on the difficulty or responsibility which the expatriate's job entails.
- In an international company, jobs will be geographically dispersed and the practical tasks of writing job descriptions, agreement with the

people concerned (job holder, superior, etc), the judging, ranking or evaluative process itself and the maintenance of whatever structure is established are much more difficult than in the domestic environment. The argument, then, might be for a simple system with more local flexibility than would necessarily be the case in a domestic company.

- The company may already have a well established job evaluation structure in operation at its home base. It needs to be sure that the slotting of expatriate jobs is done not only at a level which takes into account their particular overseas dimension, as far as responsibility is concerned, but does not exaggerate the position of the job by accounting for what is in fact 'hardship' and is compensated for separately. Thus, it is often tempting to give an individual a 'promotion' on accepting an assignment in an overseas location, which might well not be justified in relation to the employee's job responsibilities. Frequently, an individual might receive a large base salary increase when he accepts a 'tough' assignment which distorts his base salary in comparison with others. In many of these cases a more appropriate allowance and premium package is required.

THE BASE FOR OTHER BENEFITS

The list of benefits in an expatriate package directly related to base salary is considerable, for example:

- size of disturbance allowance on transfer (eg one month's base salary);
- pension contribution and benefits base (eg 3 per cent employee contribution and benefit of 1/70th final salary per year);
- risk benefit (eg four times annual base salary in the event of death);
- cost of living allowance (based on spendable income in relation to base salary);
- size of housing deduction (relative to base salary);
- amount of hypothetical tax deduction (eg income tax that would have been paid on the base salary in home country).

In a typical expatriate package, the basic salary plus expatriate premium could be 50 per cent of the total cost to the employer, other salary-dependent elements a further 25 per cent and the remaining 25 per cent determined on local costs.

BASE SALARY STRATEGIES

A company must first decide in which market it is recruiting, for what nationalities, and what skills it requires, and also at what level it will enter the salary market. In other words, how much can it afford to pay and will it choose one or many salary structures?

Although a majority of companies are concerned solely with sending an individual from his, and the company's, home base to work overseas, there is a growing trend towards a broadening of the recruiting base and the employment of other nationalities – towards the so-called third country national (TCN). A TCN may represent a special case for an American company whose expatriate workforce is 95 per cent American; nevertheless in many companies TCNs are the rule rather than the exception. Some authorities consider TCNs as a separate group but in our view the integration of these people into an overall analysis of salary strategies is the more logical approach.

A company has to recognize its own expatriate employment situation. In each case, a somewhat different base salary structure strategy is indicated.

Typical types of employees are:

'First country'
An employee in his home country.

'Second country'
The typical expatriate situation ie the employee works for a company from his home country in an overseas branch, eg an American working for an American company in Nigeria.

'Third country'
An employee from a different home country to that of the company he works for, eg an American working for a French company in Nigeria.

For second and third country nationals, the local salary markets in less developed countries are seldom useful as points of reference. The comparisons are much more likely to be with expatriate salaries in those countries and, as in the Middle East, these may be very high salaries indeed. If a company operating worldwide wishes to establish a consistent salary structure markets such as the Middle East need to be approached as exceptions. A company will have to provide a competitive package but this should be in the form of allowances and premiums rather than in the form of an inflated base salary.

In the base salary strategy, account has to be taken of the kind of expatriate careers that are anticipated. There are a number of quite distinct patterns each with its own implication for the base salary:

- short-term expatriation during a career which is otherwise in the home country (eg an Englishman sent for two years to an overseas subsidiary as part of his career development) will usually stay in the home country base salary structure;
- expatriation on a permanent basis – if this is to one country (eg an American who manages the company's subsidiary in Spain for 15 years) it is usual to use the host country base salary structure;
- mobile career expatriates, particularly with a large number of different nationalities, are probably best dealt with by an 'international' base salary structure. Where they are all of the same nationality, by far the most common situation, they tend to stay within the home country base salary structure;

- ○ short-term contract employees will tend to have their base salaries fixed either in relation to the host country going rate or home country plus additions, whichever is the better for recruiting.

Host country salary structure

Using the host country salary structure as a base has the clear advantage that base salary relativities between the expatriate and local employees are set at an appropriate level in relation to job responsibility. One problem is that there may be enormous differences between salary structures and salary levels in the countries of origin of the expatriates working there. These often lead to complicated systems of allowances and add-ons which effectively render what seems, at first sight, a straightforward approach rather ineffective. A host country salary approach works best when the salary/tax/price levels of the assignment countries and countries of origin are similar.

SALARY LEVELS IN RELATION TO NATIONALITY – HOME COUNTRY SALARIES

One of the major decisions that any multi-national employer has to make is the degree to which it is prepared to reward different nationalities different rates of pay for what are essentially the same jobs in the same location. For any given job there is a very wide difference within the developed world, between gross salary, net salary and the quality of life that can be purchased by that net salary. The construction and oil industries in the Middle East have discovered that it is in fact cheaper to recruit British engineers than their French or American counterparts. Not only have the British experienced domestic unemployment problems, but, more important, the prevailing salary and purchasing power levels are low. This complexity is compounded by substantially different levels of wage inflation in the different countries in which international companies recruit and the recent rapid variations in currency exchange rates. Although, in the long term, there appears to be a strong tendency for exchange rate fluctuations to reflect inflation rates, this is by no means true in the short to medium term as governments are able to manipulate the external value of their currency.

There are a number of different approaches to this problem which have been used by major international companies and which can be categorized as follows.

'Quasi' single nationality employer

A company which has perhaps 90 to 95 per cent of its expatriates of one nationality, may simply consider the other 5 to 10 per cent of its employees to be of the same nationality. Thus, a German company which employs British engineers on a construction project in Indonesia will treat them, from a salary viewpoint, as if they were German and pay all their expatriate employees in DM. This system works well if the other nationalities recruited come from a lower gross and/or net salary country but not if the reverse is true (ie German expatriates working for British companies overseas would not expect to be paid on a British salary structure). To a large extent, this is still the approach taken by many American companies to their TCNs, the assumption being that they would be content with US base salary levels. This was less true during the late 1970s, especially during the period of the weak $US.

Dual nationality employer

A company with two predominant nationalities, each representing a substantial proportion of its workforce and together forming the majority, may set up two quite separate base salary structures. Each structure could be defined in the currency and set at a level appropriate for the nationality group concerned. Employees of other nationalities are considered to belong to one or other of the two major groups.

Multi-nationality employer

With a large number of different nationalities, companies either create an individual base salary structure appropriate for each nationality, or they create a wholly artificial 'international' base salary structure into which the entire population is absorbed. Of course, the first option involves a very large amount of work in setting up and maintaining a rational structure for each nationality and rapidly becomes impractical unless, as is the case with companies who use the approach successfully, there is a well established domestic salary structure in each country. Where the pattern of expatriation is one short-term assignment outside the home country during a career, this may indeed be an appropriate system.

The 'international' structure suffers by being purely theoretical. Thus, the relative value of it will be different for each nationality and will vary over time with currency exchange rate fluctuations and alterations in domestic salary levels. Whatever level of salary is used and whatever currency it is paid in, there is no way to avoid this problem.

International salary comparisons

The difference between salary levels for the same job in different developed countries is striking. Taking as an example a personnel director, an MCE survey in 1980 gave the data shown in Figure 5.1

Figure 5.1 illustrates the problem an international company has when it compares the basic salaries of people doing the same job in different countries. Even if comparisons can be made correctly just once, the dynamics of exchange rates and inflation make comparison impossible over a period of time. In addition, the relativity between the median salary of a personnel director and that of the chief executive also showed a considerable variation (see Figure 5.2).

Figure 5.1 *Results of the 1980 MCE survey on salary levels in 11 countries*

Country	Median annual salary in local currency	Median annual salary in $US	% of USA
USA	$ 56,000	56,000	100
Austria	SCH 571,000	41,900	75
Belgium	BF 1,724,000	55,400	99
France	FF 240,900	53,900	96
Holland	DFL 95,300	45,400	81
Italy	LIT 31,200,000	34,000	61
Portugal	ESC 818,000	35,400	63
Spain	PTS 3,140,000	40,000	71
Switzerland	SF 110,000	63,000	113
UK	£ 17,570	42,700	76

Figure 5.2

Country	Personnel director's salary as percentage of chief executive's
Austria	42
Belgium	50
France	52
Germany	51
Holland	54
Italy	54
Portugal	69
Spain	56
Switzerland	52
UK	48

What is important is the effective purchasing power of this salary, ie how much is the net and what can it buy? Quoting data from the same report again, we must first look at the median annual net salary after tax for the same personnel directors (see Figure 5.3).

In order to show how much purchasing power these salaries are worth, if the American personnel director has $37,100 net, the equivalents in other countries adjusted for local cost of living, again in late 1980, is shown in Figure 5.4.

The conclusion from this data is that there is a wide and inconsistent spectrum of rewards for the same job in different countries – and a wide range of differentials between different jobs in the same country. In addition, there is a different structure of salary distribution for the same job between countries.

The detailed analysis has been restricted to salary structures within the developed world. If the analysis is extended to the executive salary market outside

Figure 5.3

Country	Median annual net salary in local currency	Net in $US	Net $US = 100
USA	$ 37,100	37,100	100
Austria	SCH 337,000	24,700	67
Belgium	BF 1,004,000	32,300	87
France	FF 193,900	43,400	117
Germany	DM 61,700	32,000	86
Holland	HFL 59,200	28,200	76
Italy	LIT 24,530,000	26,700	72
Portugal	ESC 592,000	11,300	30
Spain	PTS 2,591,000	33,000	89
Switzerland	SF 84,100	48,100	130
UK	£ 12,360	30,000	81

Figure 5.4

Country	Median purchasing power ($US = 100)
USA	100
Austria	46
Belgium	60
France	84
Germany	60
Holland	52
Italy	59
Portugal	27
Spain	75
Switzerland	87
UK	58

these areas there are more complexities and a marked tendency towards increasing differentials. In other words, in a developed country, the trend of salary as a function of responsibility is usually that shown in Figure 5.5. In undeveloped countries, the relationship is more frequently that of Figure 5.6.
In other words, the senior manager in a developing country will often be paid many times more than middle rank executives – at an accelerating rate, in the developed world there tends to be a diminishing marginal differential.

ONE SALARY STRUCTURE OR MANY?

The company has two choices: giving all expatriates, in a particular country and doing a given job, the same base salary, regardless of origin (which has the merit of simplicity and of relative fairness); or alternatively, relating each nationality to its home country salary levels and providing each with the same relative advantages when working overseas in comparison with working at home, but with different absolute rewards.

Figure 5.5 *Graph showing base salary as a function of level of responsibility in a developed country*

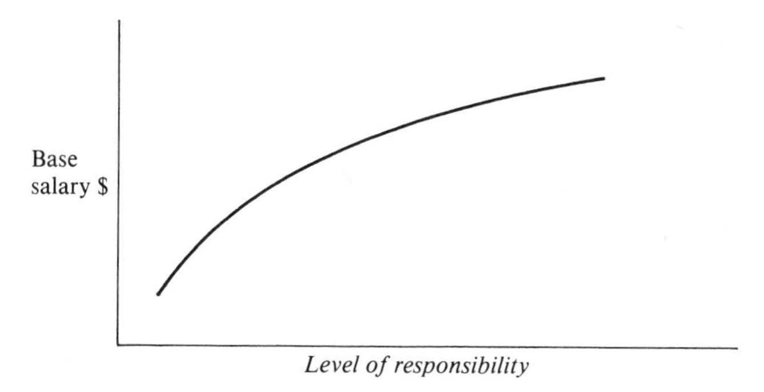

Figure 5.6 *Graph showing base salary as a function of level of responsibility in a developing country*

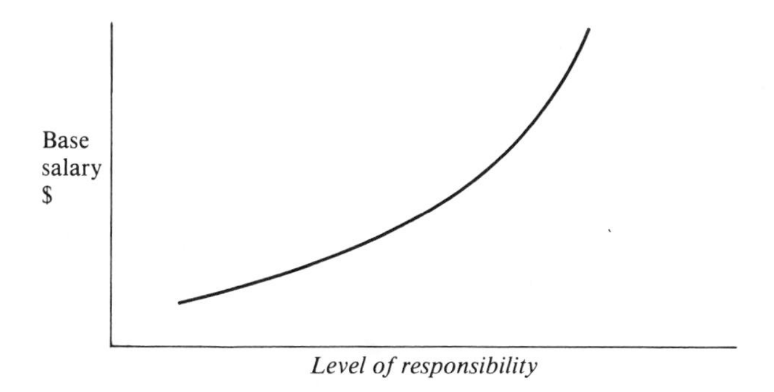

Every possible alternative between these two extremes seems to have been chosen at some time by major international companies. The appropriate response clearly depends on the particular needs of the individual company, its current and projected financial situation and its nationality distribution. Establishing a single international salary structure for all nationalities will cost considerably more for a given nationality mix than, for example, tailoring base salaries to each nationality. Salary levels will have to be set at a level necessary to attract and retain the highest paid nationality and above what is needed to attract and retain the rest. On the other hand, many companies appreciate that paying all nationalities the same rate cements a social cohesiveness which is extremely important overseas. They would find great difficulty explaining to their expatriates differences in pay for the same overseas work. Other companies take the view that, since different nationalities would expect to have different net salaries and purchasing power in their home countries, the same criteria should apply overseas.

Deciding on policy

Without being dogmatic, the following table summarizes the normal base salary strategy chosen by companies in different employment situations:

Type of salary system	Normal situations in which the system could be appropriate
One salary structure based on home country salaries	Expatriates are all or almost all of one nationality
Several different structures based on each individual's home country salaries	Large proportions of a few different nationalities and/or one short expatriate assignment during domestic career
'International salary'	Large number of different nationalities, each a relatively small proportion of total and high degree of international mobility during expatriate career
Host country salary structure	Long-term expatriation in host country

It is also conceivable that no base salary structures exist and a package is put together for expatriates either on an *ad hoc* basis or as a combination of all the approaches which have been listed (only possible with a small number of very senior expatriates). Some budget approaches to the total expatriate package effectively do this, but may be impracticable for large numbers of expatriates.

Where a company has more than one base salary structure, each must be managed separately – albeit within similar salary guidelines. It is not possible, either in theory or practice, to apply the same salary administration programmes to the base salaries of Frenchmen paid in FF, Americans paid in $US and Englishmen paid in £ sterling. As the quoted survey shows, the underlying markets call for major differences in basic salary levels – even if relative relationships are 'correct' at any one particular time they will not necessarily be correct at any other time because of exchange rate and inflation differences.

DESIGNING THE STRUCTURE

The key steps in designing a structure in an expatriate context are no different from those in a domestic environment, ie a company must:

- ○ grade jobs by some process of job evaluation;
- ○ assign a minimum and maximum salary to each grade from salary survey data (typically a 40 to 60 per cent range);
- ○ decide the inter-grade differentials (typically 10 to 20 per cent which may be constant or vary depending upon differences in levels of responsibility in jobs in adjacent grades and impact on expatriate net salaries);

- set up a series of salary administration policies to govern the way in which an individual salary is defined and develops (ie hiring salary policy, merit and promotion increase policy, general salary adjustment/cost of living increase policy);
- set up a system to maintain the structure.

Although management seldom publish salary lists employees often have a very clear idea of what they look like and their own ideas of what others earn. In any event it is what the employees believe rather than the 'facts' which matter. A good, if theoretical, objective could be to have a salary structure so logical and fair it could be published without any controversy.

Without exhaustively considering salary structures in general we look now at one or two of the key concepts which are useful in the administration and control of expatriate base salary structures. The international salary administrator has to concern himself not only with the relativities within the base salary structure but also with those having a direct impact on the rest of the expatriate compensation package. The base salary of a manager in Lagos, in addition to his net salary, discounting relative cost and hardship, needs to be in correct proportion to that of his subordinate in Accra.

PRESENTATION OF DATA

One of the simplest ways is to present graphically the grade ranges or salary brackets on semi-logarithmic graph paper. This allows simple manipulation since a percentage increase appears as a straight line. Figure 5.7 shows a typical structure on which has been plotted the grade mid points and median salaries. Ranges plotted could be those set as the salary brackets or the actual salaries of the job holders (see Figure 5.7).

Another approach is to show, for each grade, a breakdown of the total grade population. This can be as sophisticated as those making use of the data care to make it. Figure 5.8 shows how grade 6 in the above structure could be used to show the number of people in each tenth of the range.

These approaches try to show how the grade range is used, how this changes over a period of time and how merit and promotion policies are established. Statistical measures used are medians and the ratio between mean salary in a grade and grade mid point.

Within a grade population a frequent presentation (often the most effective and logical basis for the relative positioning of individual salaries) is the plotting of salary against experience.

Time can be measured by: years of company service, years in the grade, years of professional experience and even in terms of the age of the individual. This type of plotting should be used to identify different groups of people as shown in Figure 5.9 which shows clearly the salaries which are out of line.

Many companies find that this kind of representation is a key tool in salary management. This kind of graph can be shown to an individual to demonstrate and explain where he is located in the structure by comparison with other people.

Figure 5.7 *Example of a company base salary structure showing grade ranges*

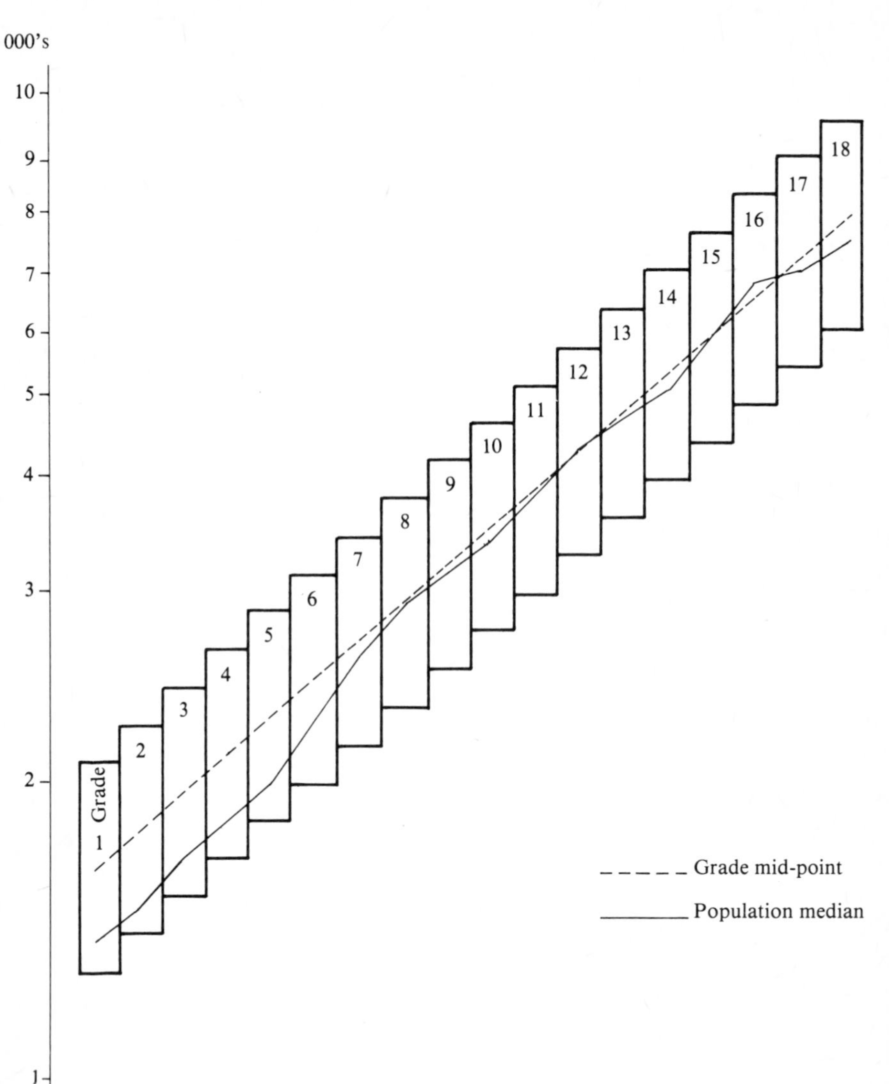

GENERAL BASE SALARY ADJUSTMENTS

Most, though not all, companies apply the results of a salary survey, compensate for the eroding of the value of the currency in which the salary is paid, or compensate for inflation by increasing all base salaries in a general adjustment. Some companies, however, prefer to use the merit increase mechanism and not apply any general adjustment.

Figure 5.8 *Breakdown of total grade population by one grade*

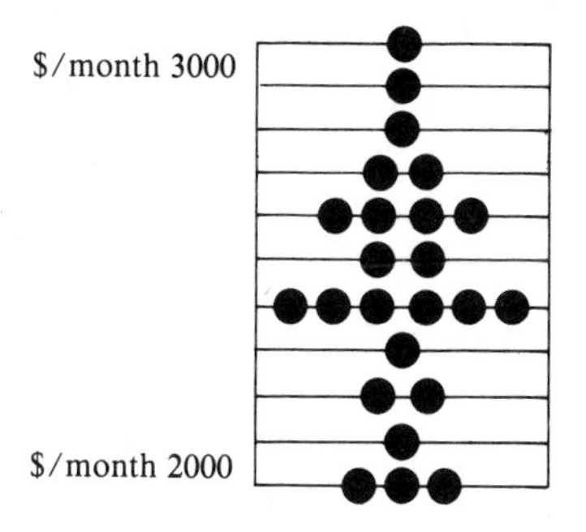

Figure 5.9 *Salary ranges expressed as a function of time, experience and age*

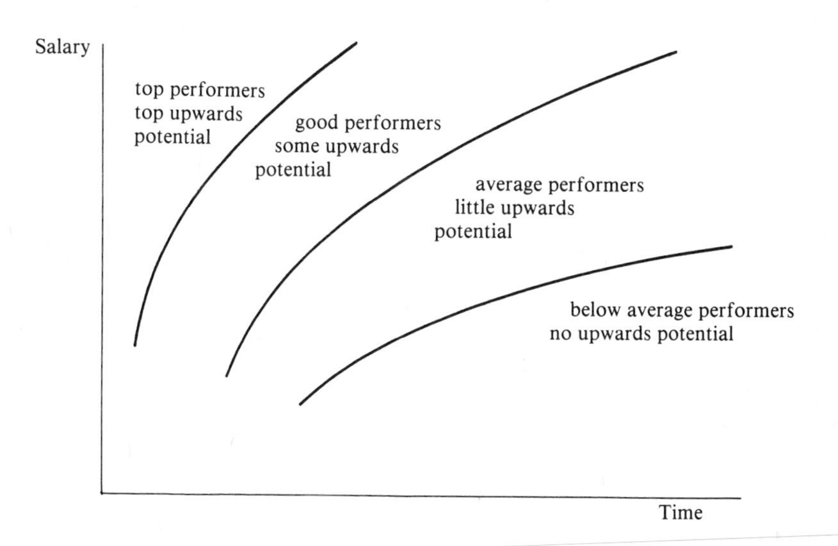

Typical general salary increases are applied as either:

- a percentage increase – eg 10 per cent of base salary;
- a percentage increase with a ceiling – eg 10 per cent of base salary with a maximum increase of $4500 per year;
- a percentage increase with a 'knee' and a ceiling – eg 10 per cent of the first $30,000 per year of base salary, 5 per cent of the next $30,000 per year with a maximum increase of $4500 per year.

Often individuals whose salaries are above the maximum of the grade (for historical or other reasons) receive zero general salary adjustment (GSA). This has the effect of rapidly restoring them to the level of the rest of the population in a painless way.

Inflation can, and indeed should, be used by the salary administrator as an excellent tool to correct the relative positions of individual salaries.

The entire structure (grade by grade) should be raised by whatever is the basic percentage of the general salary adjustment. If this is not done, the logic of the structure and the pattern of differentials within it can soon be destroyed.

When inflation begins to move beyond 10 per cent per year, either nationally or as a measure of worldwide inflation, it becomes essential to maintain the dynamism of the salary structure, consistent with the employer's ability to pay. The greater the rate of inflation, the more difficult it is to maintain a policy of no general adjustment, and the greater the level of general adjustment, the more difficult it is to have a meaningful merit policy.

In the expatriate context, much of the cost of living element normal in a domestic GSA is often absorbed by the local cost of living compensation. However, the deterioration in the exchange rate of the currency in which the base salary is denominated can have a very serious impact and require substantial adjustments. Many companies with a base salary structure denominated in $US and set at levels which were appropriate in a US context, experienced major problems, during the last period of weakness of the $US (1978-80) in recruiting and retaining non-American expatriates. On the other hand, correcting base salaries for currency weakness can lead to problems later when the currency strengthens (eg $US in 1982).

MERIT INCREASES

Most companies have a merit increase programme by which above average performers are rewarded with individual salary increases. The amount and frequency of the increases are given as a function of performance. Some companies make these increases at the same time as a general salary adjustment, others do not adjust salaries on a general basis and give only a merit increase. Where there is a merit programme, it should be separately identified and an employee must be clearly aware of how much of his salary increase results from his own performance. However, in an international context other increases in net (because of a geographical move or review of allowances) may be far more significant.

In general, the higher the level of the job in the hierarchy, the greater the impact the job holder can have on the results of the organization. So, it is not surprising to discover that, with the application of ceilings on general salary adjustments, merit increases play an increasingly important role as a function of salary. Consider a company which gives a 10 per cent general increase with a maximum increase of $4000 per year. The effective increase is shown in Figure 5.10 – we have imagined that people above $80,000 per year base salary are excluded from a general increase.

Clearly, the average individual at a base salary of $60,000 needs at least a 2.5 per cent merit increase if he is to retain the same relativity within the structure. To the extent that merit increases for higher paid people do not compensate for the shaded areas in the graph, compression occurs in the salary structure. This compression creates serious problems in providing a proper differential between an individual and his staff. Even for good performers with high salaries, experience suggests that senior management have great difficulty in giving the size of merit increases necessary to reward employees properly in times of high inflation and where ceilings on general increases are in existence.

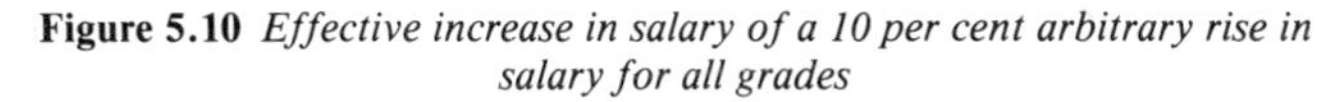

Figure 5.10 *Effective increase in salary of a 10 per cent arbitrary rise in salary for all grades*

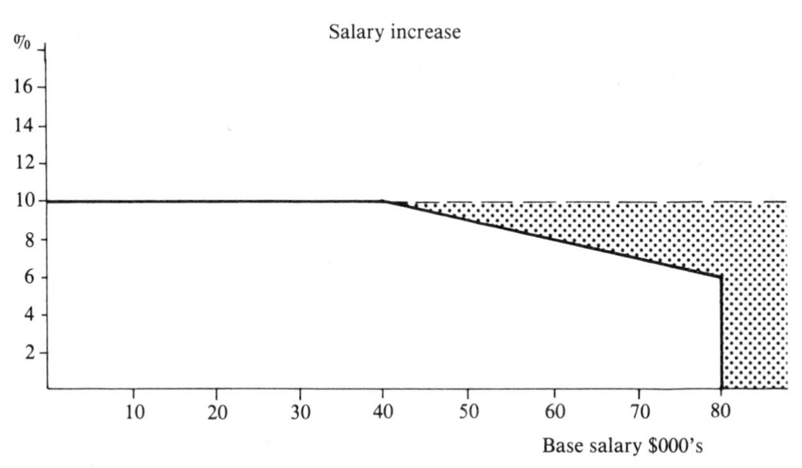

A typical approach for a given group of employees is to decide a percentage of payroll that is to be distributed as a merit increase. In a company which gives the group a general salary adjustment, this could normally be around 4 to 5 per cent in times of inflation at a 'normal' level. If a ceiling was applied to the general salary adjustment, such as in the present package, the merit increase amounts could be modulated for different groups as follows:

Group A $ up to 40,000	adjustment 10 per cent	merit 4 per cent
Group B $ 40,000 to 60,000	adjustment 8 per cent	average merit 6 per cent
Group C % over 80,000	adjustment zero	merit 14 per cent

A merit increase of 4 per cent of payroll of the group would typically be allocated as follows: increases granted to up to 60 per cent of the population; maximum increase 12 per cent, minimum increase 4 per cent. In the example above, for group B and C up to 100 per cent of the population might receive a merit increase. This is illustrated in Figure 5.11.

Normally, the merit increases for each individual are fixed as a function of his performance and position relative to the others in his grade, using the salary plot previously discussed. Salaries are not raised above the maximum or outside the bounds of the performance/potential group to which the individual belongs.

Another approach, frequently used, relates merit and all general salary increases to position in the salary bracket and performance. This one constructs a matrix as follows: the higher the performance and the lower the salary, the larger the increase.

Figure 5.11 *Effective increase in salary as a result of a specific merit related increase*

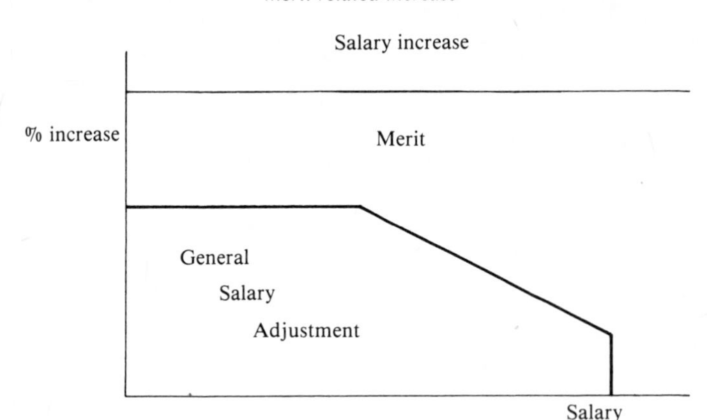

Figure 5.12

		Performance in the job			
		Outstanding	**Above average**	**Average**	**Below average**
Position in salary bracket	Top quartile	8	4	0	0
	Third quartile	10	6	0	0
	Second quartile	12	8	4	0
	Below quartile	14	10	6	0

Clearly, by multiplying the amount in each cell by the number of people in each cell, the cost of the increase is arrived at quite simply. It is easy to do this with a decent personnel statistics EDP system. The company then merely decides how much it wants to give as an increase and the salary administrator works back through the statistics to arrive at a percentage increase for each cell. If the distribution of performance ratings is forced, the approach is much easier. Whatever method has been used to generate merit increases, their internal logic should be checked using this sort of grid.

All these considerations apply equally to domestic and international base salary structures. However, without careful controls on merit increases, there might be a temptation for managers to use them to compensate for changes in expatriate living conditions which are unconnected with job performance. Not only does a merit increase remain with the employee for ever, but the criteria of consistency in the base salary structure is rapidly lost.

CONCLUSION

We have outlined the major practical and theoretical problems involved in constructing a logical and consistent base salary policy for an MNC. As a function of the countries of assignment, countries of recruitment, number of nationalities, duration of assignment and type of career, the policy needs to be clearly formulated. A well organized base salary policy is an important tool in any organization that wants to ensure that the relative rewards of its people are in direct relation to the jobs they do and how they do them rather than in some arbitrary way. It is only from the basis of a logical and accepted base salary structure that expatriate premiums, and thus the whole expatriate package, can be constructed.

REFERENCES – books covering basic salary administration concepts

Armstrong, M, *A Handbook of Salary Administration*, Kogan Page, 1980.
Henderson, Richard I, *Compensation Management*, Prentice-Hall, 1979.
Rock, Milton (editor), *Handbook of Wage and Salary Administration*, McGraw-Hill, 1972.

6. Overseas premiums

Once a company has decided what base salary structures it wishes to adopt for its expatriates the next step in building up a total remuneration package is to introduce the concept of overseas premiums. This practice is universal on the basis that some compensation is required for the disruption of moving and separation from the home environment. Following on from this, companies usually recognize degrees of difficulty likely to be encountered in the host country and introduce some element of cost protection against price differentials that the expatriate faces in his new environment.

In this chapter each type of premium is examined in turn and the problems commonly encountered are analysed.

INCENTIVE TO WORK OVERSEAS AND HARDSHIP COMPENSATION

An incentive to work overseas rests on the assumption that this is more difficult and/or less pleasant than employment in one's own country. As expatriates are frequently a self-selected group this premise may often seem rather dubious, as they may prefer an expatriate lifestyle to their own domestic environment. However, giving a form of incentive is virtually universal practice although it is defined in different ways. These are three methods of payment:

- fixed rate;
- banding;
- two dimensional.

Fixed rate

A fixed rate system of payment implies that one level of payment is made to encompass incentive and hardship premiums. This may take the form of a percentage of base salary or a lump sum amount. In either case it is paid to all expatriates going overseas and is usually termed a foreign service incentive. This is a simple system which can be adopted easily in a situation where all expatriates come from one country of origin and go to countries which generally have similar working and living conditions. An American company, for example, will often pay one incentive rate for its expatriates working in Western Europe. Frequently, if the incentive is based on a percentage of salary rather than a fixed sum, the applicable base salary will have a ceiling, so that the incentive will only apply to a limited proportion of salary, eg the first $3000 of a monthly salary. One company calculates the average salary of all its expatriates and applies all its premiums to the dollar amount corresponding to that salary. It is difficult to give a precise range of expatriate incentives but 10 to 15 per cent is commonly used for expatriation between the USA and Western Europe. Some organizations pay the expatriate a fixed incentive on a limited time basis, expiring if he stays for longer than three or four years.

The advantage of all fixed rate premiums is their simplicity. The limitation is that they do not distinguish between different environments, and therefore run the risk of offering minimal incentives in some locations and too much in others. By offering a fixed rate foreign service premium for most locations, with a special hardship bonus for exceptional cases, limitations can be overcome. For example:

> All employees receive 15 per cent addition to salary up to a ceiling of $3000 per month as an expatriation incentive. Employees in the following locations receive a further $700 'special hardship bonus' – Nigeria, San Salvador, Libya.

This type of arrangement allows for a simple system which can be slightly more flexible where conditions are arduous.

Banding

The concept of banding is to group expatriate locations on a scale of hardship and make appropriate incentive payments in each case. There will be a base level, for expatriation itself, which is likely to begin at a 10 per cent premium. After this point incentives increase for the level of hardship encountered. The problem is that hardship is a very subjective consideration – no two people will agree on what constitutes hardship. It could be a matter of:

- Working conditions
- Security
- Climate
- Scarcity of goods
- Social contacts
- Recreational facilities
- Availability of schools
- Type and availability of food
- Health standards and medical facilities
- Cultural environment
- Political stability.

A company has three main types of approach to arrive at an effective system:

- Management decision
- Consultancy and government assessments
- Employee participation.

Management decision

A direct method of decision making concerning hardship is for management to make its own review and decision. A common way of doing this is to convene a committee of senior managers, each year, to evaluate any major changes in each of the expatriate locations. The disadvantage is that judgements are by definition associated with the management view of any location and therefore subject to criticism by expatriate employees. If the organization is decentralized there is scope to allow the decision making to be taken by regional staff ensuring views that might reflect those of the expatriate population. An upward drift of hardship ratings can be avoided by making certain that the average premium value is no higher than one stated figure. Since the application of this approach is arbitrary the mechanism for change and the logic of the structure may be unclear to employees.

Consultancy and government assessments

Consultancies undertake a considerable amount of work in defining cost of living allowances for multi-national companies. Many also undertake evaluation of hardship in expatriate locations. A consultancy will usually take a sample of representative employees on assignment at each location and then construct a desirability rating for each location. Comparing this rating for a number of locations allows a ranking to be built up. The following are examples of two such tables taken from the 1982 *MICA* report.

Figure 6.1 *1982 MICA report on hardship in Saudi Arabia*

	1	2	3	4	5
Expatriate working conditions			●		
Standard of personal living accommodation			●		
Year-round weather – for normal living				●	
– for recreation				●	
Social contacts – with nationals					●
Social contacts – with expatriate community			●		
Recreational facilities				●	
Food standards			●		
Food availability			●		
Health standards				●	
Personal security			●		
Mobility (moving around, getting away)				●	
Local educational facilities					●
Cultural environment (theatre, museums, etc)					●

Key: 1 = Excellent; 2 = Good; 3 = Satisfactory; 4 = Fair; 5 = Bad

Figure 6.2 *1982 MICA report on hardship in Geneva*

	1	2	3	4	5
Expatriate working conditions	●				
Standard of personal living accommodation		●			
Year-round weather – for normal living		●			
– for recreation	●				
Social contacts – with nationals		●			
Social contacts – with expatriate community	●				
Recreational facilities	●				
Food standards	●				
Food availability	●				
Health standards	●				
Personal security	●				
Mobility (moving around, getting away)	●				
Local educational facilities		●			
Cultural environment (theatre, museums, etc)		●			

Key: 1 = Excellent; 2 = Good; 3 = Satisfactory; 4 = Fair; 5 = Bad

Similar exercises are also undertaken by the US Department of State for its expatriate employees, and these results are used by a number of multi-national companies employing predominantly American expatriates.

The following are extracts from the US government regulations which explains their approach:

US foreign post differentials

'A post differential may be granted to US government employees working abroad on the basis of conditions of environment which differ substantially from conditions of environment in the United States, and warrant additional pay as a recruitment and retention incentive. A post differential may not exceed 25 per cent of the rate of basic pay.

'The setting of differential rates is an important morale and income factor at approximately half the foreign service posts, and is a significant expense for all US government agencies with civilian employees in foreign areas. In order that the system may accurately measure hardship, periodic reviews are conducted biannually. In the case of emergency situations, reviews are made as often as seem appropriate.

'Information is taken from post differential questionnaires completed at the post which describes environmental conditions there. Additionally, reports, intelligence data and the public media are used. Environmental conditions are divided into: *isolation, climate and housing, food, education, importation, recreation, community facilities, altitude, natural hazards, sanitation and disease, medical and hospital facilities, political violence and crime and harassment*. These categories are subdivided into about 124 factors which are given point weights, the sum of which, given to each post, determines the differential classification on an increasing scale up to the 25 per cent of basic salary legal maximum. The point weights are applied by the allowances staff in accordance with established evaluation standards. The appropriate rate is found and, if an increase or decrease from the existing rate is indicated, the assistant secretary of administration makes the final decision.

'After review of the subject, increased attention was given to aspects of isolation. However, altitude was given less emphasis and disease assessment was made more specific in relation to the actual effect on American employees. More detailed analysis is now made concerning medical, dental and hospital facilities. Housing factors are restructured to give greater recognition of the conditions under which employees of military agencies may live. Increased recognition is given to the lack of suitable local education facilities. Political violence, economic crime, and various forms of harassment are analysed in greater depth than before.

'The Department determined that 10 per cent should continue to be the minimum level of differential and that the succeeding levels should continue at 15, 20 and 25 per cent as previously rather than at narrower point gradations.

'It should be noted from the above that under departmental determinations the foreign post must accrue points warranting at least the minimum differential of 10 per cent of basic pay. The maximum differential is 25 per cent.'

Employee participation

A company may not wish to take 'off the shelf' evaluations of hardship and at the same time may wish to maximize the participation of the employees involved. If this is desired, one approach that can be used is similar to the methodology of a job evaluation by paired comparisons; for example, a company that wants to decide hardship premiums in locations in Africa. It does not want many levels of premiums as this could be difficult to administer and perhaps it wishes the premium to range between 10 per cent and 70 per cent of base salary.

Africa premiums

A group of five experienced expatriates is convened to consider each location. If necessary a presentation is made on the location reminding the group of climatic conditions, housing, transport, social facilities and other conditions. Ideally the group members should have visited each location personally, if they have not worked in some or all of the locations being considered, and should come from different levels in the organization.

It is made clear that the cost of commodities should not be taken into account as these will be considered separately. The objective of the group is to generate an overall ranking of hardship which is acceptable to each of the individual members. The chosen method is to make a direct comparison between the locations comparing one against another on a basis of greater or lesser hardship. Thus if the locations to be considered are the following: Muanda (Zaire); Warri, Port Harcourt (Nigeria); Algiers, Hassi Messaoud (Algeria); Luanda, Cabinda, Soyo (Angola); Port Gentil, Libreville (Gabon); Douala (Cameroon); Pointe Noire (Congo); Tunis, Sfax (Tunisia); Abidjan (Ivory Coast), the comparison is then reduced to a series of direct judgements presented as shown:

Muanda		Warri	
Warri		Port Harcourt	
Port Harcourt		Lagos	
Lagos		Algiers	

and so on

If, as in this case, there are 16 locations this creates:

$$\frac{16 \times 15}{2} = 120 \text{ pairs}$$

This enables every location to be compared with each other. Scoring two points for less hardship (better), zero for worse and one for equal, a ranking table is constructed (in the same way as a football league table). The completed ranking is done by each member of the group comparing each location against each other location ie in this case 5 x 120 = 600 judgements. The scores for each location are summed up for all five judges and a complete ranking is obtained as shown below:

Location	*Points*
Soyo	20
Muanda	24
Cabinda	29
Warri	37
Hassi Messaoud	57
Luanda	61
Port Harcourt	80
Lagos	82
Pointe Noire	90
Port Gentil	92
Douala	96
Libreville	96
Algiers	105
Abidjan	105
Sfax	110
Tunis	116

Detailed comparisons between the judgement of different group members can identify the degree of consistency and resolve any differences.

The next stage is to plot these scores on a chart and attempt to group the locations into a number of bands. In this case the bands were:

- Very tough
- Tough
- Normal
- Good
- Expatriate minimum

Figure 6.3 *Hardship rankings for a sample of 16 African countries*

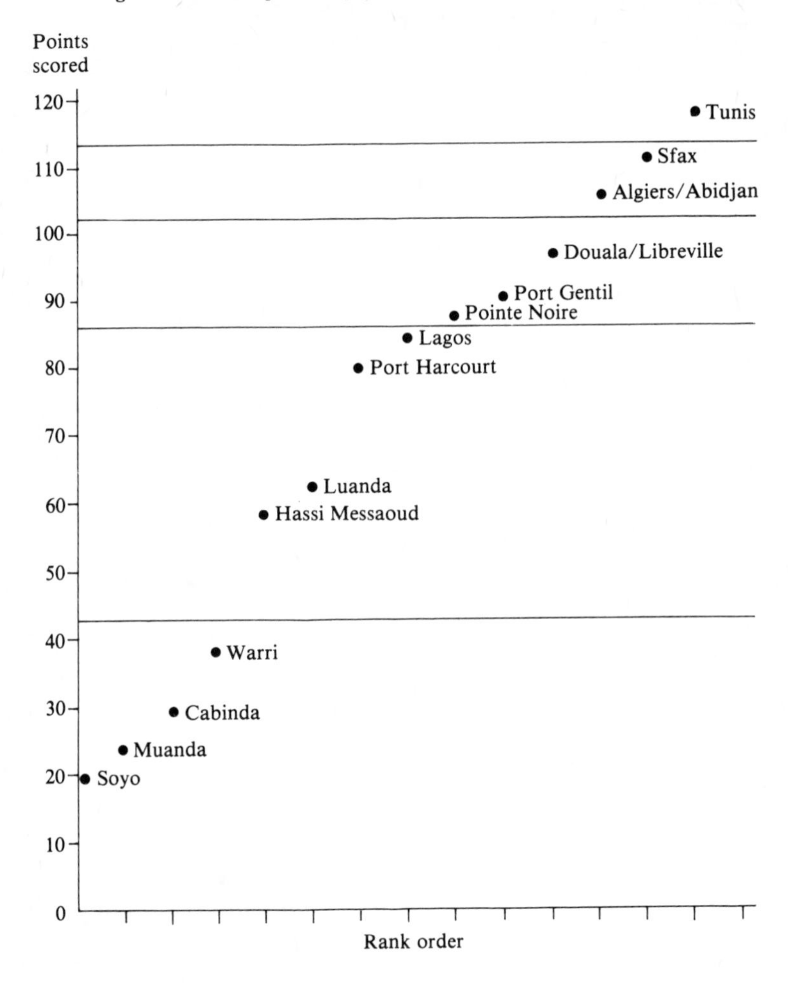

The premiums for the five bands in this case were:

Very tough	70 per cent
Tough	55 per cent
Normal	40 per cent
Good	25 per cent
Expatriate minimum	10 per cent

This type of system, although very simple, allows a consistent ranking to emerge even with a large number of locations and group members, provided that sufficient information is given and that the number of 'draws' is minimized.

The personnel manager will recognize that this process is identical to that of job evaluation using paired comparisons and that the end result could be obtained by applying any of the existing job evaluation techniques (of which the most common in this context is classification). A number of bands of hardship premium are decided and locations slotted into the appropriate band according to the chosen criteria.

GROUPED RESULTS

Many companies operating in a number of expatriate locations do use some form of grouping to arrive at a scale for hardship. Even where these locations are the same there is no consensus on what that hardship represents. This may be because the cross section of the expatriate population varies among the companies, and no two organizations have identical work and living conditions. To illustrate this point we show below a selection of premiums at present using three independent divisions of the *same* multi-national company:

Division A

	Foreign service premiums
○ Country of origin	zero
○ Algiers, Europe, North America	25 per cent
○ Singapore, Rio, Mexico	35 per cent
○ Nigeria, Gabon	45 per cent
○ All other countries	55 per cent

Division B

Foreign service incentive

Location	**Premium** %
○ France (except Paris), UK, Australia	15
○ Italy, Holland, Morocco, Tunis, Spain, France (Paris), Piedras Negras, Aruba	20
○ Reynose, Norway, Barbados, Germany, Santa Cruz, Punta Arenas, Quito, Bogota, Singapore, Philippines	25
○ Brunei, Taiwan, Rio de Janeiro, Sao Paulo, Buenos Aires, Guayaquil, Salvador, Trinidad, Mendoza, Mexico City, Aracaju, Natal, Macae, Neuquen	30
○ Sfax, Bangkok, Jakarta, Dubai, Sharjah, Jordan, Venezuela (except Morichal), Comodoro Rivadavia, Los Organos, Talara, Duri, Lima	35
○ Plaza Huincul, Belem, Poza Rica, Camiri, Abu Dhabi, Oman, Kuwait, Catu, Monclova	40
○ Villa Hermoza, Morichal, Algiers, India, Pakistan, Indonesia (except) Jakarta, Duri), Egypt (except Abu Rudeis)	45
○ San Mateus, Manaus, Catriel, Malargue, Ivory Coast, Rio Gallegos, Coatzacoalcos, Guatemala, Canadon Seco	50
○ Japan, Al Khobar	55
○ Congo, Lagos, Abu Rudeis, Cameroon, Saudi Arabia	60

○ Gabon	65
○ Iraq, Nigeria (except Lagos), Zaire, Angola, Libya	70

Division C
(Asia only)

Location	**Premium** %
○ Australia New Zealand Philippines Singapore Thailand (Bangkok)	35
○ Bahrain, Brunei Dubai Indonesia (Jakarta, Medan) Japan Korea Malaysia Taiwan (except Miaoli), Thailand (except Bangkok)	46
○ Bangladesh, Burma China Egypt, Ethiopia India, Indonesia (except Jakarta, Medan), Iran, Iraq Jordan Kuwait Papua New Guinea Oman Pakistan Qatar Somalia, Sudan, Syria, Saudi Arabia (Khobar) Taiwan (Miaoli), Turkey United Arab Emirates (except Dubai) Yemen	60
○ Saudi Arabia (except Khobar)	70

RANGE AND CEILING

In the examples shown, the premium for expatriation, excluding cost considerations have ranged from 20 per cent to 70 per cent of base salary. Such ranges are representative of most companies employing expatriates and in the final analysis are arrived at by the test of retention of staff in these locations. As was mentioned briefly in an earlier paragraph, premiums for expatriation are rarely applied to total salary without an upper limit. The most common form of limitation is to fix a ceiling; salaries above this ceiling do not carry any premium.

Another approach is to offer a reduced premium range for staff above a certain status level. For example:

Divisional managers foreign service premiums

France, UK, Singapore, Mexico, Brazil, Argentina, Holland, Peru	1.00
Indonesia, Dubai, Algeria, Abu Dhabi, Venezuela	1.10
Gabon, Nigeria, Saudi Arabia	1.20
Libya, Angola	1.30

The problem of offering lower premiums for senior staff is that it can frequently result in distorted (ie excessive) base salaries in order to make it attractive for a junior manager to be promoted to more senior levels. Unfortunately the two tier premium system probably creates more problems than it solves.

TWO DIMENSIONAL APPROACH

In the previous examples it has been assumed that premiums have been administered on the same basis regardless of the country of origin of the expatriate. Although many companies adopt this approach on the basis that most of their staff are of one nationality, or that any other approach is too complex, some organizations do try to introduce the concept of two dimensions to their foreign service premiums.

This approach is based on the theory that hardship is subjective, therefore it is not possible to make a judgement without taking account of the individual's own cultural background. In specific terms, a European moving to another European country or a South American moving to another South American country will not experience the same degree of difficulty as if they moved between continents. Alternatively, should an Indonesian moving to Aberdeen not receive an incentive similar to a Briton who works in Indonesia? Logically this might seem appropriate; the difficulty is to produce a workable system. A concept of 'cultural zones' has to be established where movement within the zones carries a relatively low premium. Moving outside your cultural zone attracts an appreciably higher incentive payment. As a result a Ghanaian moving to Nigeria may not receive as high a premium as he would have being transferred to France. The Ghanaian in France would receive a higher premium than the Belgian in France, and conversely the Belgian would receive a higher premium than the Ghanaian in Nigeria.

In commonsense terms cultural zones could be established as follows:

- Europe, North America, Australasia
- South America
- Africa (excluding South Africa)
- Arabic countries
- Asian countries (excluding Australia)
- Soviet Union (including the Eastern Bloc).

Such zones contain within them many anomalies. There exists, for example, the language problems within Europe, tribal and racial differences in Africa and Asia, and many other practical complexities. Nevertheless the concept is applied in some companies. This method does of course lead to different levels of remuneration for different nationalities doing the same job in the same overseas location.

Most organizations are widening their recruiting scope. Although their foreign service premiums are biased towards a North American or European base, in the long term the lifestyle differences between expatriates of different nationalities tend to disappear. Thus one single pattern of premiums is probably all that is needed.

COST OF LIVING

Previously, premiums have been considered in terms of incentive for expatriation and financial compensation for hardship encountered in the host country. This is only half of the picture. The other half of a company's responsibility is to compensate the expatriate for excess costs he and his family might encounter in the expatriate country. This is achieved by arriving at some sort of cost of living allowance (COLA) which can be added to the salary of the expatriate. If the host location is substantially cheaper than the expatriate's home base there could be a deduction, although this practice is rarely applied by companies ie the minimum COLA is zero.

The idea of a COLA is relatively simple but its application can involve some complicated calculations. It is an area in which many international companies spend a great deal of time and money and in which many specialist companies are highly active. It may be that the expense and time concentrated on this particular area of expatriate compensation is out of all proportion to its importance in the total package. There are four main concepts which need to be addressed:

- One or many points of origin
- Spendable income
- Arriving at a COLA system
- Maintaining a COLA system.

One or many points of origin

If a company selects its expatriates from one country, the calculation of a COLA is more straightforward. The simplest example would be if expatriates of the same nationality were going to the same host country. In this case the problem is to decide the cost differential between the two locations using whatever basket of goods is considered appropriate. Even in this situation prices and costs may range considerably inside one country, so that a common geographical location must be chosen with care. In cases where only a few expatriates come from other countries of origin it is still more effective to use one country of origin for the basis of costing. A choice has to be made between a COLA that uses a 'neutral' point of origin for all COLA differences, or one that takes into account the individual's origin each time the calculation is undertaken. To a major extent the decision will depend on the base salary assumptions. If a company uses an 'international' base salary structure there will be no obvious logic to calculate each COLA. However, if the base salary is fixed in the home country, then the logic will be to compare relative costs of living between that country and the host country.

Figure 6.4 illustrates a straightforward cost of living differential approach taken by the US State Department, intended for cost of living adjustments for American expatriates (which was used in the 1978 and 1979 IRS taxation of Americans overseas).

The 'one point of origin' approach, whilst highly effective for a homogeneous group of employees has a number of inconsistencies in other situations. For the multi-national with many expatriates of different nationalities a more sophisticated method is required.

Spendable income and discretionary income

Fundamental to a sophisticated method of calculating COLA with many points of origin is the concept of spendable income. The expatriate may not spend all his income in the host country and, moreover, the compensation package will often take care of such factors as tax and accommodation. Thus the increase (or decrease) in the cost of everyday living in the host country is only relevant to that proportion of income that is actually used in the host country. Naturally no organization can define exactly any individual's precise expenditure pattern, but most companies employing a number of expatriates do make some general assumptions.

The most direct method is to pay a cost of living allowance which only applies to, for example, the first $2500 of monthly salary, on the assumption that this is, roughly, the proportion of income used in the host country. A more detailed approach is to assemble a spendable income chart for the company's employees. This is done by taking each nationality and establishing a 'normal expenditure' pattern for each particular family size and level of income. The amount of statistical detail required is a decision for each company, as a point is soon reached where the effort spent on refining the information outweighs its value.

Spendable income is the portion of salary which, in the home location, is used for everyday living. It usually excludes income taxes, social security, pensions and insurance, together with what is usually described as discretionary expenditure. This, in broad terms, is the amount remaining of the base home country income after meeting the requirements of day to day living in the home country environment. Discretionary income is used for major purchases, holidays or saving. The level of discretionary income varies considerably from country to country depending on the relative wealth of that country, the tax structure and the particular income bracket.

From the use of government statistics or information from consultants a spendable income chart can be produced (see Figure 6.5). Whatever the country, the shape of the spendable income curve is largely similar (although it will be shifted up or down depending on family size) ie a progressively smaller propor-

Figure 6.4 *1980 qualified cost of living differentials by geographical area*

'Find the group code that applies to your geographic area and refer to Figure 6.5 for the cost-of-living differential for that group code, except group code X where no index is available from the State Department.'

Country	Group code	Country	Group code	Country	Group code	Country	Group code
Afghanistan	A	Egypt	B	Liechtenstein	M	San Marino	F
Albania	X	El Salvador	B	Luxembourg	K	Sao Tome & Principe	H
Algeria	H	Equatorial Guinea	B	Macao	D	Saudi Arabia	J
Andorra	J	Ethiopia	F	Madagascar	J	Senegal	K
Angola	B	Fiji	D	Malawi	F	Seychelles	G
Antigua	B	Finland	K	Malaysia	F	Sierra Leone	I
Argentina	K	France	M	Maldives	A	Singapore	D
Australia	F	French West Indies	K	Mali	L	Solomon Islands	A
Austria	L	Gabon	N	Malta	D	Somalia	J
Bahamas	G	Gambia	J	Mauritania	N	South Africa	A
Bahrain	J	Germany E.	L	Mauritius	D	Spain	E
Bangladesh	C	Germany W.	L	Mexico	A	Sri Lanka	A
Barbados	D	Ghana	L	Monaco	L	Sudan	F
Belgium	L	Greece	A	Mongolia	A	Surinam	F
Belize	A	Grenada	B	Montserrat	C	Swaziland	B
Benin	K	Guatemala	B	Morocco	H	Sweden	M
Bermuda	F	Guinea	I	Mozambique	C	Switzerland	M
Bhutan	A	Guinea-Bissau	H	Namibia	A	Syria	C
Bolivia	C	Guyana	C	Nauru	X	Taiwan	B
Botswana	B	Haiti	E	Nepal	A	Tanzania	E
Brazil	A	Honduras	A	Netherlands	K	Thailand	B
British Virgin Is.	B	Hong Kong	D	Neth. Antilles	D	Togo	K
Brunei	D	Hungary	A	New Caledonia	I	Tonga	A
Bulgaria	H	Iceland	K	New Hebrides	A	Trinidad & Tobago	D
Burma	E	India	A	New Zealand	D	Tr. Terr. of Pac. Is.	A

Country	Group code	Country	Group code	Country	Group code	Country	Group code
Burundi	K	Indonesia	E	Nicaragua	A	Tunisia	G
Cameroon	L	Iran	X	Niger	N	Turkey	A
Canada	B	Iraq	E	Nigeria	M	Turks & Caicos Is.	A
Cape Verde	F	Ireland	F	Norway	L	Tuvalu	A
Cayman Is.	F	Israel	F	Oman	J	Uganda	K
Central Afr. Rep.	M	Italy	F	Pakistan	A	United Arab Emirates	J
Chad	X	Ivory Coast	N	Panama	B	United Kingdom	K
Chile	H	Jamaica	C	Papua New Guinea	I	Upper Volta	L
China	B	Japan	L	Paraguay	E	Uruguay	G
Colombia	A	Jordan	G	Peru	A	USSR	I
Comoros	H	Kampuchea	X	Philippines	A	Vatican City	F
Congo	K	Kenya	E	Poland	A	Venezuela	I
Costa Rica	C	Kiribati	A	Portugal	C	Vietnam	X
Cuba	E	Korea N.	X	Qatar	K	Western Samoa	A
Cyprus	C	Korea S.	J	Romania	A	Yemen (Aden)	A
Czechoslovakia	D	Kuwait	I	Rwanda	I	Yemen (Sana)	H
Denmark	L	Laos	A	St Kitts-Nevis	A	Yugoslavia	A
Djibouti	H	Lebanon	C	St Lucia	A	Zaire	R
Dominica	B	Lesotho	A	St Vincent and		Zambia	J
Dominican Republic	A	Liberia	I	the Grenadines	A	Zimbabwe	X
Ecuador	A	Libya	I				

Figure 6.5 *Cost of living differentials by family size*

Group code	Family size (number of persons)					
	1	2	3	4	5	6 or more
A and B	No cost-of-living differential allowed					
C	400	500	600	700	700	800
D	900	1,100	1,300	1,400	1,500	1,600
E	1,400	1,600	2,000	2,200	2,200	2,400
F	1,800	2,200	2,600	2,900	3,000	3,200
G	2,300	2,700	3,300	3,600	3,700	4,000
H	2,700	3,300	4,000	4,300	4,500	4,800
I	3,400	4,000	4,900	5,300	5,500	5,900
J	4,100	4,900	5,900	6,500	6,700	7,200
K	5,000	6,000	7,300	7,900	8,200	8,800
L	5,900	7,100	8,600	9,400	9,700	10,400
M	6,900	8,100	9,900	10,800	11,300	12,000
N	7,800	9,200	11,200	12,300	12,800	13,500
O	8,700	10,300	12,500	13,700	14,300	15,100
P	9,600	11,400	13,900	15,200	15,800	16,700
Q	10,500	12,500	15,200	16,600	17,300	18,300
R	11,400	13,600	16,500	18,100	18,800	19,900

Source: Copyright © 1980 by The Bureau of National Affairs, Inc., Washington, DC 20037

tion of gross salary is spent on daily essentials and therefore an equivalent and increasing proportion becomes discretionary spending.

Figure 6.6 *Spendable income chart – Italy*

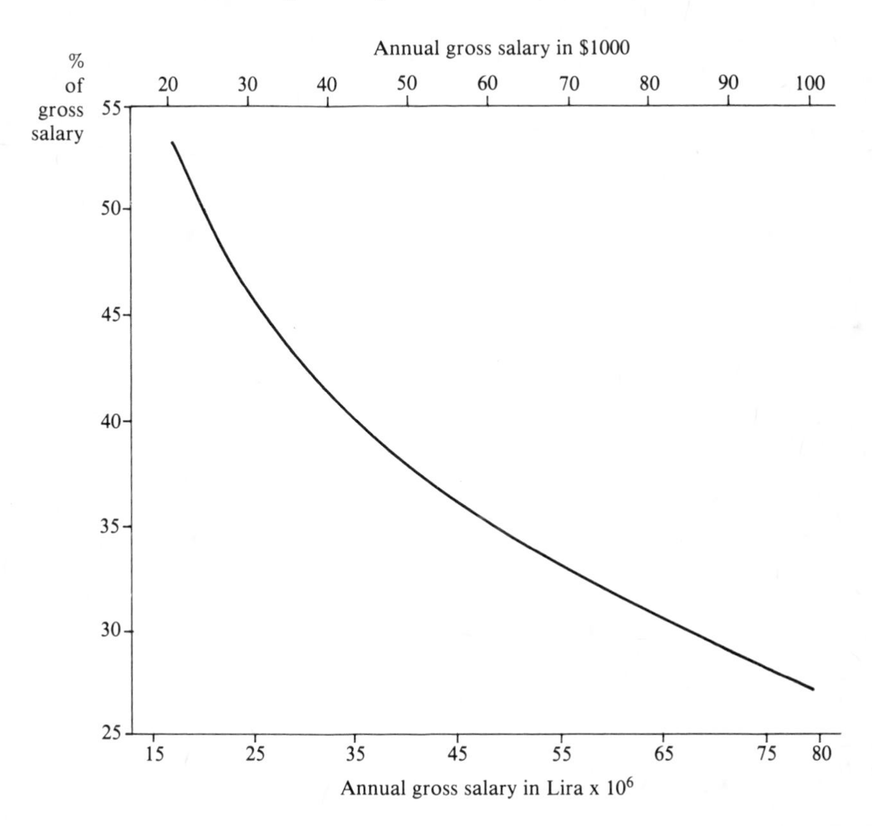

In this example an Italian executive married with two children and earning 32 million lire per year will have 41 per cent of his salary as spendable income. If he earns 80 million lire per year he will use only 26 per cent of his salary as spendable income. (The equivalent figures for an American executive are 43 per cent and 27 per cent.)

Taking as an example a married US employee with two children, to arrive at spendable income the following elements are separately identified:

- personal income tax (assuming a separate tax equalization policy);
- employee contributions to social security, pension plans, insurance and medical plans in the USA;
- personal accommodation and utilities (assuming a separate policy);
- discretionary spending:
  - savings and investments
  - vacation and holiday costs

– major purchases
– charitable contributions.

This can also be shown in graphical form (see Figure 6.7).

Figure 6.7 *1981 US income breakdown for a married expatriate with two children*

Gross salary:
(a) $30,000 pa

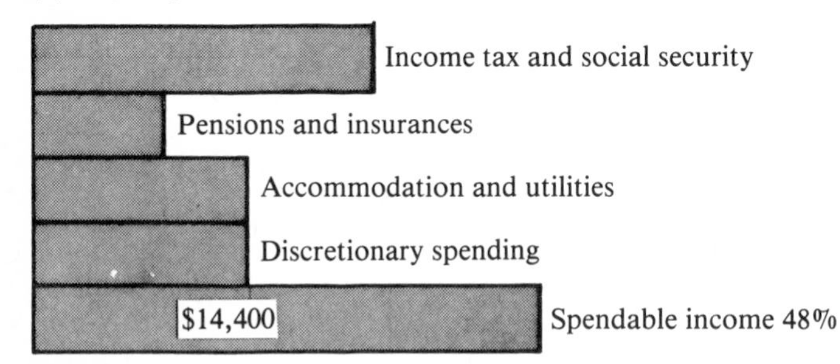

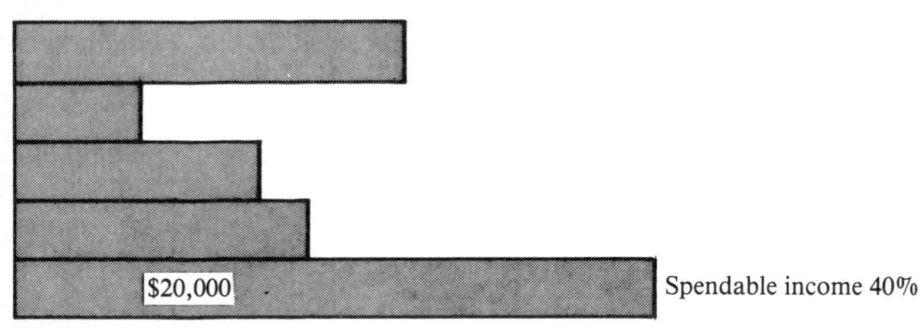

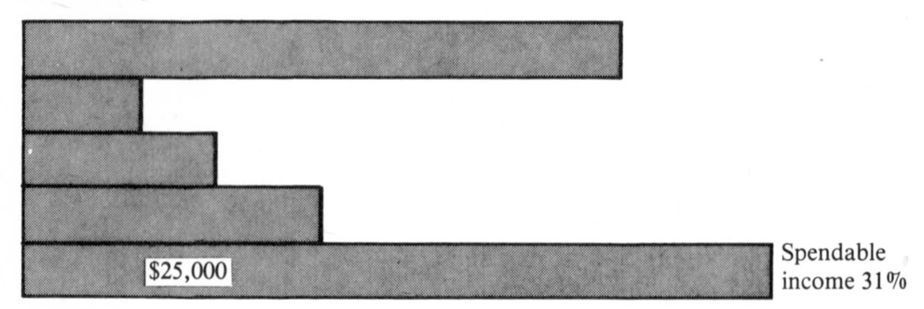

Given that the statistics used, either from government or consultancy sources, are reliable, the company should be able to build up an accurate picture of spendable income for each nationality of expatriate at each salary level. It should be stressed that this can only be an average expenditure pattern; no individual or family would produce exactly the same figures but the majority of employees would fall into a range of plus or minus 10 per cent of the figures. In some countries the element of discretionary expenditure is low. In these cases companies who base their compensation on home country salaries apply a minimum discretionary expenditure (15 to 20 per cent) so that discretionary expenditure among different nationalities remains within certain parameters.

Living costs

Once spendable income has been established the exercise of protecting the expatriate against excess living costs in the host country is relatively straightforward. The objective is to price the goods bought by spendable income in the home country, then repeat the exercise in the host country to arrive at an index by which the spendable income is multiplied. Although the concept is simple, major problems arise with the statistical measurement. The cost of living survey normally applies to the following:

- Food and drink consumed at home
- Meals away from home
- Home entertaining
- Household services
- Transportation
- Recreation
- Clothing
- Furnishing and household equipment (if not elsewhere included in the company policy).

For each category of expenditure a selection of items would need to be listed which mirror as closely as possible items of expenditure in the particular home country. The price of each item multiplied by the relative importance (weighting) of expenditure on the item in the total expenditure package will provide the total cost. The relative weighting of items will be different for different nationalities (eg nationals from both hot and cold climates) and the expenditure pattern and weighting of items will be different for expatriates and people in their home country.

All governments publish retail price indexes; while these may be useful to show relative price movements over time they do not help expatriate compensation calculations as they are normally based on the expenditure pattern of the average family in the country. Each major group of expenditure can be further broken down and analysed as sub groups. A diagrammatic illustration of this is shown in Figure 6.8.

Figure 6.8 *Typical cost of living survey groups and food spending sub groups*

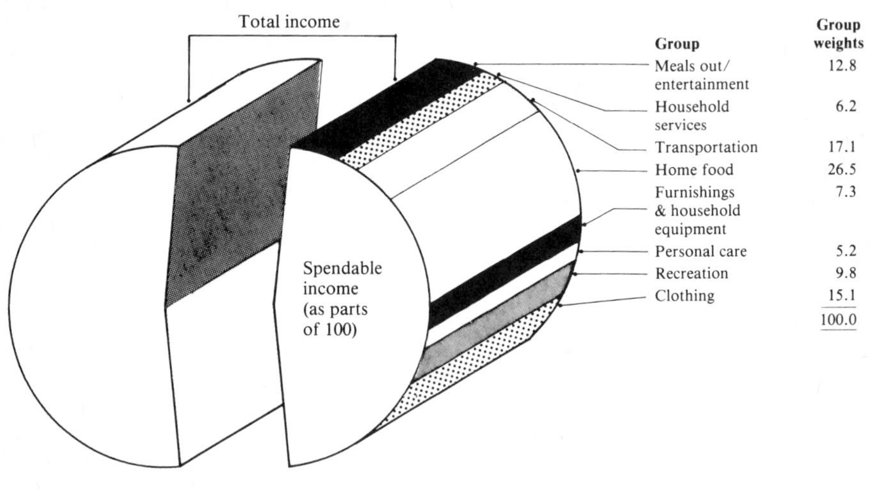

Group	Group weights
Meals out/ entertainment	12.8
Household services	6.2
Transportation	17.1
Home food	26.5
Furnishings & household equipment	7.3
Personal care	5.2
Recreation	9.8
Clothing	15.1
	100.0

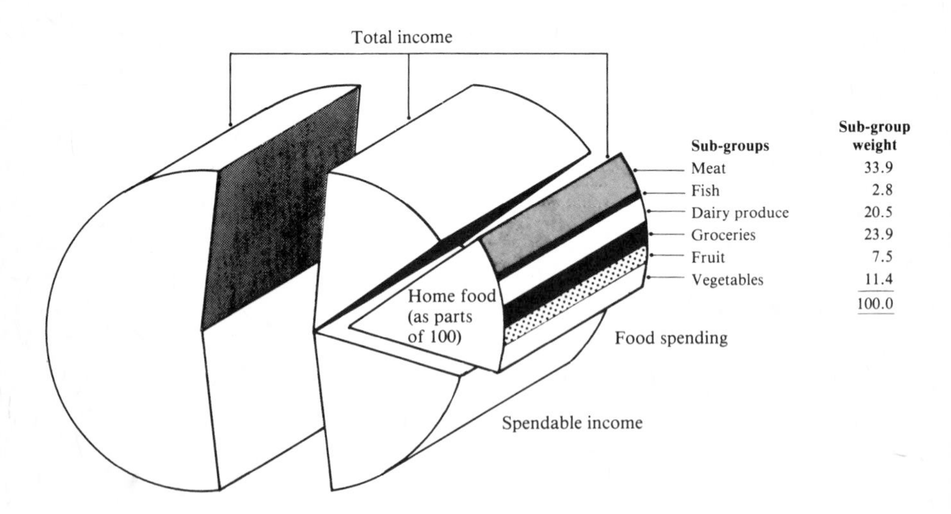

Sub-groups	Sub-group weight
Meat	33.9
Fish	2.8
Dairy produce	20.5
Groceries	23.9
Fruit	7.5
Vegetables	11.4
	100.0

Given that a similar comparison is made in the home and host country a cost of living index can be produced with the home country as 100; for example, for a Frenchman for whom Paris is 100 (see Figure 6.9).

Figure 6.9 *Cost of living comparisons, 1981*

Paris = 100.0	Married employee with two children		
Abu Dhabi	146.2	Houston	89.7
Al Khobar	157.0	Jeddah	154.7
Athens	100.1	Lisbon	82.8
Bahrain	154.7	London	108.9
Brussels	99.8	Madrid	83.8
Cairo	155.4	New York	95.0
Copenhagen	118.4	Oslo	132.3
Dubai	139.2	Riyadḥ	154.1
Dublin	94.5	Rome	88.8
Frankfurt	113.3	Stockholm	124.6
Geneva	130.2	Vienna	115.1
The Hague	109.8	Washington	94.4
Helsinki	118.7		

Calculating the cost of living allowance

Having obtained a spendable income figure for the employee and the cost of living differentials, a cost of living allowance can now be calculated.

As an example, a Frenchman working in Riyadh with a family of two children:

Annual base salary (in FF)	FF 300,000
Percentage of spendable income (from statistical information)	40 per cent
Spendable income (40 per cent x 300,000)	FF 120,000
COL index (from above table)	154.1
COLA (excess 54.1 per cent applied to spendable income amount)	FF 64,920

The COL index can be adjusted simply for different family size, eg in this case multiply by the following factors (devised by similar cost surveys):

Single employee	74.3 per cent
Husband + wife	87.5 per cent
Married couple and one child	96.3 per cent
Married couple and three children	105.1 per cent

MAINTAINING A COLA SYSTEM

By their nature cost of living allowances are dynamic not static, as each element can change over a relatively short period of time. For example, changes in:

- ○ Domestic circumstances; a larger family
- ○ Home currency prices
- ○ Host country prices
- ○ Spendable income curve and discretionary expenditure (as salary changes)
- ○ Currency relativities.

Any company using such a system must therefore commit itself to reviewing all the variables on a six monthly or quarterly basis. Unless a company has many thousands of expatriate employees it is unlikely to undertake such an exercise internally, thus making a regular update from a consultancy an attractive proposition. In practice, many companies find it difficult to reduce a COLA even where statistics indicate this to be an appropriate course of action (eg with higher inflation in home country prices than host country).

PREMIUMS: A QUESTION OF COMPLEXITY

A manager looking for a logical system of expatriate premiums, who has followed the analysis to this point, may be tempted to construct a policy incorporating:

Hardship
- ○ Two dimensional hardship allowances
- ○ Measuring hardship with a number of weighted factors
- ○ Decided by representative committees annually.

Cost
- ○ Spendable income worked out for each expatriate's home country
- ○ Weighted cost of living indexes specially constructed for each country
- ○ Costs in home and host country reviewed each quarter
- ○ Currency adjustments made as required.

To install a system of this complexity is almost impossible in practical terms. The reality is that very few companies take the calculation of premiums to this logical extreme; it is not worth the effort and time for the final results. In practice, companies select the elements of a premium system that suit their particular needs, ie cross section of expatriate employees, work patterns and pay philosophy. Any manager setting up a system for the first time should always ask the following:

- ○ Is the system easy to understand and can it be explained to the expatriates involved? A very sophisticated system may logically be the fairest solution but, if the calculations are difficult, it is likely to be unpopular and misunderstood.
- ○ Is it valid and up to date? There is no point designing a scheme which cannot be kept up to date, or allows one variable to get out of line.

- Is it worth it? No company will come up with the same system for a group of ten expatriates as it will for 10,000. One well known company does indeed have a computer and an entire department dealing exclusively with premiums. It is worth it for them as they are one of the world's largest expatriate employers with over 4000 expatriates. Not many other companies would have such a requirement.
- Who does it? An 'in-house' system means that a company retains more control and may demand more participation from the employees but balanced against this the use of consultants may provide a more convenient and objective source of information.

7. Expatriate benefits

INTRODUCTION

In the last three chapters the remuneration of expatriates has been discussed. While money is an important factor for those going overseas it would be wrong to assume it is the only consideration. Only the most hardy or inexperienced of employees will not concern themselves with the general living conditions they are likely to encounter in an overseas assignment. Furthermore, the employer too should pay great attention to this aspect as it plays a crucial part in the success, or lack of it, in retaining expatriate employees.

COST, COMFORT AND SECURITY

Experienced expatriates who have already worked overseas usually examine expatriation benefits packages (excluding salaries) from the point of view of cost, comfort and security although not necessarily in this order of priority.

Cost

The total cost of an overseas assignment is of great importance to the employee. Promises of high salary mean very little if substantial amounts of money are essential to obtain and sustain reasonable standards of living in the host country. Companies without detailed knowledge of the local scene can often present their employees with impossible problems of cost which will result either in an expensive revision of the original package or a high wastage among expatriate staff. Also, expatriate employees may have certain domestic commitments – such as the upkeep of houses and certain social security costs, and they may not envisage additional costs in the overseas location. The expatriate may not expect to live rent and overhead-free during an overseas assignment, but at the same time he should not be expected to have to bear the full economic cost.

Comfort

In the days when working overseas was considered an adventure, it may have been possible for the employer to have expected his expatriates to 'rough it' as part of their assignment. This practice is now rare, except for certain military

tours of duty and some single person assignments, which pay particularly high premiums because of hardship. Expatriates now expect reasonable arrangements in working conditions and in living arrangements particularly if, as is usually the case, their families are expected to live with them. Comfort is often a relative consideration but certainly a 'normal' standard is quickly established in any expatriate community. This may concern the size of house, location in the town, fittings and furnishings and the availability of servants. The norm will relate to what is prevalent in that expatriate community, not necessarily those which exist 'back home'. The frequent reverse culture shock of expatriates returning home is a well known phenomenon after they have become accustomed to large houses and the provision of servants, which they have to learn to do without once the overseas assignment is finished. The concept of comfort also covers the need to provide reasonable recreational facilities.

Security

Security is as equally subjective a measure as comfort. Some employees may worry about traffic accidents or mugging wherever they are located. Other employees may never give such matters a second thought. In any event in the home country it is not in general a matter of company concern.

Overseas, the situation is quite different. The company must accept a greater degree of responsibility for the well being of its expatriate employees. An extreme example of this is the swift and effective evacuation of expatriates from war zones or from areas of extreme political instability; recent examples have been Iran, Iraq and Libya. In other cases it may be that the society itself poses greater risks, either in terms of assault, robbery or possibly traffic accidents. The company, then, has to decide whether to provide guards for expatriates' houses, provide drivers and take other steps to counter such risks. At the other end of the scale it may be simply that state or private provision of medical services of an acceptable standard are not available to the expatriate and the company must come up with some alternative arrangement. Whatever the scale of risk it is certain that the employee will be looking for arrangements that minimize it and make the stay for him and his family reasonably secure. Again, the acceptable 'norm' for such security is very quickly established in the expatriate community and the company will have very little option but to follow this if it wishes to retain its expatriate employees.

If the employee usually considers cost, comfort and security as the three most important considerations in general expatriate lifestyle, the company must look at the matter from a slightly different angle. For the long assignment expatriate it may well be that he will have to arrange his own housing, make local investments and generally integrate with the community in which he lives. For the short stay or multi-country expatriate this is clearly not feasible and the company must play a role for one or more of the following reasons:

○ moral and legal responsibility;

- time and cost efficiency;
- employee morale.

Moral and legal responsibility

By expatriating the employee a company automatically accepts some moral and often legal responsibility which does not apply in the home country. For an employee in his home country the social security system is decided at governmental level and the company's responsibility is merely to comply with it. As a result of expatriation the employee loses this security but often cannot find a suitable substitute. The host country will frequently either not acknowledge responsibility or will provide a very different standard of social security. The company must, therefore, take over the welfare provisions that under different circumstances would normally be the responsibility of the individual or the state. This may involve questions of housing, transport and medical facilities, but it can also be more general, concerning overall recreation or family security together with adequate schooling for the children. Finally, many countries require that companies take on a specific legal responsibility for ensuring that, in the last resort, the expatriate is returned to his home country and any outstanding liabilities after his departure become the company's responsibility.

Time and cost efficiency

Moral questions aside, it is not in the interest of the company to tie up a great deal of expensive expatriate time in the search for housing, transport or schools. When the expatriate arrives he may not be familiar with local practices; for example, the renting of houses or the market price for cars. Without company assistance he may waste a considerable amount of time setting up home. Furthermore, in many countries, the time, effort and frustration involved in trying to organize domestic arrangements may affect the employee's job performance. Also, in many countries, it is frequently impossible to arrange such things as house leases on an individual basis. Companies may be required to provide deposits and guarantees for their employees, thus making their involvement obligatory.

Employee morale

The expatriate employee tends to view his benefits package in terms of cost, comfort and security. If the employee considers some of the elements inadequate, serious problems could be in store for the employer. Perhaps the individual has to pay a large proportion of his living costs; he may feel his housing is inadequate or that his car should have air conditioning; perhaps the company does not provide medical cover at the local private hospital or even provide membership of the local golf club. Whatever the complaint, such shortcomings, perceived or real, will undermine the expatriate employee's morale. These are not major factors in motivating the employee but they may demotivate the expatriate and even more so his family. In short, the company is responsible for a much larger range of factors which may either motivate or demotivate employees. In the terminology of Hertzberg this means that overseas employers must pay far greater attention to the so called 'hygiene factors' than their home country counterparts.

GROUPING THE BENEFITS

The level and type of benefits will vary from company to company and country to country. Here, benefits that are normally associated with an expatriate package are grouped under six headings:

- Housing – provision of housing, cost, services, furniture and staff
- Car and transportation
- Education of children
- Vacation and vacation travel
- Medical facilities and expenses
- Recreational facilities.

HOUSING

After net income, housing is the next most important benefit for any expatriate and it is a facility which the expatriate must be provided with (excluding work-camps where the accommodation is communal, single sex and on a rotational basis). An expatriate who brings his family with him will be primarily concerned with the quality of housing.

A detailed description of housing problems on a country by country basis is outside the scope of any book, but the most important considerations to be taken into account are:

- cost of housing – bought or rented;
- facilities and furnishing;
- location and staffing;
- cost to expatriate employees.

Cost of housing

The company's policy regarding cost will depend on the type of country in which it operates. In developed countries there usually exists a recognized market in leased houses or company rented apartments. The 'company lease' will often be expensive – sometimes 50 per cent more than the market for a private individual, but the accommodation will normally be particularly suited to the expatriate in terms of proximity to work, foreign education facilities and a town centre location. Such accommodation will also have well established leasing arrangements and will normally be managed by a professional leasing agent.

In less developed countries the problems posed are quite different. Frequently, the type of housing suitable for expatriates simply does not exist or is scarce. If the expatriate community increases suddenly, as is often the case in the oil industry, then market pressure will make these houses extremely expensive. Landlords may insist on special arrangements where half or more of the rent for a three or more year contract is paid in advance in hard currency into an overseas bank account.

Faced with such terms the company may decide that it makes more sense to build its own housing, but here the problems of time and organization frequently occur. Obtaining land and planning permission, supervising the building and generally setting up in the home management business may present the company with unacceptable penalties both in time and cost. By increasing its fixed assets in any country its flexibility is considerably reduced.

Even if the company decides to enter the market on a rented basis and more than half a dozen houses are involved, this will invariably necessitate the employment of some sort of housing administrator, either as an employee or as an agent. The housing administrator must be able to understand contracts, both from a linguistic and a legal point of view, and must ensure that effective housing management exists in reference to payments to landlords, the provision of services, and the general upkeep of property.

Facilities and furnishing

In many expatriate communities most socializing is done at home and only a very small proportion of women work. Careful attention is needed to the conditions in which families are housed. Obviously it is difficult to have consistent company-wide standards if the business operates in many countries. The expatriate, say, in central Rome, will be expected to accept much less floor space than his counterpart in Australia. Insisting on individual houses rather than apartments or flats may be reasonable in Aberdeen but would be very hard to justify in central Paris. The head office can hardly lay down that all houses must have central heating and carpeting when the demand in some of its tropical areas of operations will be for air conditioning and swimming pools. Housing policies must be flexible in approach in order to obtain the correct procedure for each location.

Clear and consistent guidelines on housing policy must be established early on if companies are not to be plagued with complaints of inconsistency in such policies. They should decide, at an early stage, whether they are to allocate housing on the basis of seniority or on family size. In practice, most companies base their policies on a mixture of the two criteria.

Where house furnishing is concerned, similar problems may exist. Companies have the choice of either providing furnished accommodation or providing unfurnished accommodation with the provision of some sort of furnishing grant. Both policies have their drawbacks: employees may not be satisfied with the aesthetic quality of the furnishings provided; the provision of furnishing grants can be very costly, coupled with the problem of disposal of furniture bought, upon completion of the overseas assignment.

A popular compromise is the provision of housing with 'hard furnishing' – the basic kitchen items and major pieces of furniture. This policy can be combined with either a lump sum in cash as a relocation allowance and/or a freighting allowance for the transfer of furnishings and fittings from the home country (see Chapter 3).

The choice of which policy to adopt must be decided by the circumstances in the host country and by consideration of the type of overseas assignment. If the employee is beginning a long-term assignment (three years plus) in a country where furniture is readily available, it may well be more satisfactory to allow the family to select their own furnishings. In cases where the assignment is of short-term duration or where satisfactory furnishings are very hard to obtain, it is clearly more practical to provide fully furnished accommodation which can be handed on from one expatriate family to another.

Location and domestic staff

Expatriate families have a tendency to group together – for reasons of mutual assistance, security, closeness to work, international school facilities or for social organization. In many countries this means that employers either have to organize 'compound' accommodation or, at the very least, acquire housing in the vicinity of the rest of the expatriate community. In large cities this frequently means difficult to find, and expensive, city centre locations. In countries where the standard of living is poor it means obtaining housing in areas with better standards of roads and sanitation, etc. In these cases the problem is again one of cost, since good quality expatriate housing will often be at a premium and may be controlled by a cartel of developers. The employer probably has only two choices: of either paying up; or of taking the major decision of developing his own compound on a new site. This is only really feasible when associated with major projects (oil refineries and civil engineering construction) in undeveloped countries and would not be feasible for the smaller expatriate employer with perhaps less than a dozen staff.

The provision of domestic help for expatriates is largely a case of what is the accepted custom and practice in the host country. Throughout Asia and Africa domestic staff, cooks, cleaners, chauffeurs and security guards, are the rule rather than the exception. The supply of plentiful labour demanding relatively low wages means that such staff form a low percentage of overall costs and so provision of them can be justified. In other areas, particularly the Middle East, where such domestic staff themselves will be immigrant workers, the use of servants will be much less widespread. The company will need to establish a policy as to what, if any, domestic staff can be employed. In most countries this is the responsibility of the expatriate although the domestic staff will sometimes, for legal reasons, need to be on the company payroll.

Cost to expatriates

Housing in the home country represents a substantial proportion of total expenditure for the employee. To the employer, with the exception of salaries, it is likely to represent the major element of employee cost in the overseas country.

There are four common methods of allocating the cost of such housing:

- Employer responsibility
- Housing deduction from salary
- Housing allowance/reasonable housing costs
- Marginal costing.

Employer responsibility

The most straightforward method of allocating housing costs is for the employer to bear the whole responsibility. The provision of free housing then becomes part of the whole employment package and is naturally a very attractive benefit to the expatriate. From the employer's point of view such a provision may simplify administration and generally benefit recruitment and staff motivation. Obviously, and in addition, many expatriate employees will retain home country accommodation which, if rented, can represent an attractive (additional) financial proposition.

Housing deduction from salary

In many cases the company feels it necessary to recognize the cost of housing it provides to its expatriates in the form of a specific deduction from the monthly salary. This will normally be in the form of an overall percentage figure deducted at source – usually between 10 per cent and 15 per cent. This represents equalized costs – not related to the country of assignment (where actual costs may vary considerably) and demonstrates to the employee a measure of the magnitude of the benefit involved.

Housing allowance/'reasonable housing costs'

A more sophisticated costing approach, but with more attendant employee relations problems, is the concept of reasonable housing costs where the onus is on the employee finding his own accommodation. Where choice is plentiful, this has the attraction of giving expatriates more freedom. At the same time the company may take into account the fact that expatriates are likely to encounter artificially high prices. Accommodation may have to be found quickly and without sufficient time to obtain the most economical rent. There may also be a preference to be near an international school, in close proximity to other assignees or to areas that fetch a high price. In these cases surveys, using local housing agencies, are usually undertaken to establish reasonable housing costs and to ascertain any inflationary trends in the market. The full costs of the housing, as indicated in the survey, will then be paid in the form of an allowance.

A typical example, in this case for London, is:

	Family size £ per month			
	Single	*Married no dependants*	*Married one dependant*	*Married two or more dependants*
Division manager and above	1100	1300	1400	1500
Other grades	900	1100	1200	1300

Marginal costing

Using any of the above methods, marginal costing may be introduced to take account of what the expatriate does with his accommodation in the home country. One well known international company's manual states: 'We will provide a housing cost allowance based on the difference between the amount our survey indicates each assignee statistically spends on housing in his home country and the amount shown by the work location survey.' A survey has, therefore, to be obtained for housing costs in each of the areas of origin for each expatriate. Our feeling is that such an approach is probably not worth the effort, and it is far more realistic either to capitalize on the benefits of free housing or to make a straightforward, easily understood, percentage deduction from salary.

Other housing considerations

Even when the housing issue has been resolved there are other factors that must be considered. Should services, such as electricity and telephone charges, be paid in full by the company? If not, should it be on a cost share basis or with a maximum ceiling? The same considerations apply to the payment of local taxes (or rates in the UK). A frequently encountered problem is the expatriate family who leaves accommodation in a poor state of repair. Should the employee pay a contribution or should it be another company overhead? There are no hard and fast answers to these problems but it is important for the company to attempt to define and maintain a consistent policy.

Finally, there is the question of household insurance. In many cases, where the family has shipped out its furniture, the local insurance market may not provide adequate insurance cover. In this situation the company can arrange, with several of the world-wide networked insurance companies, to provide group cover regardless of the country of location. This is clearly a very useful arrangement when expatriates frequently change location and have neither the time, nor the opportunity, to take out a local policy.

CAR AND TRANSPORTATION

The provision of a company car is no less an emotive issue for expatriate employees than for home country based staff. Giving a car to an employee may not motivate him to improve his job performance, but the potential for demotivation by not providing a car, when the employee considers he is entitled to one, can be considerable.

The company car question involves a number of issues not always apparent in the employee's home country. It is crucial for the company to decide whether the provision of a car is essential or merely a benefit. The pick-up truck for the oil field hand may be a clear-cut case of an essential tool but the saloon car for an employee based in a regional headquarters is a much less obvious case. The employee is normally expatriated without his own vehicle (unless he ships it in with foreign plates – a procedure which is not to be recommended) and many companies do provide a car, particularly if local prices are very high and/or vehicles are very difficult to obtain. Expatriates in most developing countries will seldom be prepared to make use of local transport arrangements, assuming of course that they exist. As a useful guide, a common policy in American companies is that if the employee would not be provided with transport at home, he will not receive it in the expatriate location.

If a car is provided this in itself raises certain issues. The most obvious consideration is whether it should be restricted to the employee's own use. Most companies, if only for insurance purposes, usually insist on this. A second car for the employee's wife is normally the sole responsibility of the employee. Some sort of decision also has to be taken on whether the vehicle can be used for trips on days off or even made use of during periods of extended leave. The expatriate will naturally wish to visit places of local interest during his tour of duty – but should this be extended to allowing the employee to take the company vehicle on an extended two weeks' safari?

If the employee drives there is always the possibility of involvement in local accidents, resulting in death or injury. In many countries this can be a sensitive issue as concepts of guilt, punishment and compensation vary a great deal between different cultures. The expatriate in Papua New Guinea who kills a local inhabitant in a car crash would not be well advised to discuss insurance liability with the relatives. Equally, Arab countries normally jail everyone involved in a motor accident, frequently for long periods, whilst ascertaining what sort of compensation and/or punishment is considered suitable by the relatives involved. It would be impossible to enter into a country by country discussion of this issue, but if the company allows its employees to drive it must be aware of the probable consequences of any resulting accidents.

Some expatriate locations are considered to be so hazardous, in terms of driving conditions, that companies will not allow their expatriate staff to drive vehicles. This was certainly a common feature in Tehran before the revolution and is not unusual in some African or Asian countries, particularly where urban driving is considered to be very dangerous. In these cases the provision of a local driver removes the expatriate from immediate involvement in any ensuing accident. It also assumes, but not always correctly, that the driver's experience of local driving conditions will reduce the chances of an accident. A related issue to this is where, because of local customs, the expatriate's wife is not allowed to drive (eg Saudi Arabia). The company is then faced with a choice of either providing a car and driver for the wife (common only for the families of senior executives), or of organizing car pools and children's school buses, etc. The obligation to do this may not at first be obvious, but low morale among the families, who may feel trapped without transport, will soon reflect on the expatriate's own work performance. If the company does not provide cars it is common to have some sort of car loan scheme. This usually takes account of local market prices and sometimes seniority. Such loans are usually repayable in interest free instalments over the period of the assignment.

EDUCATION OF CHILDREN

For married employees with children, the most common and difficult problem encountered is how to ensure that their children's education does not suffer. The potential difficulties can be summarized as: coping with the new cultural environment, choice of syllabus and cost.

Cultural environment

Sudden changes in cultural environment can be very disturbing for any expatriate and there are many views on its effects on children. One school of thought sees the disruption of schooling and resulting insecurity as damaging. Others consider that, all things being equal, children adapt easily to a new environment, and the stimulation offered by travel and exposure to new languages and culture is positively beneficial to a child's development. Whatever the view of the parents, regarding the benefits of travel, they will naturally be concerned that their children should enjoy at least a reasonable continuity of education, obtaining qualifications which will be recognized at home (for the purposes of higher education and job hunting). Here the expatriate is frequently faced with two choices – finding a suitable school in the host country or separating the child from the family so that he can continue his education at home or elsewhere at a boarding school. For large nationality groups, educational needs are frequently catered for in the host country. American, British and French nationals, for example, can often find schools for their children which offer home country syllabuses leading to recognized examinations. Generally, most capital cities are well catered for in this respect along with the major Middle East petroleum centres with large expatriate communities.

If acceptable schools are not available, the parents have to decide whether to integrate their child into the local school or organize a boarding school arrangement in the home country. It is, however, a somewhat insensitive employer who insists that the company's expatriates accept overseas assignments on family status, where no school is available.

Costs

For expatriate employees, a company normally provides assistance regarding children's education in two ways. It will obtain information concerning education facilities in the country of assignment and will also offer some sort of financial assistance. The logic behind financial assistance stems from the company's increased economic and moral responsibility for the expatriate during an overseas assignment. Normally, education will be a matter for parents and the state in each home country. In the majority of developed countries parents would expect that the education of their children was provided free by the state and private education would be a matter of choice and not of necessity. By expatriating parents, the company has to recognize the increased cost of either keeping the child in its home country and away from the family, or meeting the cost of a predominantly private system in the expatriate location which may be expensive.

Typical company policy in this situation will be to stress that while a child's education is fundamentally the responsibility of the parents, it must recognize that adequate schooling may entail unduly high expenses for employees overseas. The policy will then set certain conditions to avoid the more obvious abuses.

Generally, direct costs of tuition in the foreign assignment are met in full, but in some cases companies may impose a maximum amount or require the employee to contribute towards the cost of schooling.

Where the expatriate is obliged to educate his children away from the overseas assignment, different reimbursement rules normally apply. This element of reimbursement ranges from 50 per cent to 100 per cent and usually includes a maximum ceiling. Such ceilings are adjusted regularly to take into account inflation rates. For example:

Company	**Reimbursement**
West German	75 per cent up to DM9000 a year
French	Primary school maximum FF1150 a term Secondary school max FF1400 a term (16 years)
Franco-American	50 per cent of indirect school expenses to $4000 per calendar year
American	Normal education, including room and board up to a maximum of $6000 per dependant per school year

From the information given it is evident that there exists a considerable range of reimbursement policies for school expenses. In most companies reimbursement of university or higher education is not included in the expatriate benefits package, since in the home country the parents, state or even the students themselves would normally bear the cost of higher education. In addition, such higher education is by nature selective and therefore not easy to offer as overall policy. However, an expatriate, non-resident in his home country, will often find that state scholarships are not available to his children for tertiary education and this can lead to serious financial problems.

Travelling costs

Children who are educated away from the expatriate location can naturally be expected to spend at least two holidays with their parents. In view of this, nearly all companies allow two paid return economy air fares for each dependent child per year. A third discretionary trip may be allowed if for some reason the parents are not able to take their own vacation between July and September, ie coinciding with school summer holidays in the northern hemisphere. Such a travel policy is often extended to children at university, even though the company does not bear the actual education costs.

The following is a typical education assistance policy:

Education assistance

1. While recognizing that a child's education is the fundamental responsibility of his parents, the company accepts that adequate schooling may entail unduly high expenses for international staff employees overseas.
2. The company participates in educational expenses under the following conditions:
   (a) Reimbursement applies to children under the legal custody of international staff employees
   (b) Reimbursement applies to unmarried children between the ages of five and 19, and is extended until the end of the secondary school year when the child reaches 19.
   Expenses (except as described in paragraph 4(c) incurred by children attending post-secondary or university level education are not reimbursed.
3. In countries where acceptable schooling facilities are available and attendance at a particular school has been approved by the regional manager, the company reimburses registration and tuition fees, the cost of the school books and daily transportation to and from the child's residence and, where applicable, compulsory school insurance.
   The regional manager must approve the type of transportation to be used.
   All other school expenses (board, stationery) are paid by the employee.
4. When local schooling is deemed inadequate by the regional manager and the child attends a school away from the employee's place of assignment, the company will reimburse:
   (a) The cost of tuition, registration fees and school books.
   (b) 50 per cent of the indirect school expenses (room and board) or $100 per month, per child, when the child lives with relatives or friends.
   (c) One round-trip fare per calendar year per child, in addition to the vacation trip, at the lowest rate (economy, student), between the school and the employee's place of assignment, provided the trip is actually taken.
   Employees are expected to bear the cost of any other travel by their children over and above the four single or two round trips (vacation and one other) permitted. This reimbursement applies up to, and including, the year in which the child reaches 21.

(d) The maximum reimbursement is limited to $4000 per calendar year, per child (exclusive of the cost of the round trip fare). Reimbursement for a child starting and/or finishing school during a year will be pro-rated.
(e) If, for personal reasons, including resignation or request for transfer, an employee leaves an assignment after an advance payment has been made by the company, the employee is responsible for any forfeiture of pre-paid tuition.

VACATION AND VACATION TRAVEL

An employee's expectation about time off will naturally depend on a number of factors: seniority in the company, common conditions in the home country, the custom and practice in the industry and type of work. For example, a senior executive will traditionally work longer hours, regardless of the domestic legislation concerning the length of the working week. Employees in the United States receive considerably shorter vacation allowances than do their counterparts in Western Europe, and oil industry or airline workers will be more accustomed to working 'unsocial hours' than will bank or insurance firm employees.

Expatriation in itself should result in a higher accrual of vacation than would normally be expected in the home country. Living in a foreign country can entitle the employee to a longer period of home leave because of the social isolation of the posting, the lower frequency of holiday taken and the length of travel time involved in returning home. Hardship encountered in an expatriate environment is frequently compensated by longer and/or more vacation. Thus, a 'tough' assignment, in a desert or jungle, or perhaps in a very different cultural environment, might earn additional hardship leave.

One policy or many?

If the company is employing expatriates of only one nationality, it is relatively easy to design an effective vacation policy. The usual approach is to adhere to the home country vacation entitlement, together with a bonus allowance for expatriation. Such a policy is more difficult to sustain if the expatriate employees come from many countries with different vacation practices. There are two solutions to this predicament – companies can either allow employees to adhere to their home country vacation plan or they may prefer to produce a compromise plan which will satisfy all expatriate employees. The problems of having groups of expatriates working together with different leave entitlements can be considerable.

Even more than salary differentials, such leave entitlements are very noticeable and can cause considerable friction to develop among the staff involved. Furthermore, from a planning and administrative viewpoint, the scheduling of various entitlements can present considerable difficulties. Because of this home country reference, such vacation plans are comparatively rare and most multinationals adhere to a unified system.

Vacation accrual

Companies that apply a unified system of vacation frequently distinguish between 'European' assignments and other overseas locations. They also commonly recognize service seniority. Given these factors, Figure 7.1 shows a typical vacation accrual structure for a sample of seven companies.

It is apparent from this sample that there is considerable variation in vacation allowance policies, although an average of 30 days a year for 'good' conditions and 60 days for 'difficult' conditions seems to be representative.

Figure 7.1 *Example of a company vacation accrual policy*

	Europe	
Company	**System of accrual**	**Calendar days per 12 months worked**
A	Within 12 months service period Western Europe 25 working days plus travel time Eastern Europe 33 working days	 38.7 52.6
B	42 calendar days after 12 months	42
C	Less than 20 years service: 28 calendar days/year Between 20 years and 29 years: 35 calendar days/year For 30 years and more: 42 calendar days	28 35 42
D	Less than 20 years service: 20 working days 20 years or more: 25 working days (or grade 24 to 28)	31 35
E	26 working days plus 3 for split vacation within 12 month service period	46
F	Within 12 months 38 calendar days	42
G	3.25 days/month	39

Frequency of vacation travel rights and vacation salary

Most domestic employers have some stipulation that holidays must be taken in a number of 'blocks' rather than in individual days. Employers of expatriate staff have to refine their policies rather more than their counterparts in the home country. With the cost of transport and the necessity of establishing a stable expatriate workforce it is common practice to limit vacation periods to once or twice a year. Often a vacation cannot be taken before the employee has completed a year of expatriation.

Overseas	Calendar days per 12 months worked	Rest days
After 12 month period 30 working days minimum, 44 working days maximum In Saudi Arabia 22 working days in 6 months – average 4 days travel time	42 minimum 61.6 maximum	5 days work/week plus bank holidays
Acceptable conditions 48 Desert tropical 54 Extreme conditions 60	48 54 60	5 days work/week plus bank holidays
Same as Europe	28 35 42	5 days work/week plus bank holidays
Same as Europe	31 35	5 days work/week plus bank holidays
+ 1 day/month for Middle East and Far East + 2 days/month for black Africa and China from 2 to 4 days travel time	56 66	5 days work/week plus bank holidays. If public holiday is worked it is made up later. For each week offshore – one day vacation
from 4.3 days/month to 5 days/month depending on location – travel time 1 to 3 days	52 60	5 days work/week plus bank holidays
4 days/month	48	48 days of rest/year guaranteed

Invariably employers provide free return travel to the home location on a once a year basis for the expatriate and his family. This will include a specification of the class of travel (normally economy) together with excess baggage allowances. An issue which is commonly encountered concerns the situation where the family wishes to travel to a location other than their point of origin. Frequent practice is to allow a cash payment up to the value of the economy ticket which the expatriate may then spend on such travel arrangements as he wishes, provided he actually leaves the overseas assignment.

Vacation salary usually includes an element of international compensation, although some companies provide holiday pay calculated only on base salary.

Other considerations
(local holidays, field breaks and compassionate leave)

Whilst all employers are obliged to observe holidays based on local laws and customs for their home country staff, they often feel that they do not have such an obligation where expatriates are concerned. In operational circumstances the contract may stipulate that such local holidays do not form part of the contractual obligation. In such cases the policy may simply state that regular days off are scheduled locally in order to provide breaks in the working year. This could be based on a five or six day work schedule allowing for four to eight rest days per month. It was mentioned earlier that extremely arduous conditions are commonly considered a good reason for providing additional or more frequent vacation entitlements (some companies include this element in the overall annual vacation rights). Other employers prefer to distinguish this entitlement from normal vacation and use the terms 'field break', 'hardship leave' or 'R and R' – rest and recreation leave. Practices vary, but they generally take account of the degree of hardship, the marital status of the employee and the travel involved in reaching the nearest acceptable vacation centre. A typical field break policy could appear as follows:

a) Field breaks are granted to permanent expatriate staff in the following locations – A (tough)
B (very tough)
b) There is no change in salary during the field break and this leave does not affect normal vacation rights.
c) Field breaks do not accrue if not taken and cannot be saved or pooled with annual vacation.
d) An economy return air ticket is supplied to the nearest point of interest to be selected by the local regional manager.
e) Field breaks are:

	Married	*Single*
B	21 days after 6 months	15 days after 110 days
A	No field break	15 days after 6 months

A final aspect of a personnel policy, involving leave and vacation for expatriates, is the provision of compassionate or emergency leave. When the employer has moved the expatriate family thousands of miles away from home, occasionally domestic emergencies may occur in the home country. These could include a death in the family, problems with children remaining at home, or simply domestic business affairs which require urgent attention. In these cases it may be possible to take regular vacation, but if not, the company normally allows some sort of leave of absence (generally, leave of absence infers that the employee is unpaid but remains on the payroll for insurance, medical and pension purposes).

MEDICAL FACILITIES AND EXPENSES

In the home country an employer is usually only involved in the medical care of its employees through a private medical insurance programme which may be provided in countries where health services are inadequate or non-existent. Overseas, the company's responsibility is invariably increased.

Expatriation itself can lead to certain medical problems because of climate, food and hygiene. This situation forces an employer to define a policy for a number of problems its expatriate employees may encounter, eg the availability and cost of medical facilities, sick leave and medical repatriation.

Availability

Most developed countries pose few problems for the provision of medical services. Prior to expatriation most families should have undergone a thorough medical screening at the employer's expense so the expatriate workforce is generally healthy. There will of course be language and sometimes cultural difficulties, even in developed countries, that result in the expatriate's preferring treatment from a home country doctor based in the host country. In some less developed countries however, particularly in Africa and parts of Asia, adequate medical attention will simply not be available. In this case, the company has to make a choice of either bringing with it medical services – an expensive option open only to large expatriate projects – or designing a reliable evacuation policy that can ensure medical treatment in another location within a reasonable period of time. There are specialist insurance companies that provide this service worldwide, for example, Europassistance, who provide services in Europe, Africa and the Middle East.

Cost of medical facilities

Expatriates will come from countries where either all medical treatment is paid for at source, in the form of direct taxation (as in the UK through National Insurance contributions); where there are compulsory private insurance schemes in operation (France, Germany), or where there is an optional private medical insurance market (the United States). The expatriate employee will sometimes be in a situation where the host country reciprocates free medical treatment (EEC nationals), but will more often be faced with the full economic cost. In such circumstances the employer will offer either a full reimbursement of medical costs (directly or through an insurance scheme to which employees subscribe as well as the employer), a cost share system or a 'topping up' scheme to equalize with the home country cost.

The following table shows the schemes offered by six multi-national companies:

Company origin	*Payment by employer*
Anglo-Dutch	100 per cent (if no company facilities)
German	100 per cent
American	100 per cent prescription drugs 100 per cent hospital charges – 120 days 80 per cent thereafter (maternity not included) Maximum aggregate $100,000 per employee family per career
American	80 per cent up to first $500 then 100 per cent
French	100 per cent reimbursement through local social security and complementary insurance policy jointly subscribed by employee and employer
American	Difference between medical cost in work country and home country medical plan

Medical cover invariably includes the employee, the spouse and all dependent children. The applications of operating a medical insurance policy to cover expatriate employees in a number of countries are discussed in Chapter 11 which deals with insurance programmes.

Exclusions to the medical plan

To protect themselves against excessive costs most companies name some sort of exclusion clause in their medical plan. The most obvious case is where the expatriate can obtain free medical treatment, as in the UK. In such cases the company may not be prepared to meet the costs of private medical treatment. A more complex case is where the employee or a member of his family contracts a condition which requires long-term medical treatment and then subsequently leaves the company. The company must decide whether it should undertake a long-term responsibility for an ex-employee for medical costs incurred as a direct result of employment with the company. This may be more clear-cut in cases of work related accidents, but not nearly so evident in cases of, for example, recurrent bouts of malaria.

Other exclusions, or partial exclusions, are usually encountered in areas of dental care, eye care and psychiatric treatment. While the company may pay for dental inspections and treatment necessary for dental health, it will rarely cover the whole cost of cosmetic dentistry for the expatriate and his family. The same applies to eye care where inspection and the provision of lenses may be covered, but not the cost of frames. Such exclusions are based on the distinction between genuine medical treatment and cosmetic surgery.

Psychiatric treatment may be another area of exclusion. Most companies will classify nervous breakdowns or nervous exhaustion as physical ailments – particularly if it seems to have a work related cause. On the other hand, paying for a family member to undergo a course of expensive psychoanalysis may, to many companies, appear to be stretching the limit of corporate responsibility.

As with all benefit policies a consistent policy covering these eventualities is needed. Over a period of years the company will certainly be faced with a decision on every conceivable aspect of medical treatment. The company needs to reserve the right, in employment contracts, to limit the reimbursement of medical and associated costs to those 'generally prevailing' and for treatment of a 'normal standard' and above all to what is 'reasonable and actually incurred'. An example of a typical expatriate medical plan follows:

Medical expenses

1. Medical expenses are not refundable in the case of:
   - dental treatment outside the scope of the dental plan;
   - eye care outside the scope of the eyecare plan;
   - aesthetic treatment (cosmetic surgery, etc);
   - psychiatric treatment.
2. Only medical expenses incurred during the employment of the employee are reimbursed.

3. Medical expenses are refunded only against presentation of properly documented bills.
4. The company refunds the medical expenses after deduction of any reimbursement made by social security or workmen's insurance. It is incumbent upon the employee to take the necessary steps to secure these refunds.
5. No restrictions are imposed as to the choice of doctors, laboratories, hospitals, clinics, etc. However, the company reserves the right to limit the reimbursement of medical and associated costs to that generally prevailing and of normal standard in the country where the patient is treated and in any event to what is reasonable and actually incurred.

Medical check-ups

6. Employees, wives and children must have a medical check-up at least once every two years. The company will pay reasonable expenses for such a check-up. One extra day of vacation is given for this, provided the check-up is taken and the medical reports received by the company.
   Innoculations and vaccinations, judged by the company to be necessary, are taken by the employee and his family at company expense.

Dental plan

7. Expenses for dental treatment are reimbursed by the company in the following manner:
   ○ 50 per cent of the costs of covered dental services up to a maximum of $1000 reimbursements per family per year.

   Dental services covered include:
   (a) periodic oral examinations (maximum two per year)
   (b) dental treatment and surgery necessary for maintenance of oral health

   The plan does not include:
   (a) dentistry for cosmetic purposes
   (b) replacement of lost dentures
   (c) gold fillings, crowns and bridge work

Eyecare plan

8. Expenses for eye care are reimbursed in full by the company in the following manner:
   ○ up to two eye tests a year
   ○ provision of one set of lenses (sunglasses excluded) per year (safety lenses should be selected when appropriate)

   No payment will be made for the provision of additional lenses or for the cost of frames.

Sick leave

Sick leave policies for expatriates are usually concerned with repatriation, whether the accident or illness was work related or not. In cases of short absences from work there will be no question of repatriation, but where the employee's illness is likely to last for a long period the company usually reserves the right to send him to a country where medical facilities are readily available or of sending him back to his country of origin for medical treatment.

Many companies will also distinguish between absence which is work related, as against absence for other medical reasons. This may involve a different scale of sick leave and salary payment. The difficulty with this approach, however, is defining which illnesses are work related and which are not. For example, is a heart attack caused by the pressure of the expatriate job or by smoking too much? Therefore, the trend is to include all types of medical absence within the limits of the same sick pay policy.

Length of payment and follow-up

While the definition of a reasonable length of provision of sick pay is a perennial problem for all personnel managers, the higher costs of expatriate employment make this an expensive issue for the expatriate company. Some companies will simply state that their decision is based on each individual case. Others will give a scale, on a progressively diminishing basis or related to length of service. For example:

Company	
A (American)	100 per cent of base x overseas premium for up to six months 60 per cent of base x overseas premium for up to a further six months
B (French)	up to three months base plus COLA then up to one year 100 per cent of base salary
C (German)	three years seniority – up to three months base salary more than three years – up to five months base salary more than ten years – up to seven months base salary

Whatever the scale chosen, the company at some time will have to consider termination on medical grounds. This can often be tied to an insurance scheme where the insurance company will provide further payments and possibly make a lump sum payment for permanent partial disability (see Chapter 11 on insurance programmes).

RECREATIONAL FACILITIES

In addition to housing, education, vacation and medical facilities, the expatriate employer cannot avoid considering recreational facilities. Indeed, such facilities can often be considered one of the most important elements of expatriate living. The expatriate and his family are after all in a strange culture and often without access to any local leisure facilities.

The list of potential facilities the company may offer is almost limitless but the most commonly encountered are social club, swimming pool, tennis and squash courts, sailing club, golf club and the provision of a country house.

For each of these the company must consider the existing facilities, judge the value of employee morale and the cost of providing its own resources. What should be realized by a manager new to expatriate employees is that what might appear unwelcome paternalism in the home country may be seen as a clear company responsibility in the expatriate community.

CONCLUSION

The benefits described in this chapter are an essential part of the expatriate employment package. The company cannot avoid becoming involved in many more aspects of the life of its employees than in the domestic situation. The benefits are extremely expensive (in Chapter 14, dealing with administration and control, such aspects are fully examined) and while their provision is most unlikely to motivate employees, dissatisfaction with them will almost certainly be a major demotivation. One of the most common causes for expatriate dissatisfaction is the quality of housing and related benefits provided overseas. The policies need to be evolved in relation to the other expatriate groups in the overseas location, be clearly defined and communicated to employees and operated on a consistent basis.

8. Worldwide income tax

INTRODUCTION

Income tax structures are an important area of concern for the expatriate compensation and benefits manager. Not only does he attempt, in the same way as his domestic counterpart, to produce a tax-effective package but net salary, ie after deductions, is his major concern. The expatriate company needs a good understanding not only of general taxation concepts but also of the specific tax legislation of the countries in which it works and from where it recruits.

Many domestic employers take the view that the impact of taxes on their employees is a matter of private concern. As citizens they discharge their civil responsibilities by paying their taxes and in any event benefit from the welfare state, education system, infrastructure and so forth purchased by these taxes. An expatriate, however, is most unlikely to benefit from much of what the taxes levied in the host country are specifically intended to provide.

Income taxes themselves may be levied by either national or local government and there are frequently wide variations between different regions (eg in the USA). In many countries expatriates are able to achieve a highly favourable tax treatment, although in others no distinction is made. Many countries tax their residents on all worldwide income, although favourable tax treatment can often be obtained where a significant part of the year is spent outside the country concerned. Finally, there are a few countries (notably the USA) which tax their citizens living and working overseas on their foreign service income.

This chapter discusses some of the basic concepts of income tax with which the compensation and benefits manager should be familiar, looks at the variety of income tax structures around the world, and then focuses on the expatriate tax issues and the solutions which have been adopted.

GENERAL TAXATION CONCEPTS

Taxation of individuals can be either direct, in relation to earnings, or indirect, in relation to expenditure. The ratio of direct to indirect taxation varies widely from country to country as a function of the prevailing political-economic philosophy. In addition to direct taxation, most countries require employees (and employers) to contribute to a social security system which may be funded either entirely from these contributions or partly from general taxation.

The expatriate compensation package is concerned both with direct taxation, in so far as it affects the way and the amount of taxation of salaries and benefits, and with indirect taxation, to the extent that it affects prices and thus the cost of living part of the package. In addition to taxation on earnings, countries also impose taxes on capital gains (usually ignored in expatriate tax considerations) and property taxes (which are normally dealt with as part of the housing cost consideration of the expatriate package).

This chapter is concerned almost entirely with the taxes on income, in the form of salaries and benefits, earned from expatriate employment, whilst other tax elements are discussed briefly at the end of the chapter. In a short overview it is impossible to do more than touch on the major elements of expatriate tax planning, and professional advice must be sought in specific cases. Some reference works that give more detailed information are indicated but as tax law is complex and also highly changeable, such works require frequent updating in order to be useful.

FISCAL ASPECTS

In most cases a company will take full responsibility for the completion of tax returns for individual employees, within the scope of the tax equalization or protection programme. Where an individual is responsible for paying his own tax, a company should provide the expatriate with access to tax advice from an external professional source and reimburse the professional fees (with perhaps a ceiling on what is reimbursed).

Where the company is responsible for an employee's income tax, the responsibility is normally more fiscal than personal and usually a tax manager is responsible for what is disclosed and how taxes can be minimized. The problem that multi-national companies face is that they want a single set of compensation and benefit policies for expatriates to apply in a wide variety of countries, each with greatly different tax laws and, therefore, varying degrees of tax efficiency, as far as different elements in the package are concerned. The levels of maximum marginal tax rate on earned income show considerable variation between countries (see Figure 8.1, data correct as at mid 1981).

In the context of tax protection or equalization systems, this gives an indication of the costs of disclosure for the company. It will also indicate areas where serious problems (ie excessive tax cost) will be anticipated with particular expatriate benefits.

PERSONAL INCOME TAX SYSTEMS

The variety of personal income tax systems in different countries is vast. There are some general similarities however – particularly in ex-colonial countries where much of the previous taxation philosophy remains.

In general taxable income is arrived at by an addition of earned salary and the taxable value of benefits furnished in kind (to the extent that these are declared). From this amount, deductions and exemptions are made on either a standard basis (eg as a function of family size) or itemized (eg interest on house

Figure 8.1 *Tax rates on earned income for an expatriate married with two children*

Country	*Maximum tax rate %*	*Taxable income at which maximum applies $*
Australia	60	39,600
Austria	62	88,941
Belgium	76.32	101,885
Bolivia	35	30,000
Brazil	55	48,031
Canada (Ontario)	62.78	98,993
Denmark	70	20,187
Egypt	50	90,361
Finland	51	68,460
France	60	49,000
West Germany	56	116,667
Hong Kong	15	29,227
India	66	11,390
Indonesia	50	28,800
Iran	90	75,000
Italy	72	462,000
Japan	93	383,970
Kenya	65	21,814
Malaysia	60	43,290
Mexico	55	102,249
Netherlands	72	75,056
New Zealand	60	18,996
Nigeria	70	46,428
Norway	65.4	28,300
Peru	65	86,667
Portugal	77.5	35,000
Singapore	45	349,325
Spain	65.6	112,000
Sweden	85	37,870
Switzerland (Geneva)	42	50,000
Taiwan	60	83,333
Thailand	65	47,619
Trinidad	70	25,000
UK	60	57,712
USA (New York)	64.3	60,000
Venezuela	45	1,860,465

loans, charitable contributions) to arrive at taxable income. The applicable tax rates are then applied to determine the tax liability, which could be paid currently (Pay As You Earn – PAYE) or in arrears as a lump sum, or some combination of the two. Social security contributions may be made before or after arriving at taxable income.

Most tax structures are progressive and some are highly so, ie there is an increase in the percentage of tax deducted as income rises. The average tax rate, which is the percentage of taxable income taken in taxes, should be distinguished from the marginal tax rate, the percentage of tax paid on the last monetary unit earned. The difference between the gross salary and the taxable income, which may be considerable depending on the level of allowances permitted, must be considered. Thus, in France a percentage deduction from gross salary is allowed before taxable income is arrived at, whereas in many other countries all that is allowed is a flat monetary amount, the relative proportions of which thus rapidly diminish as the salary increases.

Each year governments normally adjust tax brackets to take account of inflation. Usually this adjustment is less than the inflation in taxable earnings so that the government tax taken increases in real terms. This is known as *fiscal drag*.

The personnel manager, who is not usually a tax specialist, needs to take a step-by-step approach towards understanding the tax structure of a given country, both for expatriates and locals:

1. What is counted in gross salary? ie which fringe benefits are considered to have a cash value for the purposes of taxation, and how much does the cash value amount to? The following points should be borne in mind:
   - some countries ignore a large number of the normal expatriate benefits such as housing;
   - some elements of remuneration such as overtime, bonuses and statutory payments are either excluded from gross income for tax purposes, or are taxed at a lower rate;
   - special arrangements may apply for such benefits as cars or entertainment.
2. What is the basis on which a foreigner resident in the country is taxed on his earnings in that country?
3. What deductions are allowed from this gross salary in order to arrive at taxable salary? The possibilities are virtually endless in the various systems that the multi-national company will be concerned with. Some examples are:
   - standard deductions of a fixed monetary amount depending on family size;
   - standard deductions of a percentage of earned income – also varying in relation to family size;
   - social security contributions by the employee;
   - pension fund contributions by the employee;
   - special deductions for expatriates;
   - deductions for income earned in respect of activities outside the country of residence;
   - medical and other insurance contributions by employees as a deduction;
   - actual medical expenses as a deduction;
   - deduction of interest on loans (for special purposes such as house

purchase or as in USA for any purpose).

4. What is the tax rate structure and hence the average tax rate applicable to the level of taxable income arrived at? How much are local taxes levied on income?
5. How are taxes paid – PAYE, in arrears, quarterly estimates?

This will give a broad understanding of the way a local or expatriate can be expected to be taxed in a given country. It will also allow the personnel manager to compute the tax efficiency of each element of the compensation and benefits package, and decide whether any major problems exist in the case of tax protection or equalization policies. He will also be able to judge the attractiveness of the package for employees paying their own tax.

A HYPOTHETICAL EXAMPLE

Take the example of a country with the following income tax rate structure, suppose that a 20 per cent standard deduction is allowed before calculating taxable income, with no ceiling on salary to which this deduction applies.

Taxable income $	*Percentage tax rate*
0- 5000	25
5001-10,000	30
10,001-15,000	35
15,001-20,000	40
20,001-25,000	45
25,001-30,000	50
30,001-35,000	55
35,001-40,000	60
40,000 plus	65

Tax paid on $28,000 taxable income is thus computed as follows:

25% of first $5000	=	$ 1250
30% of next $5000	=	$ 1500
35% of next $5000	=	$ 1750
40% of next $5000	=	$ 2000
45% of next $5000	=	$ 2250
50% of next $3000	=	$ 1500
$28,000		$10,250

So the average tax rate is 10,250/28,000 or 36.6 per cent. The marginal tax rate is 50 per cent.

So, for this country a simple graph can be drawn which shows the average and marginal tax rate for any *taxable income* (see Figure 8.2)

Figure 8.2 *Average and marginal tax rates for a given taxable income*

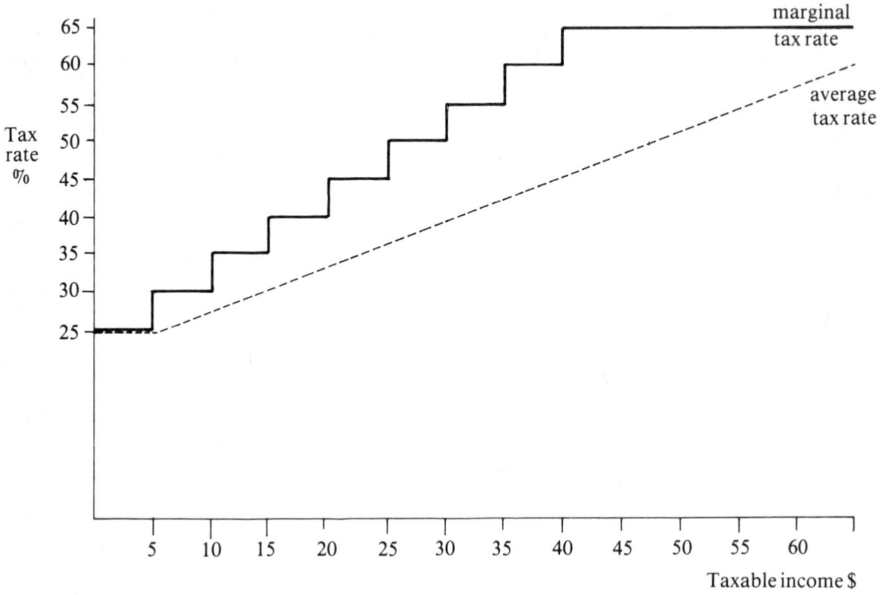

By taking account of the 20 per cent standard deduction, a graph of marginal and average tax rates against *gross salary* can be drawn (see Figure 8.3).

Figure 8.3 *Average and marginal tax rates for given gross salaries*

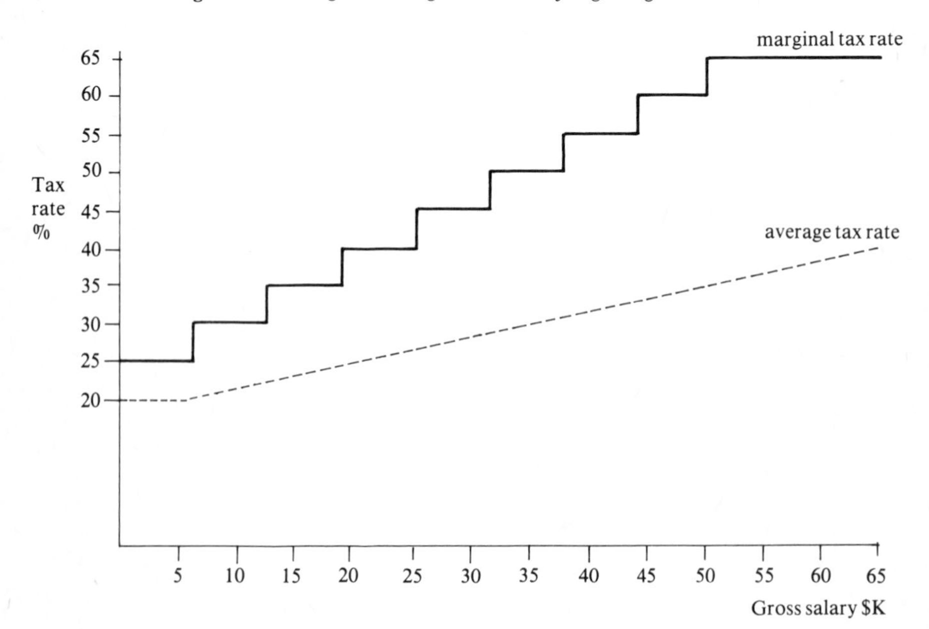

The impact of this type of percentage deduction clearly favours higher salaries. When analysing the tax structure of a country, it is important to grasp the relationship between average tax and actual gross salary – as opposed to taxable income. The final graph is the key one which shows gross salary against net salary (see Figure 8.4).

Figure 8.4 *Net salary as a function of gross salary*

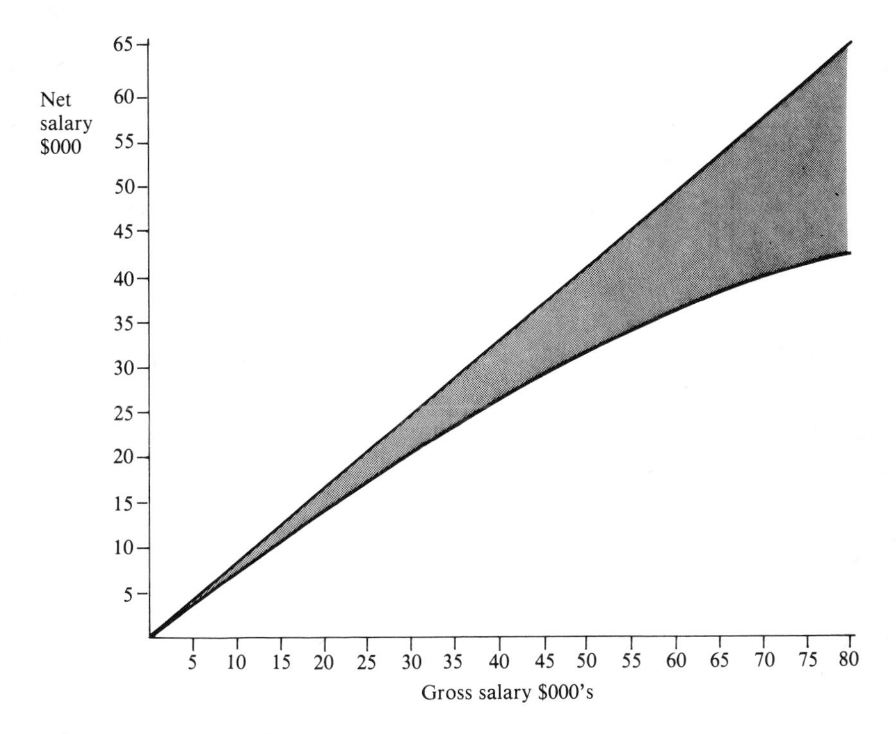

The straight line represents no tax paid, where gross equals net. The curve represents the net salary after tax corresponding to a given gross salary in this country. The shaded area between the lines is the amount of tax paid.

The graph shows the very great difference between marginal and average tax rates. The more progressive the marginal rate structure, the steeper the graph will be, and the greater will be the difference between the marginal and average tax rates.

WORLDWIDE TAX STRUCTURES

The following figures show the differences in the effects of taxation on expatriates in some 40 different countries (excluding social security contributions and assuming the 'normal' deductions only – correct as at mid 1981).

Figure 8.5 *Average tax rates for a married expatriate with two children (gross salary $50,000)*

Average tax rates – gross salary $50,000			
Country	*Percentage rate*	*Country*	*Percentage rate*
Sweden	63.8	Mexico	32.7
India	60.2	Bolivia	31.1
Portugal	54.6	Italy	30.4
Denmark	53.1	West Germany	29.3
Kenya	52.6	Nigeria	28.3
Trinidad	51.8	Belgium	27.9
New Zealand	50.6	Egypt	23.5
Finland	48.7	Singapore	23.1
Thailand	42.2	Japan	22.5
Peru	40.4	Switzerland (Geneva)	22.5
Iran	38.9	Holland	19.7
Greece	37.7	France	16.7
Austria	37.2	Hong Kong	15.0
Norway	36.9	UK	12.5
Malaysia	36.5	Venezuela	11.7
Indonesia	34.8	Kuwait	0
USA (New York)	34.6	UAE	0
Australia	34.3	Saudi Arabia	0
Brazil	33.5	Oman	0
Canada	33.5		

From countries with zero personal income tax such as those in the Middle East, to those such as the UK which have very high tax for resident British but low taxation for expatriates, to the high tax European countries, there is a wide variety of tax levels, with significant implications for expatriate compensation and benefits planning.

Figure 8.6 shows the impact of family size, comparing the tax paid by a married expatriate with two children to that paid by a single expatriate, both earning a gross salary of $50,000.

Figure 8.6 *Ratios of tax paid per salary in a sample of 17 countries for a married expatriate with two children*

Country	*Ratio*
France	0.57
West Germany	0.71
Switzerland (Geneva)	0.81
USA (New York)	0.82
Japan	0.86
Portugal	0.89
Norway	0.91
Canada	0.92
UK	0.93
Peru	0.93
Bolivia	0.95
Brazil	0.95
Holland	0.95
Malaysia	0.95
Mexico	1.00
Iran	1.00
Hong Kong	1.00

Few countries thus make much of a differentiation although in those that do, the difference can be very large indeed. In fact the latest French tax changes are likely to reduce this major advantage for individuals with high salaries and large families.

Finally, Figure 8.7 shows the effect of doubling the gross salary for the married expatriate with two children to $100,000.

Figure 8.7 *Effect of a two-fold increase in gross salary for a married expatriate with two children*

Country	*Ratio* (tax on $50,000 to tax on $100,000)
Italy	3.50
Belgium	3.26
France	3.18
Holland	3.17
Nigeria	3.15
Iran	3.14
UK	2.87
West Germany	2.83
Australia	2.75
Switzerland (Geneva)	–
Venezuela	2.67
Canada	2.64
Malaysia	2.64
USA (New York)	2.63
Mexico	2.62
Brazil	2.55
Peru	2.55
Thailand	2.54
Singapore	2.55
Trinidad	2.06
Hong Kong	2.00

Thus, if an expatriate's salary is doubled in Hong Kong, the tax is doubled, whereas in Italy the tax more than trebles.

These tables show that there are major and significant differences between the taxation of expatriates in the various countries within which a multi-national company is likely to work. There is no substitute for the compensation and benefits manager acquiring a good working knowledge of the tax systems of the countries with which he is concerned.

Depending upon the family status, salary levels and allowable deductions, the expatriate may be subject to widely different tax rates in the same country, let alone comparing one country with another. If a company is trying to apply a consistent set of expatriate policies for all expatriates in all countries, it has no alternative but to become involved in some sort of equalization programme.

EXPATRIATE TAX POLICY CONSIDERATIONS

There are, broadly, two approaches that multi-national companies take to the taxation of their expatriates. Either the expatriate pays tax in the country in which he is assigned on the same basis as a local resident, or the company provides some form of tax protection for the employee.

Like the rest of the compensation package, the tax policy has to be looked at not only in the context of the total package but also in relation to the kind of employees and types of assignment, using the same analysis as outlined in earlier chapters.

Thus, an approach which requires the expatriate to pay the tax in the country to which he is assigned, is obviously appropriate for an employee who is expected to remain for a prolonged period in that location overseas. However, for short-term expatriates this approach can lead to major problems such as:

- gross unfairness between assignments in high and low tax countries;
- random factor of the date of arrival in countries which tax on a complete year basis, eg France.

TAX PROTECTION

The basic philosophy of a tax protection programme is normally for the expatriate to pay tax on his base salary at the level at which he would have paid tax in his home country on that same base salary. Let us consider a typical calculation:

base salary	$40,000
overseas premium	$ 8000
cost of living allowance	$ 2000
gross salary	$50,000
taxable value of benefits in kind	$28,000
total gross salary for tax purposes	$78,000
tax paid in host country	$29,000
hypothetical tax paid on home country base	$12,000
'reimbursement'	$17,000

The expatriate is deemed to have a hypothetical tax on his $40,000 base salary of $12,000 and thus he would either pay his taxes in the host country and be reimbursed personally, or the company would pay his host country taxes and deduct $12,000 from his gross salary. The intent of this approach is to provide the employee with effectively tax free foreign assignment premiums and benefits, while maintaining his tax level on his base salary. It is an approach frequently used.

There are, of course, a number of both practical and theoretical problems with this kind of method:

- How is the hypothetical home country tax calculated? What are the standard deductions and specific deductions that the individual would have been expected to have had in his home country (such as interest on loans, insurance)?

- The tax reimbursement is also taxable, which may result in a 'pyramid' effect in some countries, where tax is paid on tax paid on tax paid (normally a single payment is negotiable in most countries).

TAX EQUALIZATION

Another approach, well suited to a workforce with many different nationalities where frequent moves are normal, or indeed to a single nationality employer who wants to avoid some of the problems inherent in the tax protection approach, is a tax equalization system.

The theory of the system is that the total tax liability of the expatriate employee is calculated, and an average tax rate as a function either of salary or overseas gross salary is applied. Thus a company might decide that its employees would be liable on the average salary (in the average country) for tax at an average rate of 12 per cent of earnings. It would then deduct 12 per cent of the gross salary (base plus hardship allowance) and pay host country taxes directly.

The advantages of the scheme are obvious:

- simple, easy to administer and understand;
- prevents an employee having an especially 'bad' (eg Sweden) or especially 'good' (eg Saudi Arabia) tax break, so treating all expatriates in the same way;
- the gross salary structure is in direct proportion to the net salary structure (avoiding the problems posed by the diminishing marginal attractiveness of salary increases) and thus very easy for salary management purposes.

However, there are disadvantages:

- if expatriates remain for prolonged periods in the same location the system can give them either an especially bad or good deal by comparison with local taxation;
- the benefit provided becomes an increasing function of salary, which is hardly sound management. An example would be a 20 per cent tax equalization programme applying in the hypothetical country's tax structure already discussed in this chapter (see Figure 8.8).

Figure 8.8

(a)				*(b)*	
Gross salary $	*Average actual tax rate* $	*Net salary after tax* $	*Net salary with 20 per cent tax equalization* $	*Gross that would be needed to achieve this* net $	*Ratio gross b/a*
20,000	24.5	15,100	16,000	21,000	1.05
30,000	27.5	21,750	24,000	33,000	1.10
40,000	31.5	27,400	32,000	47,500	1.14
50,000	34.0	33,000	40,000	64,000	1.28
60,000	37.5	38,100	48,000	92,500	1.54

It is clear that the result of this kind of equalization on higher salaries produces equivalent gross salaries at a rapidly escalating and increasingly unrealistic level. This leads to obvious difficulties when trying to repatriate people with high salaries and there are exaggerated differences between highly paid expatriates and equivalently paid local employees:

- The systems may be made more sophisticated to deal with this problem; either a progressive percentage may be used or a different percentage can apply to different grades in the organization. Neither of these approaches is satisfactory, bearing in mind that they have a highly arbitrary element;
- The initial intention of such a system is to equalize the cost, ie make the scheme self-balancing. This is rarely the case in practice since, even if it were self-balancing originally, a scheme would rapidly become out of balance because of progressive tax structures and fiscal drag, quite apart from the impact of the changing distribution of salaries within a changing distribution of countries, eg moving a highly paid group of expatriates from a regional headquarters in a low tax country to one with high tax. Of course, a progressive and regular increase in the 'company' tax rate could certainly accommodate this but it would be hard to administer (since many countries' systems do not readily allow tax liability to be accurately determined on a current yearly basis) and is difficult to gain acceptance;
- Most of these equalization systems do involve a significant net cost to the company. There is thus a benefit to the employees which is in effect invisible. It is not a good practice for the employee to have a substantial benefit of which he is not aware.

AMERICAN EXPATRIATES

The taxation of expatriate American citizens' foreign earned income has changed radically four times within the period 1976 to 1982. Although the United States has always taxed its overseas citizens' foreign source income, the effect of deductions was to give Americans working overseas virtually no US tax liability on their overseas earnings. In the late 1970s the domestic reaction to the popular image of the affluent expatriate resulted first in the 1976 Tax Reform Act which reduced, retrospectively, many of the expatriates' tax benefits. The Act was subsequently delayed, modified in 1977 and in 1978 a completely revised tax law was passed. The objective of the 1978 Act was to allow US citizens working abroad to deduct from income only those excess costs related to overseas employment, together with certain allowances for hardship areas but not, through a system of exclusions, to benefit beyond this level from the normal US tax system. Finally in 1981, the Economic Recovery Act, which was started as an incentive to encourage American citizens to accept expatriate employment, re-established a major exclusion for foreign earned income. One of the major criticisms of the 1976, 1977 and 1978 Acts was that by making it less attractive for expatriate US citizens – or more expensive for expatriate employers with US citizens in tax protection plans – a major reduction in the numbers of expatriate Americans would result. This would create a substantial reduction in the competitive position of US exports of goods and services.

In broad terms existing legislation means that US citizens, who can demonstrate that they are bona fide residents of foreign countries (for a period of at least 12 months including a calendar year) or have been physically present overseas for 330 out of any 360 day period, can qualify for special treatment under the 1981 Economic Recovery Act. For example:

- exclusion of the first $75,000 of foreign earned income (rising by $5000 per year to $95,000 in 1986 and beyond), including salaries and all benefits in kind;
- exclusion of the difference between foreign housing expenses and basic housing cost, set each year by the IRS as 16 per cent of the salary of a particular grade of government employee (eg in 1982 it will be $6059 per year).

The general effect of the latest tax reform is that few US citizens abroad will, for practical purposes, pay any US tax (since, in addition to the exclusions, the majority of foreign taxes paid can be taken as a US tax credit). It is probable that the only locations which could present tax problems for Americans would be those with typically very high overseas premiums and low personal income taxes, eg the Middle East.

US tax law is extremely complex. Where a company has a tax protection programme which provides the employee with an overseas net salary and protects his total tax at the level of the national tax on a home country base salary, it is a matter for the employer to manage the US citizen's tax return. Where there is no such programme and the expatriate US employee is responsible for his own US taxes, a company should ensure he takes competent professional advice. The company could reimburse the cost of tax advice from an 'approved' advisor up to a dollar limit. The impact of incompetent self-help or of using domestic US tax advisors who are not fully conversant with expatriate US taxation, can be a financial disaster for the expatriate.

There are one or two other nationalities who tax their expatriates on foreign earned income even as non-residents, eg Switzerland and Korea, but the level of taxation is low in these cases.

RESIDENCY QUALIFICATIONS – NOT MET

One area of both complexity and importance relates to the taxation of expatriates who do not meet the non-residency qualification of their home countries. This can happen in the year of initial expatriation or of repatriation. It can also happen to people who work on rotation cycles (although this latter group seem in practice to escape the tax net).

A common practice for employers, whether or not they have a tax equalization programme, is for home country taxes in these kinds of situations to be the employee's responsibility. This is related to the belief many countries have, which has already been explained, that people should pay the taxes levied on them by their governments almost as a moral responsibility as citizens. However, there is another school of thought which attempts to manage net salaries and to ensure that the incidence of home country taxation does not thwart the structure it is trying to achieve. A great deal depends, as usual, on the basic company philosophy, the kind of nationality mix and types of assignment. The implication is that when an individual is moved in or out of his home country, careful tax evaluation is needed.

OTHER ISSUES

The working wife

If a wife works in an overseas assignment and the company has a tax protection or equalization system, their joint filing would obviously raise the tax liability of the employee. In this context a company will want to calculate the theoretical tax liability rather than provide the employee with a needless windfall benefit.

Benefits

Many countries provide regular cash payments in the form of child allowances and family benefits funded out of either taxation or social security contributions. In some countries this can amount to a relatively substantial sum. A number of companies when calculating their tax equalization, balance sheet or other computations take full account of these payments. Others ignore them.

TAX ON WORLDWIDE INCOME

Some countries tax residents – even if foreign nationals – on worldwide income, ie in the case of an expatriate, income which arises from sources other than that relating to direct employment in the country concerned. This could be income paid overseas in respect of work performed outside the country, and obviously any income from investment or rents arising outside the country concerned and declared for tax purposes. In most cases where this foreign source income is subject to income taxes in the country in which it is earned, tax treaties allow for tax paid on the income to be taken as a foreign tax credit or as a deduction, in order to eliminate the possibility of double taxation. In other cases taxes are only levied on foreign source income remitted to the country concerned.

Aside from the practicalities of a country obtaining full disclosure from its non-domiciled residents, this area of tax is seldom one in which a multi-national company is involved so far as its tax protection programmes are concerned.

CONCLUSION

Income tax is a complicated and sophisticated area in which the expatriate compensation and benefits manager must acquire a working expertise, a knowledge that is generally not required of his domestic counterpart. Since much of expatriate compensation is concerned with net salaries, companies cannot avoid deep involvement with the tax liabilities their expatriates are likely to face in their different countries of operation.

9. Integration of the salary package

INTRODUCTION

For the purpose of clarity each element of the expatriate remuneration and benefits package has been separately described. In each case – for the base salary, premiums and benefits – there are several alternatives. The employer may decide to base his structure on home country salaries – he may decide to offer expatriation, hardship and COLA payments. There is also the choice of whether to provide free housing in the location or whether to make a deduction from salary. Tax liabilities must be examined to see how both host and home country rates should apply to the expatriate's salary. Finally, the employer must decide in what currency the salary will be paid and to what extent he is prepared to protect the expatriate against fluctuations in exchange rates. All these elements, most of which are subject to changing circumstances, must be integrated into a total salary package which can be updated and maintained with reasonable ease.

In this chapter the major approaches used to construct integrated salary packages are examined. Some are relatively simple, some very sophisticated. The employer, in choosing any system, must balance sophistication against flexibility and should allow for the particular needs of the company itself.

Each of the principal methods of integration have now become associated with a particular title. Companies have their own descriptions of the techniques – causing the same approach to emerge under a variety of titles. The most common techniques are as follows:

- Assignment country, sometimes known as 'going rate'
- Home country – balance sheet, sometimes known as the 'build-up method'
- Modified balance sheet
- Safety net or umbrella
- International base pay or global compensation plan.

There are many hybrids of these methods and many companies have designed their own individual variants.

ASSIGNMENT COUNTRY

In a given situation a company may find that paying the going rate is the most effective approach to structuring expatriate salaries for people spending a prolonged period in the same country. If this works without problems most of the complicated procedures regarding allowances and tax become unnecessary.

The 'going rate' philosophy is likely to be effective when salaries in the host country remain attractive in comparison with the expatriate's own employment market. For many years it was possible to attract Europeans to work in the USA by offering them USA salary rates, taking into account reasonable cost of living and relatively low tax rates. Equally, a British employee would have been happy to work in most continental European countries at market salary rates as this would provide him with a substantially higher purchasing power than he might have enjoyed at home. Some companies apply assignment country salaries and also allow a small element of allowances. The three most common types of allowance are:

- Once-only allowance for transfer – a lump sum for settling into the country of assignment
- Location premium, usually a percentage of base salary or a sum which is reduced over time (the logic behind this is that the expatriate will adjust to the foreign location after a number of years)
- Housing allowance, free (or subsidized) accommodation – again for a limited period.

The company will usually also provide some assistance with excess educational costs.

The advantage of such a package lies primarily in its simplicity. The employer does not concern himself with currency fluctuations or tax equalization programmes. The expatriate is paid wholly in the local currency and is responsible for his own tax and social security payments. Salary administration follows the same lines as that for local employees, particularly with regard to general increases and merit payments. The expatriate is, except for some small allowances, on an equal level with local employees and with other expatriates paid in the same way.

Nevertheless there are some major disadvantages to this policy. If the company employs expatriates in many different countries, then using the assignment country approach may result in a large variation in purchasing power and discretionary income between nationals. If two Englishmen are expatriated to undertake the same job, one in Switzerland and one in Portugal, they will end up with substantially different standards of living. If one of these expatriate's is transferred to another location there will be no consistency between his salary levels in the two countries.

An assignment country approach implies that the expatriate will contribute to, and benefit from, the host country social security and pension arrangements. This approach may be suitable for the long-term expatriate in one country, but is inappropriate for short-term expatriation or an employee who works in a number of foreign countries. Employees will be unlikely to benefit from the two or three years' contributions made in the host country and may have problems maintaining his home country payments. Equally, if he maintains commitments in the home country – mortgage or insurance payments, he may find them becoming an unacceptable burden if the currency of the host country depreciates against that of his home country. The recent rapid, major currency realignments following the 1973 oil price upheaval created substantial problems in the relative attractiveness of going rate salaries. A change of over 50 per cent in the $/FF exchange rate which occurred between 1981 and 1982 dramatically affected the attractiveness of FF salaries for US expatriates. A further difficulty is that of repatriation after several years when, using this system, there may be no clear criteria regarding the position of repatriated employees in the home country salary structure.

Such difficulties may be overcome by the use of specific policies, particularly if the company has only a few expatriates in only one overseas operation. The assignment country system is, however, wholly unworkable in most non-OECD countries when the going market salary rate is much less than that in the expatriate's home country. Given this situation considerable adjustments would need to be made to make the salary of interest to the expatriate. If this is brought about then the object of such a salary system is defeated, causing a destruction of the relationship to both host country and home country salary structures.

HOME COUNTRY – BALANCE SHEET METHOD

The balance sheet method is undoubtedly the most popular method of integration for most established multi-national companies employing large numbers of expatriates. At its most sophisticated it provides a logical basis for the whole salary package for each expatriate. Essentially, the balance sheet method takes the home country salary structure for each expatriate and then proceeds to calculate the total net salary in the host country. The job to be performed abroad by the expatriate is evaluated in the home location salary structure and the home base salary defined.

Home country social security, pensions, insurance and similar provisions are frequently maintained on the basis of this salary. Using this base salary an expatriation and/or hardship premium is calculated together with the cost of living allowance. The company must then decide whether to make a deduction for housing and the method of applying tax equalization. Thus, for a British expatriate working in Saudi Arabia the sample balance sheet would be as shown in Figure 9.1.

In this sample the entire net salary is converted at the current rate into Saudi Rials and paid in Saudi Arabia. No tax is payable (in fact the company operates a tax protection programme and would pay any local tax liabilities).

Figure 9.1

		£ *per year*
Basic UK salary		12,000
Less hypothetical UK tax (Note 1)		2891
Home country net		9109
Foreign service premium at 35 per cent of basic salary		4200
Hardship allowance at 20 per cent of base salary		2400
Cost of living adjustment (Note 2)		3168
Overseas housing deduction (Note 3)		(1200)
Total overseas net salary		17,677
Note 1 Basic UK salary	12,000	
less pension, associated security contribution	1200	
less personal allowances	1165	
taxable salary	9635	
tax paid at 30 per cent	2891	
Note 2 Spendable income (from spendable income curve) is 48 per cent of home country base: £12,000 x 48 = 5760		
COLA is at 55 per cent: 55 per cent x 5760		
Allowance	3168	
Note 3 Housing based on 10 per cent of UK base salary		

If the company is providing the balance sheet calculation for one nationality or treating its expatriates as though they are all from one country – a common practice of US multi-nationals – a composite schedule of the balance sheet can be built up. For each salary level the following calculation is made:

Base salary
plus
Foreign service premium
plus
Hardship allowance
plus
COLA
minus
(Home country hypothetical tax)
minus
(Housing deduction)
to arrive at
Overseas net salary

Figure 9.2 illustrates how a composite schedule can be derived for a variety of locations. In the higher salary ranges the allowances diminish rapidly because of the higher home country 'hypothetical' tax rates and because the COLA is only being applied to the spendable income part of the salary (proportionally smaller on higher salaries).

Figure 9.2

	Location				
Monthly base salary ($)	*Abu Dhabi* %	*Algeria* %	*Argentina* %	*Bahrain* %	*Brazil* %
1500-1699	42	40	18	42	27
1700-1899	41	38	17	41	25
1900-2099	40	37	16	40	24
2100-2299	38	35	15	38	23
2300-2499	37	33	14	37	22
2500-2699	35	32	13	35	21
2700-2899	34	30	12	34	19
2900-3099	33	29	11	33	18
3100-329′	31	27	9	31	17
3300-3499	30	25	8	30	16
3500-3699	28	24	7	28	14
3700-3899	27	22	6	27	13
3900-4099	25	21	5	25	12
4100-4299	24	19	4	24	11
4300-4499	23	17	3	23	10
4500-4699	21	16	2	21	8
4700-4899	20	14	1	20	7
4900-5099	18	13	0	18	6
5100-5299	17	11	0	17	5
5300-5499	15	9	0	15	3
5500-5699	14	8	0	14	2
5700-5899	13	6	0	13	1
5900 and above	11	5	0	11	0

To arrive at the overseas net the home country base is enhanced by the percentages in the table corresponding to each salary range.

INTRODUCING CURRENCY VARIATIONS INTO THE BALANCE SHEET

The results obtained from a balance sheet calculation can be translated into appropriate salary amounts using the home country or host country currencies. Given widely fluctuating currency rates, however, the original calculations will only remain valid for a limited amount of time. For example, if an American expatriated to Mexico is paid in dollars and the peso weakens against the dollar, the expatriate will find himself progressively better off each month when his salary is paid. If, on the other hand, the dollar starts to weaken against the peso he will have less spending power in Mexico. In practice the balance sheet method usually pays a portion of the expatriate salary in the host country, the rest being paid in the home country currency. The balance sheet shown below illustrates how compensation is broken up into the portion paid in the host country and in the home country, using the previous example (see Figure 9.3).

Figure 9.3

	Home country currency £ sterling	*Host country currency rials*
Compensation summary		
Base pay	12,000	
COLA	3168	
Foreign service premium	4200	
Hardship allowance	2400	
Hypothetical tax deduction	(2891)	
Housing deduction	(1200)	
Net compensation (X)	17,677	
Method of pay		
A. *Portion paid in host country*		
Host location spendable income		8928 (Note 1)
B. *Portion paid in home country*		
Remainder of base pay plus allowances	8749	
X = A + B		

Note 1 – Host country spendable income is home country spendable income + COLA

A better solution is to calculate and fix the host country spendable income in local currency and then pay the salary in two quite separate portions. In the example shown the £8928 would be converted to Saudi rials and the amount paid in local currency would not change, except where local inflation causes a review of the cost of living. This is the only fair and effective way of compensating for an adverse currency shift without the employee suffering and equally avoiding windfall gains because of devaluation.

ADJUSTMENT MECHANISM IN HIGH INFLATION COUNTRIES

An expatriate may complain that very high inflation in the host country will reduce his purchasing power over time. If regular adjustments are not made, to take into account inflation and currency fluctuations, the expatriate may feel his salary is somewhat arbitrary. The solution to this is the use of an inflation adjustment factor, applied directly to the cost of living allowance. So, if the COLA was 100 per cent and the monthly cost of living increase in the host country was 10 per cent, while in the home country it was 1 per cent, then a 9 per cent factor would be applied each month to the COLA. (This assumes that the host country currency remains stable.)

This system protects the expatriate's foreign spendable income until such time as it is formally adjusted by the full recalculation of the balance sheet.

MODIFIED BALANCE SHEET

The modified balance sheet method uses essentially the same approach as that employed in the balance sheet system, but the definition of cost differences between home and work countries is simplified. As the handbook of an international corporation using this method comments:

> As the group employs 50 or so nationalities of expatriate worldwide, it would call for the use of as many base salaries and sets of cost of living assessments as there are nationalities in each location, a daunting administrative task and one which would result in unacceptable difference between the remuneration of staff originating from low pay and high pay base countries.

To overcome this problem the company selects a basic reference salary to act as a yardstick for all nationalities. The currency of such a base salary must be relatively strong and stable and linked to a large group of currencies (eg the Swiss franc). Salary levels in the country where the reference salary is fixed must be realistic and competitive.

The reference salary is then used as a yardstick against which variations in the cost of living in host countries can be measured. This produces a spendable income to meet day-to-day living expenses in each host country, in exactly the same way as the standard balance sheet system. All expatriates at the same job level and family status in each location receive the same spendable income regardless of nationality. A standard expatriate and hardship allowance is also applied. At this point only, the modified balance sheet approach takes account of the expatriate's country of origin. A discretionary expenditure index is compiled for each expatriate's home country as a function of salary. In other words, it is accepted that the level of discretionary expenditure varies widely from country to country, reflecting differences in standards of living in different countries. Thus, each expatriate's net salary is made up of a mixture of spendable income – standard for each location, and discretionary income – depending on the country of origin. Figure 9.4 shows the effects of such an approach.

> Consider the same expatriate in three different locations overseas – X, Y and Z. Hence, the same expatriate receives the same discretionary income in each location and different nationalities receive the same local spendable and expatriate allowance in the same location.

The modified balance sheet incorporates two approaches. It adopts a standard comparison for hardship and COLA for all nationalities. At the same time, each nationality is given a different discretionary income based on statistical information obtained from his home country.

Figure 9.4

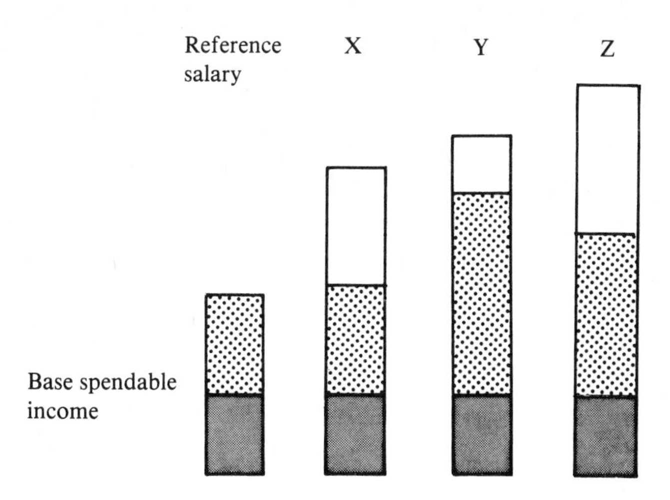

and for three different expatriates in the same location

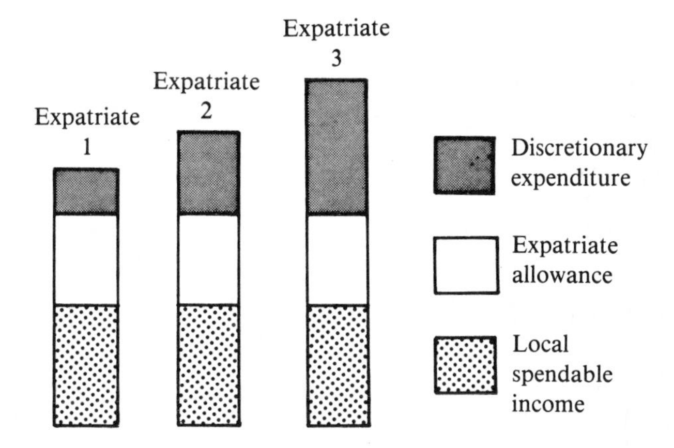

The advantage of such an approach is that it simplifies the cost of living comparison, while at the same time retaining an element which recognizes that expatriates come from countries with different standards of living – a factor which is often ignored in the global compensation plan. Theoretically, it is sufficiently flexible to accommodate expatriates from many different countries without being impossibly difficult to administer. Furthermore, although different nationalities receive different net salaries in the same overseas location, there is a defensible logic for doing so.

The problems with the scheme are the same as those encountered with all balance sheet methods – they rely on indexes which are generalizations and are not always understood by the expatriates involved. For the multi-national company that wants to adopt the balance sheet method, but at the same time employs expatriates from many different countries, the modified balance sheet may be a viable alternative.

Optional spending power

Another variation of the balance sheet approach is the introduction of an element of choice for employees regarding their spending power in the overseas location. The standard balance sheet approach pays the spendable income converted to the host country currency. It may also provide a housing cost element and any other specifically foreign allowance in the host country currency. (The remainder being paid in the home country currency.)

There may be situations where the expatriate wants to make larger expenditures in the host country, eg buying a second car. To do this he must use the part of his salary paid in his home country currency. In doing so the expatriate will pay exchange rate transaction costs and may lose heavily if the host country currency moves adversely against the home country currency.

One solution to this problem is to pay all the expatriate's salary in the host country currency, but guarantee that the portion considered to be discretionary will be protected against currency fluctuations.

The company may also give the expatriate a choice of how much of his total income he wishes to be paid in the host country. Having made this choice, the company then guarantees this element in terms of the home country rate.

In spite of all the company's efforts the expatriate may still feel badly treated in terms of comparisons between the home and host country. This is because, after several years, he and his family tend to forget the actual prices at home and ignore the fact that inflation has occurred there, as well as in the assignment location. The company must work hard to demonstrate that the balance sheet approach adopted does take into account the level of inflation and currency devaluations.

Safety net payment system

There may be cases where the company has chosen either the home country or the host country structure as a general guide for salaries, but has found that in some countries, the reference cannot apply. For example, if the expatriate is transferring from a low to a high salary area it may be found that basing this salary on home country rates and adding incentives and allowances still does not bring him anywhere near market salary rate in the host country. Equally, if the company generally uses the host country rate for the job there will be countries where, even with overseas incentives, the package will still not be sufficiently attractive to the expatriate when compared with the home country base salary. A solution to such a problem is for the company to apply the safety net approach; the expatriate receives whichever is the higher of:

- the host country salary together with an element of incentive for an

overseas assignment; or
- the home base salary plus COLA.

Figures 9.5 and 9.6 illustrate this approach:

Figure 9.5 *Transfer from a higher to a lower salary area*

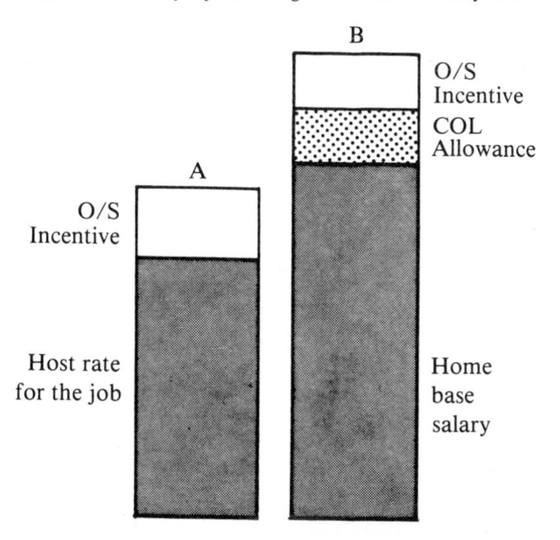

A Swiss expatriate in India would be given salary structure B because A, plus a normal overseas incentive, would still leave him worse off than in his domestic market.

Figure 9.6 *Transfer from a lower to a higher salary area*

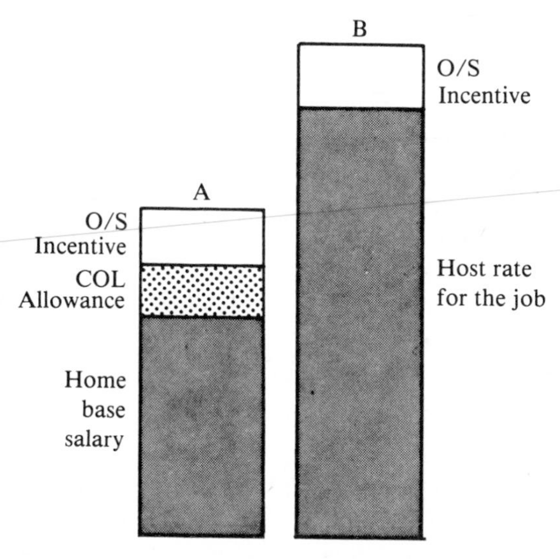

The Indian expatriate in Switzerland is given salary B since the host country rate is more attractive to the expatriate than the home basic salary plus allowances.

The advantage of providing this sort of option is that it can give salary administration considerably more flexibility in a wide variety of countries. If the company employs expatriates from countries having very high salaries it is going to find it hard to accommodate them by basing salaries on local rates, assuming of course that these rates are available. If it employs expatriates from low salary countries, it could base its expatriate package on a host country basis.

Such a scheme does have certain disadvantages. It is a complicated approach requiring simultaneous measurement of the home base salary, the foreign rate for the job and every other element of the balance sheet system. Equally, when applied it can result in several expatriates, working in the same job and in the same location, receiving quite different salaries. It is most likely to be used where, for example, the balance sheet method can be applied for most of a company's expatriates, but there are one or two locations where this leaves the expatriate less well paid than the local employee. In this case the company may decide it is worthwhile offering extra allowances to provide an incentive for expatriates to go to that country, at the same time maintaining the balance sheet approach in other locations.

INTERNATIONAL BASE PAY

Most multi-nationals have one or two nationalities who predominate and who are most frequently expatriated. Because of this the balance sheet approach is often favoured as it will only involve comparisons with one or two home countries. However, some multi-nationals have a genuinely international expatriate workforce with up to 50 nationalities. Working out a full or even modified balance sheet for every nationality is a daunting task. The company may choose to opt for a global compensation system which removes expatriates both from the home and host countries for salary purposes. The key to such a scheme rests on determining a 'representative' base salary for the jobs being undertaken, together with the use of a 'neutral' currency through which payments are made. (This differs from the modified balance sheet in that no home country reference is made.)

Establishing international salaries can only be achieved by looking at representative markets. In the oil industry the market could be a composite of the US, European and Middle Eastern markets. In banking it could be a selection of American and European salaries. This enables the company to obtain a representative figure of the levels of net salaries that are current in the industry. An expatriate pay scale can then be established which is separate from any one home country structure.

Using the base salary structure a system of overseas allowances can be established. These would be hardship premium (since the base salary is intended to take account of expatriation) and COLA (based on an arbitrary reference point), together with a deduction for housing and tax equalization. This method differs from the balance sheet system since these allowances apply equally to all nationalities of expatriate. To achieve this one must assume that hardship applies equally to expatriates from different backgrounds. As a result the cost of living adjustment must be taken from a fixed point – the price impact of living away from, for example, Washington DC. Clearly, the base used will affect the cost impact in different locations, but it will protect the expatriate against the extremes in costs encountered. Because all expatriates are being treated on an equal basis it is possible to produce a composite premium system which combines hardship and COLA. Using this type of system only a very approximate spendable income is used, premiums normally apply either to the whole base salary or make use of an arbitrary figure as a ceiling.

Housing deductions are dealt with on a standard basis for all expatriates; thus a standard deduction (normally 10 to 15 per cent) would be adopted or housing might be provided free. The logical way of dealing with tax is for the company to evaluate the average tax liability of the average expatriate in the countries in which it operates and then apply an average figure to all its expatriates, thus equalizing the load. Tax equalization schemes of this nature tend to be between 10 to 20 per cent of base salary. All salaries and allowances are normally expressed in a common currency. In practical terms this is either US dollars or Swiss francs – or any other currency with a relatively stable history which is easily convertible into other currencies (and, obviously, one in which the company receives a substantial part of its revenue).

A global compensation plan is complemented by long term benefits on an international basis. This implies that savings plans and pensions should not be orientated to one particular nationality. A common approach is to establish 'offshore' schemes free of national taxes and have all international staff eligible for such schemes. This concept will be further discussed in Chapter 12.

For a multi-national company with mobile expatriates of many nationalities, the global compensation approach has many advantages. From the outset it guarantees genuine parity among the different nationalities of expatriates, who will all be in the same salary structure and paid in a common hard currency. There will also be parity between assignments, with a common premium for each expatriate location. Problems experienced with the other approaches of distinguishing between the company's own nationals and TCNs disappear. It is administratively very straightforward and can be understood by the whole expatriate workforce.

Global pay offers advantages for a large, mixed and highly mobile expatriate workforce. But, as with the other approaches, some problems exist. The most obvious of these is that over the years the 'neutral' currency that is chosen to pay all expatriates can vary against national currencies. Taking the example of the US dollar during the early 1970s, and taking a constant dollar income, the income of a Briton and a German in home currency terms would have varied considerably (see Figure 9.7).

Thus, whatever had been defined as the 'international average salary' in 1970 would be relatively more attractive to the UK expatriate in 1976 than to the German expatriate. The result of this sort of currency movement, together with different salary inflation rates, has many implications for recruitment policies.

Figure 9.7 *Result of a fluctuation in exchange rate on expatriate salaries*

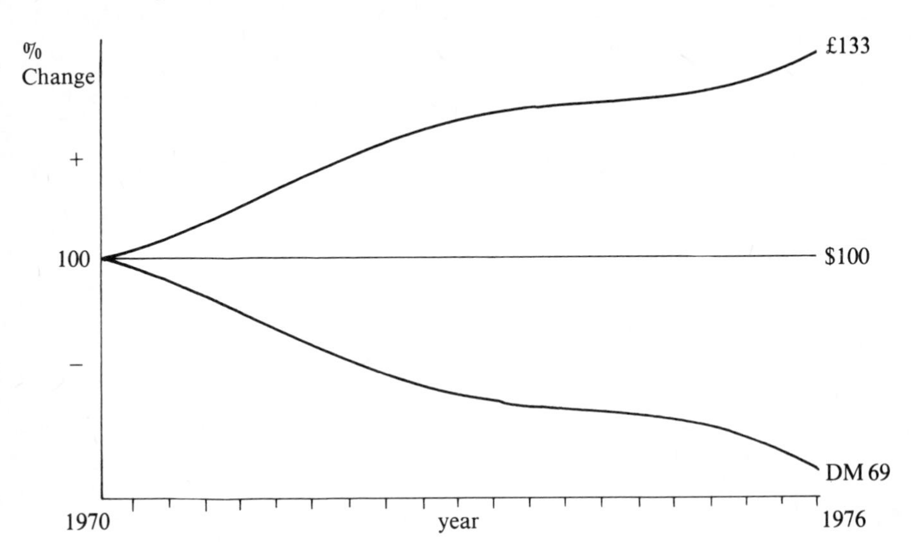

In the above example it will be very easy to recruit UK employees and more difficult to find Germans. If the international salary is set sufficiently high to attract German and, say, Swiss recruits, it will become unnecessarily high for other nationalities and prohibitively expensive for the employer. This is particularly so with expatriates from developing countries, who on this basis will be paid many times their domestic salary when they expatriate.

Another problem with international base pay is that it often results in very high salaries compared with local staff. The expatriate, undertaking the same job as a local, will have a salary package worth many times that of the local which can cause resentment and bad feeling. Moreover, when the expatriate returns to his home country he may feel that his new, much lower home country salary is unacceptable. Finally, a system of 'offshore' long term benefits suits a career expatriate but is quite unsuitable for the individual who undertakes one expatriate assignment only. In this case an expatriate will undoubtedly prefer to be kept in the home country scheme rather than have a short term membership of an international scheme. Overall, the international base pay programme is suited to multi-nationals who employ a large mobile expatriate workforce, coming from a mixture of OECD countries, many of whom spend most of their careers as expatriates. Otherwise it is a superficially elegant solution which may result in more problems than it solves.

INTEGRATING THE PACKAGE – CONCLUSION

Integration of the expatriate salary and benefits package has been discussed after examining the constituent parts – the base salary, premiums, tax and benefits. The personnel manager designing an expatriate package must consider an overall logic consistent for all nationalities and all locations. This is, of course, easier said than done. No one approach is likely to be ideal for all situations and there will always exist a temptation to create a 'special deal' to meet an individual case. The danger of 'special deals' is that they have a tendency to proliferate and quickly corrode the logic of the expatriate package. When this happens consistent administration of the expatriate workforce becomes impossible with a resulting drop in morale. The overall policy must be selected carefully and adhered to.

Selecting a policy implies finding a solution that is appropriate to the particular company, not necessarily one which is the most complex or sophisticated. A simple but consistent approach may be much better than a sophisticated package even when it contains some anomalies. Indeed the full balance sheet system, in terms of sheer complexity, can only be suitable for the medium or large scale expatriate employer.

The profile of the expatriate workforce is also important. As a generalization the following policies are appropriate for the different types of expatriates:

Expatriate type	*Compensation and benefits approach*
Short-term contract	Assignment country rates or balance sheet
Career development posting	Balance sheet or safety net
Long-term, one country	Assignment country
Long-term, many countries	Modified balance sheet, international pay plan.

10. Expatriates on rotation

INTRODUCTION

This book is concerned with expatriates – people living and working outside their home country. However, in many cases, foreigners are used on a rotating basis, where they remain based in their home country and spend time in the foreign location without their family on a regular on-off schedule. In many industries, such as the oil industry, this pattern of work for oil rig personnel, for example, is the normal rule. This type of working pattern implies a mixture of home country and expatriate compensation and benefits characteristics.

At the outset, it is appropriate to outline why these work systems are used and some of the major problems they create.

ADVANTAGES

- It is clearly cheaper for an employer not to have to bear the expense of housing, education and other typical expatriate costs. Expatriates on this work schedule are normally accommodated in camp environments (since rotation systems imply the overseas location is unsuitable for family living).
- In theory, since the expatriate employee is without his family, he is available for work continuously throughout the 'on' period of the schedule. Generally a job that requires the employee to work continuously may suggest a rotation schedule.
- In locations that are considered by the employer to be 'unsafe', it is necessary only to consider the security and possible evacuation of the individual employee rather than of an entire family.
- Where local conditions are such that expatriate families would not be able to have a 'normal' life, poor medical facilities, no school, very substandard accommodation, no recreation, and major cultural barriers to contact with local people, rotation can evidently minimize the problems.
- The opportunity is presented to give people working in hard environments a predictable rest pattern – not by any means always possible for people on a resident basis. The company will in effect employ two complete workforces.

- ○ Companies must conform to local labour laws, such as the regulation of the number of working hours.
- ○ A highly mobile employee has the opportunity to provide stable education in the home country for his children, as opposed to changing schools every few months.
- ○ The opportunity for wives to continue to work in the home country; however difficult it is to have a two career family in a home country context, it is even more so overseas.

For an employer, assigning an expatriate on a rotation schedule can be a far less expensive and risky approach than transferring the employee and his family to an overseas location on a resident basis.

The jobs for which rotation represents a practically acceptable system are those which are basically operational and where it is possible for two people to cover the same position; in other words, directly analogous to shift working. It is rather unusual to find expatriates in managerial or professional jobs working on a rotation system.

DISADVANTAGES

There are a number of disadvantages which in the view of some companies outweigh these advantages:

- ○ Break in continuity of work with consequent effects on maintenance, on-the-job training of employees, contact with a client (vital in the case of a service company), and general sense of job responsibility.
- ○ Travelling time (eg Americans working in the Middle East), jet lag and costs and complexity of personnel planning.
- ○ In many countries, relations with local authorities and local clients are clearly impaired by the implication that the country is not acceptable for expatriate families.
- ○ The risk of creating a highly mercenary attitude in an employee who is likely to have vacation periods of up to half the year and may begin to see the job as a regrettable necessity in order to earn money to finance leisure activities.
- ○ Developing immature attitudes to social relaxation (eg no other recreation in a camp environment except drinking).
- ○ Lack of integration of the expatriate and national employees who are on different working patterns.
- ○ Communications with employees are made extremely difficult – managers may seldom see employees.
- ○ Lack of flexibility – both in bringing the employee back early or altering his departure for time off.

Each company will have to make its own judgement based on the location, type of occupation and level of the employee as to the relative weight of each of the advantages and disadvantages. Thus typical rotation assignments are:

- expatriates in 'war zones', eg Iraq and Angola or where there are serious internal political problems such as Iran in recent years or Nigeria during the Biafran war;
- expatriates working in operational positions in the Middle East, particularly in countries where facilities are limited and strict enforcement of Islamic law makes the assignments unattractive for expatriates and their families;
- oil company personnel working on rigs including offshore installations; even those expatriates working in the North Sea tend to rotate rather than be permanent residents in Aberdeen or Stavanger;
- people in, for example, the aviation industry where working hours are strictly limited.

When a job requires continuous work from an employee, to the detriment of a normal family life, a rotation pattern is frequently used, since it is difficult for families in an expatriate situation to deal with the continuous absence of the husband.

TYPES OF SCHEDULE

There are many different possible schedules which all to some extent depend upon the particular requirements of employers. Indeed, some companies give their employees a choice between several different systems, each with a different level of compensation.

When an employee returns to work after a break of several weeks, there is likely to be a settling-in period and, at the end of the work period, he is likely to be more concerned with anticipation of the forthcoming next break. Thus, from an employer's viewpoint, the work period must be long enough to minimize the proportion of time these elements represent while recognizing that the nature of the assignment will induce fatigue after a certain time. The employee will probably want to have breaks as long as possible, especially if travel time is taken as part of the break and if long-distance air travel is required.

The following schedules are commonly used and are considered to be the most effective:

Even-time

- Usually as a four weeks on/four weeks off (occasionally five weeks on/five weeks off) schedule; this effectively requires two people for each job.
- In some cases, the individual has to wait until his relief arrives, in others, the schedule is arranged as an effective 30 days on/26 days off to allow for overlap.

Other types

- six on/two off – generally not very popular with employees especially those with long air journeys. Six weeks is a long time to spend working every day in a hard environment.

- ○ six on/three off – three men for two jobs.
- ○ five on/three off – a development of even-time which gives an awkward deployment pattern.

SALARIES

If a company has both rotation and permanently resident expatriates in the same location, there needs to be a clear policy to define the relative compensation and benefits packages attached to each working pattern.

In general, in a rotation assignment, the expatriate employee has few expenses in the location – housing, food and transport normally being provided by the company. Thus his costs are unchanged from what he would be expected to spend in his home country, were he working there.

The basic salary will be established using the methods described in previous chapters (home country salary or 'international' salary). The only other element of compensation – an overseas premium – is usually a function of the type of rotation pattern rather than the location. The supposition is that the locations will all be equally demanding from the viewpoint of living and working. A company which offers different rotation schedules may calculate the amount of this premium in order to arrive at the same cost per man/week worked. In addition, companies will survey the expatriate market as part of the process of defining the level of premium.

Thus, a company operating several different schedules could have the following policy, assuming a base salary of $2000/month:

System week on/off	*Premium during on period*	*Premium during off period**	*Average premium*	*Cost of one week's work to the company* $
4:4	30%	zero	15%	1200
5:3	75%	zero	47%	1176
6:3	90%	zero	60%	1200
6:2	110%	zero	83%	1220

*ie base salary only

In some cases a company might add to this premium an additional payment for especially hard assignments, eg the company pays 75 per cent for Libya on the work period of a 4:4 rotation, equivalent to an average of 37.5 per cent premium over the eight week cycle. Other companies may pay an average premium for a rotation cycle that does not change between the on and the off period.

A company must ensure that the relationship between what is paid as a rotation premium and the overseas premium paid in the same location is attractive to permanent expatriates. No problems are likely in hard assignments where the permanent expatriate's overseas premium is high, eg the Middle East, but can create serious difficulties in 'pleasant' assignments, eg Aberdeen, especially at the level of net salary. The permanent expatriate who has to bear substantial living costs in a low hardship premium assignment may well resent the rotation employee, with no local costs, on a more attractive financial and time off package.

Generally, employees are paid in either their home country currency or the currency preferred by the employer, but in either case the salaries are normally paid outside the country of assignment.

TAX AND SOCIAL SECURITY

Country of assignment

The normal practice is for the employer to bear any of the tax or social security costs for which the employee may be liable, since he is almost certainly never going to be in a position to benefit from these contributions.

Home country

It is customary for employees to be fully responsible for any home country income tax liability they might have on money earned overseas during rotation. Such liability is seldom covered by tax protection programmes since the employee is able to benefit from any contributions which he may make. If the employing company is not resident in the country from which the employee comes, it may be very difficult to acquire social security coverage; this area requires careful study to ensure that the employee is able to participate in what may be valuable and irrecoverable benefits.

Tax treatments vary from country to country and their application depends on the degree to which the employee reports his income (since a non-resident company has no obligation to report what it pays its employees).

- A Frenchman, working on rotation and spending over 50 per cent of his time overseas, can normally deduct all his overseas earnings from his taxable income.
- An Englishman on rotation would not be taxed as a non-resident (since he would spend more than 63 days per year in the country) and in theory could only deduct 25 per cent of his earnings from his taxable income.
- An American would be taxed on all his earnings and could not claim overseas allowances.

In practice few countries appear to have a sufficiently sophisticated tax collection system for this to present any serious problem for the individual employee.

BENEFITS

Vacation

It is normal for rotation work patterns not to include any vacation – the on/off cycle is intended to allow for this.

Housing

Housing in the home country is not provided.

Medical benefits

Whenever possible, the employee and his family should be covered by the social security health programme in the home country. This is not difficult to arrange when the employer is a resident company in that country. For a non-resident employer, coverage might be arranged on an individual basis (perhaps to be reimbursed by the employer). Another approach is to give the employee and his family the same medical benefits in their home country as the company's normal expatriate policy.

Other benefits

While the employee on rotation normally receives the same risk benefits as a permanent expatriate, he is usually given membership of the company home country pension plan, where such a plan exists. Otherwise he has the same benefits as permanent expatriates.

'THE TICKET PROBLEM'

Although most people on rotation tend to go back to their home country for their breaks (especially if they are married), single people often prefer to travel widely throughout the world rather than return to their parents' home. This is frequently the case with young men in the oil and construction industry. An American bachelor working in the Middle East might prefer to take his breaks in Bangkok, Kenya or the Côte d'Azur than in his home country, and the cost of air fares would be much less for the company.

Most companies provide either a ticket to the point of origin by the cheapest available fare with a reputable carrier, or provide money up to this cost or reimburse actual costs to the same degree. Where a cash payment is permitted problems may occur. For example, if two single expatriates (on rotation assignments), one French, the other American, take their break simultaneously in Bangkok the French expatriate will have to pay most of the cost of the ticket. The American will not only pay nothing but will have spending money left over. There is no clear solution to this kind of problem, short of providing a non-refundable, non-alterable ticket to the point of origin. (However, most expatriates are able to exchange even these kinds of tickets.) It is usually poor policy to give, in cash terms, the value of the return ticket, but whatever policy is chosen, anomalies are bound to occur.

CONCLUSION

Rotation represents an important option for a company, and one which may be used in specific circumstances. While a company would normaly prefer its expatriates to be resident, there are circumstances when rotation represents a solution to questions involving cost, facilities, security, etc. In situations where rotation systems apply, the personnel manager needs to be able to construct a compensation package which is not out of balance with the system applied to permanent expatriates.

11. Insurance and risk benefits

INTRODUCTION

Risk insurance attempts to compensate the employee or his dependants for the loss of income suffered as a result of specific events occurring which prevent him working for his employer on a temporary or permanent basis. This is quite different from damages that may be awarded by a court against an employer in the case of incapacity arising out of the employer's negligence. The amount of such damages will not be affected by the level of life or accident insurance. It is also quite different from the compulsory employer's liability insurance which is a requirement in some countries.

Conventionally, an actuary will look at three factors when setting up an insurance plan for a given risk: the manner in which it occurs, for example, occupational or non-occupational, accident or illness; the amount of the loss (generally expressed as a function of salary); and the requirements of the dependants (generally defined in terms of family size). For the expatriate plan, the country where the event occurs is not normally a factor to be considered.

Whereas in the home country an employee is frequently covered by a workman's compensation or social security structure which can provide in many developed countries a substantial benefit to dependants, it is certainly not the case in developing countries. To all intents and purposes the expatriate employee's risk benefit package is that provided by the employer (supplemented by anything he might want to provide for himself).

This chapter looks primarily at risk insurance, covering death or disability of the employee. Benefits are provided either by lump sum payments funded from an insurance policy and/or by survivor or disability pensions paid out from the company pension plan. One or two other areas of insurance of particular concern to expatriates and their employers are also discussed.

The compensation and benefits manager, while not being an underwriting expert or an actuary, needs to have a sufficient grasp of the concepts to be able to seek and evaluate the proper professional advice. He should base his analysis of the insurance needs of his expatriate employees on what is appropriate for his company to provide before considering the vehicle to be used to provide them. A number of the conventional wisdoms current in insurance thinking are open to question and need to be critically examined. The design and implementation of a risk benefit package is the responsibility of the personnel manager, not the insurance broker or carrier whose advice, while essential, will be influenced by commercial considerations and pays less attention to the specific needs of the expatriate group.

Why should the employer provide these benefits?

Risk benefits are usually provided by almost all major companies. To some extent this is the result of each company attempting to produce a competitive benefits package regardless of the underlying rationalization. However, there are a number of other reasons, some good, some less so, why employers should provide risk benefits – rather than merely paying a salary and letting employees do as they please. A number of points must be examined:

- It is very much cheaper per head for an employer to set up an insurance programme than for individuals – the ratio of costs can easily be over 5 to 1.
- Employers feel they have a moral responsibility to provide for their employees' families in case of death or disability; after all, this is part of the philosophy of pension provision.
- To the extent that an expatriate may be exposed, because of his job, to unusual risks because of health hazards in underdeveloped countries or the use of unreliable forms of transport, the employer will frequently feel that insurance cover is needed and recognizes that the greater the risk the more difficult and expensive will be the individual's task to insure himself.
- Where the employee is engaged in a dangerous job, such as deep sea diving, an insurance programme is a key recruiting and retention tool.
- In the developed world many countries have social security programmes that can provide quite substantial risk benefits. Expatriate employees cannot expect to find the same cover in less developed countries overseas or remain in their home country programme. Employers may feel that they need to provide this basic cover.

Who should carry the cost of the policy?

The level of contribution by employees, if any, to the cost of their risk benefits depends on the company philosophy. As with pensions, it is common for employees to contribute to the cost of risk benefits (more common in American multi-national companies than European ones). Discounting the employee tax benefit, the arguments for and against employee contributions seem fairly evenly balanced. The following points should be considered:

- employee contributions are usually relatively modest and do not represent any hardship to the employee, but they may reduce the cost to the company;
- an employee could be provided with advice as to the level of risk

benefits he wants and contribute towards it as a function of this choice;
- the employee is more likely to recognize the value (and cost) of a benefit if he pays something towards it.

On the other hand, the employee is not asked to contribute to the cost of his vacation salary nor his ticket home – benefits which typically cost the expatriate employer many times the insurance premiums.

BENEFITS SURVEY

The starting point for any consideration of expatriate risk benefits has to be a survey of comparable companies carried out in the same way as the salary and benefits survey already described, coupled with a general review of benefit levels provided in the home countries of the expatriate employees. Such a survey needs to cover both survivor and disability pensions provided from a company pension plan and lump sums provided from an insurance plan. The benefits must be compared in a common format. A pension should be expressed as an equivalent present value lump sum. The proportion of benefit coming from an employee's own contribution should be discounted, for purposes of comparison, since it is the employee himself who provides this part of his benefit.

Criteria which define what is paid tend to be:

- Occupational or non-occupational, ie did the accident, injury or sickness result from an occupational cause?
- Accident or illness. How is accident defined?
- What salary is used in computing benefit? Home country base, actual overseas gross, average base salary of all employees in the group?
- Multiples of salary paid as a function of each level of event, ie death or disability and the manner in which it occurred – accidental, non-accidental, occupational or non-occupational (all of which combinations exist in many company plans and yield a different benefit). Some companies define these lump sums in absolute monetary terms.
- Impact on this amount as a function of dependent family size. Typical companies might vary their benefits by up to six or more levels as a function of family size.

What also needs to be reviewed are complementary insurance plans, eg for occupational travel, common among US companies operating overseas.

CAUSE OR EFFECT?

Insurance in essence should look at the effects of certain events. If an employee dies, the financial requirements of the dependants are precisely the same, no matter what the cause of death. If risk benefits are intended to compensate for loss of income the circumstances in which the event occurred are not relevant; the effects of death in a traffic accident on the way to work in a Third World capital or of death from lung cancer are identical for a given individual's dependants.

However, many companies take the view that some kind of compensation has to be provided by the employer when employees suffer death or disability as a result of carrying out their work responsibilities. This is compounded by the conventional wisdom that the more hazardous the employee's work responsibilities, the more heavily he believes he needs to be insured.

In domestic employment it is usually fairly easy to define occupational or non-occupational accidents. In an expatriate environment it is by no means obvious, since not only has the employee his work responsibilities but he is forced to live in what is frequently a far more risky environment than his home country because of his overseas employment. Thus, not only is there a theoretical objection to differentiating between occupational and non-occupational causes but there are, especially for expatriates, very real practical objections. Suppose that an employee (having the same number of dependants in each case) meets his death in one or other of the following circumstances:

- killed in a car crash on the way to the office in the downtown area of a Third World capital, or killed in a taxi coming home from a night club in the same town (traditionally a higher death benefit would often be paid in the former case);
- death from malaria (of an individual who had not taken prophylactic measures recommended by his employer) in a West African assignment – a fairly obvious occupational cause – and death from a stroke in the same location;
- total paralysis resulting from a fall from a construction site overseas in which the employee was working as a civil engineer and total paralysis resulting from an accident while playing squash in the same location.

These are, of course, difficult cases around which policies are hard to construct. But they indicate the major problems which occur when a company tries to insure for the cause of an event rather than its effect.

REPLACEMENT INCOME

If the objective of a risk insurance programme is the provision of a replacement for the income of the employee, lost as a result of his death or disability, there are a number of key issues which need to be considered.

- **lump sum or pension**
  Traditionally, where the pension plan provides widows and orphans and invalidity benefits, these are in the form of a pension and are rarely commutable to a lump sum. This has the advantage of assuring a continuing form of income (albeit subject to the problems of inflation) no matter what financial profligacy the dependants may show.

Typically, insurance policies pay out lump sums for death and accidental disability and annuities for long term permanent disability. A lump sum may in some circumstances be a very advantageous method of payment in that it can allow, for example, house purchase outright. A combination of lump sum and pension represents a good compromise and it should be possible to set up a programme whereby the option is a pension of which up to, say, 50 per cent can be commuted to a lump sum.

There may be major tax implications for the beneficiaries which will need to be investigated and these will differ totally depending on the country concerned. The company will need to decide in what currency such payments will be made – an annuity paid in $US to the dependants of a German employee would have rapidly declined in value after the 1970s. On the other hand, there may be practical difficulties in purchasing, at a reasonable price, annuities in one currency with a lump sum in another.

○ **family need**

It could be argued that a scale of benefits based on dependent family size is contrary to the replacement income concept. There are few employers who set salary levels as a function of family size and it may seem illogical to apply this criterion to insurance. However, this is a very common approach. Finally, substantial insurance payouts to the estate of bachelors without dependants seem to be a waste of company money.

○ **salary**

The base salary of an expatriate is only a part of his total compensation package. The salary upon which the programme is based has to be consistent with the company's overall compensation philosophy. In other words, for a typical balance sheet package the home country base salary is probably a reasonable reference point for insurance benefit calculations. For a short-term expatriate this is certainly true. With a long-term expatriate the home country base salary may be quite inadequate a basis by comparison with accepted international norms (eg an expatriate engineer from India) and since such people frequently marry wives of another nationality there is often no likelihood of the dependent family moving to the employee's home country. In these cases some level of enhancement to a home country base is needed or an 'international' base salary needs to be used.

The premiums for particular geographical assignments should not be considered part of the salary for insurance purposes. If a company has expatriates in many places the location of the incident ought not to play any role in the calculation of the benefit.

In the context of a multi-national company with many expatriates in many countries it is common to take as the salary, for insurance purposes, an international base salary multiplied by an average expatriate's premium.

DEATH BENEFITS

Upon death, whatever the cause, the amount of benefit awarded varies as a direct function of salary and family size.

In many pension plans a widow's pension equal to half to two-thirds of the employee's prospective pension is provided. A typical UK-type scheme of 1/60 of final salary per year of service would yield a widow's pension of around a third to a half of the employee's salary at the time of death. At a commutation rate of 10 per cent, this is equivalent to a lump sum benefit of between 3.3 and six times the annual salary.

Typical enhancements for dependent children are 10 per cent of the widow's pension usually up to a maximum of four dependent children and with the equivalent lump sum benefits. How much benefit the company provides from the insurance programme will thus depend upon:

- what is already provided by the company pension plan;
- the market survey;
- the degree to which the company believes that it is the employer's responsibility to make such provision.

Typically, international companies provide death benefit in addition to the survivor pensions which can range from one to five or perhaps even six times the annual salary.

In general the needs of the survivor will be greater the younger the employee. Insurance plans should provide death benefits which have:

- little payout to the estate of a bachelor;
- either survivor pensions based upon full prospective service, with a company provision (not guaranteed) to review the pension in the context of inflation; or
- a proviso to award a substantial enough lump sum to purchase an acceptable annuity in whichever country the survivors live. It is good practice to stipulate a proportion of the lump sum which must be used to purchase such an annuity and the company needs to provide the expertise to allow the survivors to make an appropriate selection.

DISABILITY BENEFITS

These benefits tend to be of two types – a lump sum payment (as a proportion of salary and occasionally of family size) to compensate for specific accidental disablement and an invalidity pension paid during the survivor's lifetime. Either or both may be provided and the same criteria used for the calculation of death benefits should also be followed. Furthermore, since the employee survives it is normal for the amounts of benefit in case of permanent disability to be greater than in the case of death.

SOME GENERAL COMMENTS

Distinctions between permanent disability caused by accident, illness, occupational or non-occupational causes are hard to justify as far as the insurance lump sum is concerned. It is normal for the insurance plan to provide for a lump sum payment in case of permanent disability which is modulated by a percentage coefficient depending upon the degree, eg loss of both legs: 100 per cent; loss of one small toe: 2 per cent.

TRAVEL ACCIDENT PLANS

A number of companies have, in addition to the death and disability insurance plans, a complementary insurance for travel accidents for expatriates. This kind of insurance is usually extremely cheap, reflecting the rarity of the occurrence of such accidents, and can provide substantial additional benefits.

However, this kind of plan is anachronistic, dating as it does from the old fear of air travel. It is difficult to operate since it is usually restricted to common carriers. The most dangerous form of travel for expatriates, a company or private car, is usually excluded. If the level of death and disability benefit is adequate, the complementary plans mentioned are unnecessary.

INSURANCE CARRIERS

The multi-national company has three choices in structuring its risk insurance benefits. It can keep its expatriates on the home country plan wherever they work – an appropriate policy where a home country balance sheet system is used. The expatriate could join the host country insurance programme where there is a large company presence, although this can create problems on transfer. Finally, the company can organize a worldwide insurance programme for all its expatriates no matter where they work. This is particularly suitable for companies who operate an international pay plan.

Unless a company decides to insure its own risk, having decided the shape of the risk benefit package, it is necessary to select an insurer who will provide the desired cover. This will normally be a large multi-national insurance company. When selecting the company to use, the key points are:

- The insurance company should be acting on a worldwide basis and able to make payments in whatever currency the multi-national company requires. It must have experience of operating other multi-national plans and be sensitive to the particular service needs of expatriate employees.
- Since most multi-national companies have, in addition to the insurance programmes for their expatriates, a range of programmes for their local

employees in the countries in which they operate, it is highly advantageous to select an insurance company which is part of a multinational pooling arrangement.

MULTI-NATIONAL POOLING

Multi-national corporations have benefit plans in many countries around the world. Often, the insurance contracts in different countries are not related to each other and only cover very small groups of individuals. This approach can be wasteful. Such waste can arise for two reasons:

- competitive insurance rates in many countries are not available (because of legal restrictions or because of the small numbers involved);
- no advantage is taken of the bulk purchasing power of the multinational corporation.

Setting up a multi-national pool reduces the cost substantially (by up to 10 per cent or more of gross premiums). Under such arrangements each local benefit plan is insured with a local carrier that belongs to a selected 'network' of insurance companies. Each year, the network draws up an account which shows:

- total premiums paid to the insurers;
- total claims paid by the insurers;
- any other amounts paid out or received by the insurers;
- the insurers' 'retention' (ie the charge for expenses calculated on a group basis and the premiums for risk exposure taking the group experience into account).

The balance of income over payments made (if any) is then paid out as an international dividend. Local plan design and local dividends are unaffected by the arrangement. 'Stop loss' or 'loss carry-forward' provisions are used when there is a negative balance.

There are currently around a dozen major international networks, such as Aetna/Generali (often referred to as 'Generali'), IGP (John Hancock), MIA (Travelers), Vita and Insurope.

OTHER CONSIDERATIONS

The multi-national company needs to be aware of the legal exchange control and tax environments of the countries in which survivor benefits are likely to be paid. This may mean providing payments through a suitably constituted independent trust to avoid the provisions of legislation which taxes any form of capital transfer. It may require payments to be made into overseas accounts. It is important for the company to take whatever steps are needed to ensure that the tax taken on the lump sum payment is minimized, and that the local exchange control regulations are effectively dealt with.

Where company contributions to a compulsory social security programme yield significant survivor benefits, these ought to be deducted from the insurance lump sum from any company insurance programme in order to give the same treatment to all expatriates, irrespective of their location at the time of accident and to avoid wasteful double cover.

SELF INSURANCE OR EXTERNAL INSURANCE?

A company has to decide how much of the risk benefits of its employees it will meet out of current income or through some kind of internal reserve and how much will be covered through insurance policies.

The analysis has very little to do with employee relations *per se* but more to do with the nature of the insurance business, costs and probability.

There is a more or less measurable probability of any particular event occurring, based on past statistics. Thus mortality tables can give the probability of a man of a given age dying in a specified period, modulated by his state of health and lifestyle. With a sufficiently large group of people, such as the number employed in large multi-nationals, the probability of substantial variations year by year in the numbers dying is small. So, since one individual will either live or die in a given year, the chance of it happening varies from zero to 100 per cent, in a larger group the chances of a given average number dying tend to vary within a very narrow band.

With self insurance the company carries the risk; the bigger the group of people covered, the more measurable and constant the risk might be. There are several points worth consideration. These are:

- Self insurance, which could lead to uneven costs in a group which is too small – thus making it difficult accurately to demonstrate the true annual cost of running the business and leading to cash flow problems. It could also lead to excessive costs in any one period in the event of a catastrophe (so that employers with significant numbers of employees together in a potentially hazardous situations, eg an oil rig offshore, might wish to avoid self insurance).
- Stop loss insurance, where only the risk above a certain monetary amount is insured, can be a way of self insuring with a limit.
- Self insurance programmes obviously save the employer the insurance company's profit margin and the insurance company's administration costs. In a large multi-national company with employee risks benefit insurance premiums running into many millions of $US this is a major consideration. Obviously, there is likely to be a higher, if hidden, administrative cost for the multi-national company with self insurance.

In essence self insurance is only a realistic option for a very large company. If fewer than 300 expatriates are concerned self insurance is probably imprudent.

The most common forms of expatriate benefit plan that are self insured are:

Medical and dental plans

- While most North American companies have insured plans in their domestic operations and tend to extend the same plans to expatriates, this is not the case for the majority of European multi-national companies who prefer to run their medical and dental benefit plans on a self insured basis. Many expatriate employers do not want to place an insurance company in any kind of a relationship with their employees. They feel that there are too many grey areas requiring local management interpretation in the multitude of different overseas locations, and that an insurance company could never develop sufficient flexibility or local knowledge to approve or reject expenditure claims. The advantages of the arm's length relationship and undoubted control exercised by an external administration can be lost if dissent and dissatisfaction with a seemingly arbitrary decision lead to serious morale problems in the closed expatriate communities in many overseas locations.

Sick pay plans

- Most companies provide some form of self insured sickness pay on a temporary basis – moving to insured plans for longer periods of sickness (eg more than one year) or in the case of permanent invalidity.

CONCLUSION

Expatriate risk benefit programmes are normally wholly the responsibility of the employer since no social security benefits are usually available. The programmes form a part of the normal expatriate benefit package and, while not likely to be motivators, are of major importance to employees with dependants. The multi-national company must decide what structure of benefits it intends to provide and then solve the extremely complex problem of funding and paying these benefits in an international context at a controllable cost. Major insurance companies have appreciated the problem that multi-national companies face and offer comprehensive programmes tailored to their particular needs.

12. Long-term benefits for expatriates

INTRODUCTION

For employees in most western countries long-term benefits, usually in the form of comprehensive retirement plans, have come to be considered a normal part of the employment package. Such plans may be organized entirely by the state or may be a combination of both state and company benefits. In either case the company will be expected to pay a substantial contribution towards the cost of financing such schemes.

At the same time that the provision of long-term benefits has become universally accepted in industrialized countries, an awareness has grown that serious problems may be encountered. Whatever the method of funding retirement plans, a period of high inflation will cause difficulties in paying out a worthwhile pension throughout the period of retirement. Further, early retirement and longer life expectancy also mean a longer commitment to payment (averaging 20 years if the individual retires at 60 years of age). All this has to be seen in the light of changes in the demographic structure of most western countries, where fewer people of working age will be supporting a proportionally larger population of retired people.

Any employer who establishes a long-term benefit package needs to recognize that the company could be taking on a commitment for at least 60 years and that, at least implicitly, the company needs to take a long-term view of the economic environment over that period; until the youngest employee now employed has died. The wider the geographical scope, the greater this problem manifests itself.

Providing long-term benefits for expatriates poses a number of specific problem areas which are quite different from those associated with normal home country employment. It is in this area that the TCN encounters problems. Where an expatriate employee remains in the company's home country pension plan few problems are raised by expatriation.

The major expatriate benefit issues revolve around:

- The loss of social security pension benefits in the home country because of absence, and the non-eligibility of expatriate nationals to remain in some home country pension plans.
- The existence of a number of different corporate employers in the same MNC, each with their own pension plan. The expatriate may be a

member of any number of these plans. An individual who works all his life in his home country, but changes employer frequently, will accumulate a number of small and worthless frozen pensions. The same could happen to an expatriate despite a full career with one multi-national company.

- The problem of providing a single pension plan or 'umbrella' which gives benefits of the same value in the retirement countries of different expatriate nationalities.

This chapter does not examine in detail basic pension planning and design except where they have particular implications for expatriates. The personnel manager needs to understand basic concepts, such as: vesting, plan formulae, funding, the difference between defined contribution and benefit plans, career average, money purchase and final salary plans, and be aware of the basic actuarial and financial implications in long-term benefit planning. A selection of useful books is given at the end of this chapter.

THE EXPATRIATE'S CONCERNS

The expatriate employee and employer have specific problems with regard to the provision of long-term benefits. The employee's principal considerations are likely to be:

- if the employee is going overseas for a short time, whether payments to (home) pension and social security schemes can be maintained;
- if expatriated in one country for a long period, whether host country retirement plans can be joined, whether they are worthwhile and also if they are payable to him after he retires to his home country;
- for the multi-country expatriate if there is a way in which he can accumulate and combine the schemes of a number of countries or if the company offers an overall 'umbrella scheme' to protect him;
- as expatriate careers are normally somewhat shorter than those in a home country, whether he can claim a pension earlier than normal (age 50 to 55) combined perhaps with a 'second career' job in his home country.

THE COMPANY'S CONCERNS

The company will be concerned about:

- whether to provide home based, work country based or international 'offshore' retirement schemes for its expatriate population;
- how such schemes can be funded and on what salary assumptions, given that expatriates usually receive an extensive allowance system;
- how multi-country expatriates can be accommodated into these provisions;

- how a pension plan can be designed to retain employees, also possibly to encourage them to leave for early retirement when expatriate employment ceases to be attractive to them and perhaps enhance retirement benefits for people who work in 'tough' assignments.

THE EMPLOYER'S HOME COUNTRY PLAN

For most categories of expatriate continued membership of the employer's home country plan will be the most satisfactory solution for only a short period of time, or if the home country plan can be used for expatriates who have longer overseas stays, continued membership is the obvious option to follow. The advantages are that the expatriate can return to his home country and continue under the same plan without a loss in long-term benefits. Certain assumptions have to be made regarding what represents pensionable base salary in the expatriate package; either the home country base salary is used or a notional figure is selected in the home country currency and raised according to both merit and domestic salary increases.

In a company with a large number of different nationalities this approach leads to very different pensions. Formulae are radically different and apply to very different levels of salary. If the company has endeavoured to maintain broadly equivalent levels of expatriate salary and benefits for all nationalities, it may seem very inequitable for differences to arise when employees retire. On the other hand the differences in cost and inflation rates between countries are such that, for example, an Italian and a Norwegian with the same dollar pension will have very different standards of living.

Many expatriates marry wives of a nationality different from their own and retire to their wives' home or to a third country. Indeed, many expatriates opt for an overseas career in order not to return to their home country.

One of the approaches to this problem involves the company fixing a proportion of the expatriate's salary which will be used for funding pension benefits, eg 15 to 25 per cent. This would then be paid into:

- the home (or nominated) country social security plan if possible; or
- the home (or nominated) country private pension plan (if the employer has one) and the balance into some 'top-up' fund.

The problems of continued membership of the employee's retirement plan in the home country mostly concern meeting the rules that apply to such schemes. In some cases, eg France, where a substantially nationalized system exists, the expatriate and the company can continue payments to such a scheme while the employee is out of the country. American citizens employed by US companies cannot remain in the US (state) social security system while they are working abroad. Because of government policy, companies are obliged to look after their expatriate's interests in a company plan during their time abroad. British companies may be inhibited, by rules governing their domestic plans, from keeping overseas employees as active members of retirement plans after three years have elapsed.

Most home country plans are fully integrated with state pensions. Expatriates will often be unable to enjoy social security cover in their home country while working overseas, so special arrangements will have to be made to ensure that they are not unfairly penalised.

Even if a company does not operate a home country base salary structure (eg an international pay plan), it may find it convenient to maintain a theoretical home country reference salary for expatriate employees. This home country salary is easy to define where a company has a salary structure in that country (which is maintained by adding general domestic increases and any merit or promotion increases received by the expatriate overseas). This salary then becomes the base for pensions and other benefits. It also provides an obvious basis for re-entry.

'HOST' COUNTRY PLANS

Where a company applies the assignment going rate to its expatriate employees it will normally put them into the pension plan applying in the host country. This system will be effective for the very long-term expatriate who will ultimately integrate into the host country. It may also be appropriate for a short-term expatriate provided that the benefits are either directly transferable or dynamized to ensure that they are protected from inflation. If the short-term expatriate employee receives only 'frozen benefits' this approach will prove unsatisfactory. It is possible to set up a hybrid scheme, where the expatriate benefits as much as possible from the host country plans and any shortfall is made up either through a home country or offshore plan.

OFFSHORE FUNDS

The use of the 'offshore fund' has grown considerably in the last ten years as it offers particular advantages to the multi-national company. The phrase offshore fund is itself rather misleading. There is no need for the fund to be physically 'offshore', indeed Liechtenstein is one popular centre for offshore funds. Nor does the plan, of necessity, require to be funded in the true sense of the word. (Indeed, such funds may provide pensions which are promised but for which no funds are accumulated in advance.) However, the term 'offshore fund' has come to be universally recognized and is often used for financing benefits for multi-country employees.

By their very nature offshore funds are likely to be less efficient than conventional plans organized within one country. Most single country plans enjoy tax relief on the contributions made into them by both the employer and employee and on income earned by the pension fund. On the other hand such a scheme, to qualify for tax exemption, must adhere to local authority revenue rules. This implies a limit on the amount of contributions paid into the scheme by an employer and on the scale and starting age of benefits paid out of them. For multi-country employees, therefore, it is sometimes the case that conventional plans are impossible to organize.

The following examples illustrate this:

1. An Irish national working throughout his career for a US group of companies spent several years in the US (where he was a member of a US retirement plan), followed by a long period in Australia (where he belonged to the company's pension plan) and is now going to an African country, where he is expecting to work until retirement and where he is required to join the local pension plan.

When he reaches retirement his benefits will consist of frozen pensions from the United States and Australia as well as the benefits he has earned in the African plan. However, the two frozen pensions are based on salaries he was earning a long time before retirement and the three pensions, added together, fall far short of the final pay-related pension which he was led to expect when he first took up employment with the US company.

Although this employee is in a pension plan and has adequate death and disability cover in Africa, the group as a whole may well decide to build up a reserve in their offshore fund which can be used to augment his retirement benefits when they fall due.

2. A Dutch firm of consultants has a number of highly specialist engineers who move around the world wherever the firm is involved in building projects. For tax reasons they are usually employed either by partnerships in the country in which they are working or, sometimes, by local companies with which the Dutch firm has agency agreements.

Membership of the firm's Dutch pension plan would not be appropriate, even if it were possible, partly because the Dutch plan has scales of benefits for its Dutch employees which assume they will all earn full Dutch social security pensions. Occasionally, one or other of the engineers joins a local plan but for most of the time they are not eligible to join plans anywhere in the world.

The flexibility (in terms of eligibility conditions and in terms of benefit levels) which can be enjoyed in an offshore fund is ideal for this group of employees.

3. A British citizen employed in the UK by the UK subsidiary of a US multi-national is sent to Nigeria for a period which is expected to last for at least six years. In Nigeria, he will be employed by the Italian subsidiary.

The Department of Inland Revenue in the UK will partially withdraw approval from the UK plan if the employee remains a member of it for longer than the first three years of his absence.

There is no UK subsidiary in Nigeria and no company plan there, nor is there a company plan in Italy which the employee can join.

In these circumstances, it is impossible for benefits to accrue in the United Kingdom, the USA, Nigeria or Italy and it might very well be appropriate for some funding to be taking place offshore until the employee returns to the United Kingdom and rejoins the UK plan, or moves to another country where he can join another local plan.

Clearly, each of the situations described above is different and will result in a different type of benefit problem. Such problems are often extremely complicated and require the advice of specialist actuaries. The principle, however, remains simple. Where the single country solution is impossible or inadequate, the multi-national company creates an offshore fund and invests through insurance contracts, unit trust arrangements or direct investments in order to provide overall long-term benefits at an acceptable level.

In most countries any resident fund will be subject to high taxation. Because of this the offshore fund must ensure:

- exemption from high tax rates;
- access to investment media and insurance contracts;
- availability of desired currencies;
- political and economic stability.

Among the locations that meet these requirements the most common are:

Bahamas	Gibraltar
Bermuda	Hong Kong
British Virgin Island	Channel Islands
Cayman Islands	Liechtenstein
Cyprus	Panama
Dutch Antilles	

All the large insurance companies and employee benefit consultants will offer advice and information on all aspects of offshore fund locations.

CHARACTERISTICS OF EXPATRIATE PLANS

Whether the expatriate retirement plan is funded in the home country or offshore it will often have different characteristics from the typical home country plan. These are most likely to be:

- early retirement provisions;
- extra credit for 'overseas years' (years of expatriation);
- longer periods of encashment.

Many expatriate schemes will provide for retirement at 55 and in some cases as early as 50. This reflects the common shorter career pattern for expatriates when it is not expected that they will be re-employed by the same company in their home country (a very common situation in the civil engineering and oil industries). Early retirement involves some sort of actuarial reduction of the pension received, although some companies subsidize this element of the plan to encourage older employees to leave.

One scheme gives the early retirement benefits shown in Figure 12.1. Another scheme provides two different scales of pension benefits:

Overseas accrual rate	1/60 final salary per year
Home country accrual rate	1/80 final salary per year

Thus, the expatriate reaches the maximum benefit (in this case 50 per cent of final salary) earlier than his domestic counterpart.

Figure 12.1 *Early retirement benefits*

	Percentage of accrued pension payable	
Age on retirement and pension receipt	*With 20 years overseas service*	*Without 20 years overseas service*
65	100	100
63	100	83
61	100	69
59	100	59
57	100	50
55	100	40
54	96	38
53	92	37
52	88	–
51	84	–
50	80	–

In many offshore funds the expatriate has a much longer period (Pensions usually become 'paid-up' after five years in the case of home country employees.) during which he may cash in his pension before it becomes 'paid-up'. (The idea behind this is that many expatriates will return to their home country in their 40s.) A frozen pension plan without inflation protection will be of little value to them when paid out in a further 20 years. Without strict government 'vesting' provisions it is possible to offer them repayment of their (and a proportion of the company's) contributions which can be taken as a lump sum, say up to 15 years of membership in the scheme. Such an alternative is likely to be much more attractive to the employee than retaining a non-index linked offshore plan. Companies may even enhance this payment to encourage certain expatriates to leave their employment.

CASH ACCUMULATION FUNDS

A second type of scheme, commonly used by expatriate employers, is that of a provident fund (cash accumulation plan). This differs from the pension plan as it is designed to provide a cash sum when the employee leaves the company rather than when he attains pensionable age. Such a fund may co-exist with and supplement a company pension fund or it may stand on its own as the only benefit when leaving the company.

The purpose of such a fund is to accumulate sufficient funds to facilitate re-entry to the home country base without difficulty. Such funds are most common with multi-national companies that employ a workforce on a permanent expatriate basis (eg the oil industry) where the average age is fairly low and employees rarely stay with the company after their mid 40s. In these circumstances the company attempts to design a long-term benefits plan tailored for such a career pattern.

Two examples of such plans are shown below:

Provident fund (Franco-American company)	
Membership	○ all expatriate employees.
Company contributions	○ 3 per cent of base salary on employment date up to a maximum of 15 per cent after 12 years of service (no employee contribution).
Investment vehicle	○ a choice of three funds: fixed income, stock market and company stock; proportions to be chosen by the employee.
Vesting	○ immediate.
Communication	○ fund results published on an annual basis together with an individual statement.
Payment	○ on termination of employment or death.
Location	○ offshore in the Cayman Islands, administered in the Bahamas.

Cash accumulation plan (US company)	
Membership	○ all expatriate non US employees.
Company contributions	○ 5 per cent of salary each year with a 7 per cent compound interest rate guaranteed.
Vesting	○ ranging from 10 per cent in year one of employment to 100 per cent after 10 years. Payable 100 per cent on death of employee.

Clearly, the first example, using an investment vehicle, offers the employee more chance of growth, but also with more associated risks. The second plan gives a fixed interest rate and has a progressive 'vesting' encouraging the employee to stay for at least ten years.

HOST COUNTRY SEPARATION PROVISION

Most plans, which are designed to provide a cash sum to the employee on termination, are also a protection for the company. In many countries statutory severance payments exist which the expatriate employee may invoke if he leaves the company as a result of a dismissal or for some other reason. In some countries, eg South America, payment can be as high as two months' salary for every year of service. The wording of cash accumulation plans will usually stress that any severance payments claimed in the host country will be deducted from the total payable to the employee from the plan itself. This point was discussed in detail in Chapter 2.

SOCIAL SECURITY PENSIONS

In all OECD countries social security pension programmes exist, although in less developed countries such programmes are rare and insignificant. (In the future, in such countries, one would expect that they will become more common and more valuable.)

The contributions from employer and employees to the social security pension scheme and the scale of benefits are in many countries substantial. Figure 12.2 shows the situation in Europe and the USA in terms of percentage of gross salary.

Figure 12.2 *Employee and employer contributions made to state social security schemes*

Country	*Employer's contribution*		*Employee's contribution*	
	$40,000 salary %	*$20,000 salary* %	*$40,000 salary* %	*$20,000 salary* %
Austria	4.75	9.49	4.38	8.76
France	17.38	24.21	5.39	6.99
Germany	7.21	14.42	7.10	14.42
Ireland	1.21	2.41	0.70	1.40
Italy	42.25	42.25	7.80	7.80
Holland	12.14	21.61	9.15	17.19
Norway	16.50	16.50	7.12	7.68
Spain	10.16	20.32	1.77	3.54
Switzerland	6.71	6.90	5.21	5.40
UK	2.84	5.67	1.84	3.69
USA	2.68	5.35	2.68	5.35

Figure 12.3 shows the amount of pension paid by the social security programmes in these countries.

Figure 12.3 *Pension as a percentage of final salary*

Country	*$40,000* %	*$20,000* %
Austria	24	48
France	57	72
Germany	22	45
Ireland	6	12
Italy	37	74
Holland	17	34
Norway	22	37
Spain	30	60
Switzerland	21	42
UK	10	21 (after 1998)
USA	14	28

The pensions themselves are based on many different formulae and systems; some are flat rate, others flat rate with an additional pension as a function of career earnings revalued or final salary usually with a ceiling. In some countries, eg France, there exist semi-autonomous nationalized pension funds organized on an industry basis for executives where membership buys so many pension 'points' per year. These points are given a monetary value and the pension consists of the sum of the total points earned, the monetary values being revalued each year in line with inflation.

All of the state schemes are indexed against inflation, both reference pensions earned and pensions in payment. This is the major difference with respect to private company schemes, where such indexing could not be contemplated. The best a private scheme can do is to make periodic, non-guaranteed revisions of pensions in payment. The cost of fully funding pension promises that are a function of final salary and provide for updating of pensions in payment can, in times of high inflation, be unacceptably expensive.

It is a matter of judgement whether the social security pension promises (unfunded and therefore paid out of the contributions of currently active people) will be sustainable. Demographic shifts to a higher proportion of older people in a population, declining employment base in many industrialized countries and continuing inflation raise the cost dramatically. However, for many millions of people these pensions represent their only long-term savings.

In the majority of European countries it is possible for the expatriate national to remain covered by the home country social security pension programme (in some cases, eg the UK, he is able to remain a member of only the basic state scheme, not the additional scheme). This cover can be on either an individual or a company basis. A full career pension cover from social security, even with the concerns expressed in the previous paragraph, represents a good investment and should be encouraged by the employer's policies. In addition, the accrual of benefits in many of these schemes is not evenly distributed over the career. In other words, the loss of ten years' contributions to the state scheme in a 40 year career will frequently result in a loss of more than a quarter of the final benefit.

Within the EEC, reciprocal arrangements between countries make it possible for contributions paid on an EEC national expatriate employee's behalf in one EEC country to count towards the pension benefit in another. At present this covers the flat rate portion of two-tier pension plans only, but the longer term intention is to provide full interchangeability to facilitate the movement of labour provided for in the Treaty of Rome.

An expatriate who works in a country which has a social security pension plan will normally have to contribute towards it for a certain period of time before becoming eligible for pension benefits. Contributions made for less than this time are either refunded or, more usually, lost.

The following is a list of some of the minimum contributing periods necessary for employees to be eligible for pension benefit:

Austria	three years
Denmark	one year
France	three months
Germany	15 years
Ireland	average of five and a half months per working year
Italy	15 years

Holland	reduced benefit by 2 per cent per year less than 50 years
Norway	reduced benefit by 2.5 per cent per year less than 40 years
Spain	ten years
Switzerland	one year
UK	one year
USA	ten years

In conclusion, social security pensions are worthwhile benefits the loss of which is significant, and continuity in the home country social security plan is an important objective.

- High contributions are often paid by the expatriate and the employer to overseas social security pension plans which can, provided minimum contribution periods are met, provide substantial benefits. Within the EEC, for EEC nationals, these can be pooled to enhance the home country benefit. Other nationalities (outside the EEC) may have several different pensions from the countries in which they have worked which may be far from negligible.
- A company needs to keep a good record of what is paid for each of its expatriate employees to overseas social security systems and have a good working knowledge about the social security programmes in the countries where it operates and from where it recruits.

Finally, any overseas expatriate pension programme ought to integrate the social security benefits that can be obtained as part of the overall package.

THE EXPATRIATE AND HIS SAVINGS

So far we have stressed that the employer takes on a much greater responsibility for his expatriate employee than would normally be the case with his home country counterpart. This explains why many companies also offer their expatriates a variety of saving schemes in addition to pension schemes. The motivation for these schemes is usually twofold: the expatriate is earning appreciably more money than he could at home and he may be isolated from sound investment advice and information. The company may take it upon itself to provide a vehicle for the investment of expatriate savings. Such schemes can take a variety of forms but generally fall into three categories:

- stock purchase plans;
- savings funds;
- time deposits.

Stock purchase plans

Stock purchase plans are rarely designed exclusively for expatriate employees. However, they do provide a useful opportunity for the employee to purchase stock regularly without requiring access to brokers or a stock exchange. Such plans are also seen by the company as encouraging employee identification with the organization. There is always the danger with this kind of plan that the stock performs badly and as a result the employees savings suffer, with consequent effects on morale.

A typical stock purchase plan works in association with a large stockbroker. The employee authorizes automatic deductions from his salary for the purchase of company stock. The stockbroker then receives the total amount deducted from the payroll and with this purchases, for all participants, as many shares as the total fund makes possible. These shares are then allocated according to individual contributions. The employee's account may be closed at any time, at which time his shares are sold and the money refunded. The shares could be purchased at market value or at a discount (typically 15 per cent).

The advantage of such a scheme is that an expatriate can make regular purchases of stock without needing to make specific instructions. Usually the company covers the cost of any brokerage fees incurred. To keep the scheme within practical limits there is normally a minimum and maximum that can be invested each month, eg between $10 and $500. In all such schemes the company must stress that participation is entirely voluntary and that the company is making no recommendations to its employees.

A number of organizations, particularly American companies, go one step further and make a company contribution to stock purchase plans. This is largely as a result of the Federal Tax Reduction Act of 1975 which has encouraged such schemes, where companies receive tax credits if such credits are used to set up and support stock ownership plans for employees.

Under another set of legislation, TRASOPS (Tax Reform Act Option Scheme), a tax credit equal to 1 per cent of qualifying capital investments may be used to provide stock to employees on a non-contributory basis, together with 0.5 per cent on a 50/50 working basis. As a result in many US schemes the company will match the employee's stock purchase contribution up to a certain level; eg the company will match employee contributions up to a maximum of 2 per cent of basic pay.

Savings funds

Many companies, while organizing share purchase schemes, consider it necessary to provide a more general savings fund, particularly for their expatriate employees. Dependence on the price of one share, eg company stock, can result in a volatile performance which would be an unsound basis for all of an expatriate's savings. Savings funds are designed to provide more stable performance through investing in a spread of market and fixed interest investments. Such plans are usually managed by a specialist investment advisor and dividends paid are automatically reinvested. Monthly contributions are made to the fund which publishes a portfolio analysis on an annual or quarterly basis. Where a fund is designed exclusively for expatriates it will often be located 'offshore' to take advantage of the optimum tax position available. Thus, the expatriate can benefit from a long-term saving plan along unit trust lines which can be used while not in close touch with investment opportunities in his home country.

Time deposits

Stock purchase and saving funds are designed for medium- and long-term investments. Many expatriates may want to make their own investments, perhaps during leave periods in their home country. In this case they need a savings vehicle that makes the most effective use of their money on a short-term basis. A popular solution to this problem is the time deposit offered by some banks to employers with large numbers of employees using the same bank. In such schemes the bank automatically invests all funds in current accounts above a certain balance. The funds are combined with the funds of other participating employees to form a single minimum 30 days time deposit at a competitive rate of interest. In all other respects the account will function as a normal current account which can be used by the expatriate employee. This is a much more effective method of saving salary over short periods of time than placing the money in a current account that does not attract interest.

There are many other saving schemes and investment approaches offered to expatriates through private investment programmes. The plans discussed above are the common approaches sponsored by the companies themselves. Other investment ideas (property and commodities) are described in publications which are specifically aimed at the expatriate market, eg *Resident Abroad* (see Chapter 16).

CONCLUSION

In many respects the expatriate's objectives towards long-term benefits are the same as in his home country. He wants the company and/or the government to provide a secure retirement income protected against inflation. If his career term is likely to be shorter than normal he will require a cash sum payable on termination to re-invest or help him begin a 'second career'. Finally, the expatriate wants to be able to place his savings where they will obtain a reasonable return on investment.

Where the expatriate differs from his home country counterpart is that he relies much more extensively on the company to meet these objectives. If he moves around the world he cannot rely on governments to provide his retirement income. With a shorter career span a termination benefit becomes increasingly significant when it helps him re-enter his own country and re-adjust to the diminished job market that might be available to him. During his working career abroad, he must have access to short- and medium-term saving schemes when he is living in locations where local and/or international investment opportunities are not available. The expatriate employer must take all these objectives into consideration when designing long-term benefits for its employees. Inadequate planning will have two results. The younger expatriate employees which the company wishes to retain may leave because, although their current salary may be attractive, they are deterred by poor long-term benefits. Conversely, the middle aged employee whom the company might like to encourage to return to his home country may be unable to do so because he has inadequate savings or a poor pension plan. For these reasons the general trend for multi-national companies is to ensure that their own nationals and third country nationals are adequately provided for with respect to long-term benefits.

REFERENCES

Melove, JJ and Allen, ET, *Pension Planning*, Irwin, 1972.
Pitch, M and Wood, V, *Managing Pension Schemes*, Gomar Press, 1974.

13. Repatriation and re-entry

INTRODUCTION

In many if not most cases the expatriate employee returns to his home country within three to five years, usually to work for the same employer. It is only a minority who have a full career as expatriates.

This chapter is concerned only with expatriates returning to work for their employer in their home country. Contract employees returning home and people who return home and do not work for the same employer will no longer be the concern of the overseas employer.

Repatriation may be at the request of the employee or the employer – or it may be an amalgam of both. In many cases repatriation will have been planned at the time of the original expatriation. The foreign posting may have been a 'one-off' career development assignment or the company's intention may be subsequently to transfer an individual overseas again at a later date (in which case they may want him to remain 'mobile').

An expatriate employee may want to return home for common personal reasons, eg children's education, wife's career, health and general stability, in which case the company's major preoccupation is to find him an appropriate position in the home country organization.

Where an employee is expatriated for only one assignment he will expect and anticipate his return home. However, where an expatriate employee is anticipating an overseas career with the company an appointment in the home country may be most unwelcome and may require considerable persuasion and substantial inducements.

Many employees of international companies have dual nationalities and spouses of another nationality. A normal expedient is to consider as nationality the country of passport of the individual when he is recruited and not change it. This is not a perfect solution (since it can lead, for example, to an Englishman who was born in Australia of English parents and spent his entire life outside the UK, being considered to be repatriated on transfer to the UK) but is probably the fairest overall policy. Lastly, there are a number of companies who consider as the employee's home country their corporate headquarters and integrate even expatriates directly into the headquarter's country compensation and benefits package.

PERMANENT REPATRIATION

Key compensations and benefits issues for permanent repatriation are:

- salary;
- what to do with expatriate benefits accrued overseas;
- children's education.

A company should guide its repatriating employees towards professional financial advice in the context of their individual tax and investment position. Return to the home country after many years of highly paid, somewhat artificial, expatriate life-style (servants, closed affluent societies and high quality of housing) will obviously make reintegration difficult and it is important that a company does what it can to minimize the impact of these problems on its employees.

Salary

A 'permanent' repatriate will be reintegrated into the compensation and benefits structure of his home country. This will be facilitated if the company has maintained either a home country base salary structure or a home country reference salary. In other cases, however, the home country salary structure and levels will bear no relation whatsoever to the expatriate salary package.

Where the home country salary levels are relatively high, eg USA, Switzerland, and/or tax rates relatively low, eg France, the reintegration problems may be less acute. In other countries, typically the UK with relatively low salaries and high taxation and most non-European countries, the problem is much greater.

The approaches to repatriate salaries tend to be either:

- to do nothing, ie direct and immediate integration;
- to pay a lump sum bonus at the time of repatriation (which could be tax protected).

BENEFITS ACCRUED OVERSEAS

When an expatriate has contributed to an overseas social security programme he may have acquired worthwhile long-term benefits which can either be paid to him on retirement or be pooled to increase his home country benefit entitlement. Benefits for the French social security pension plan, for example, are inflation proofed and payable worldwide. A company has to set up an administrative system to ensure that a record is kept for the employee of the contributions made and the benefits accrued in overseas social security systems.

The benefits accrued in an overseas or offshore pension fund may either be transferred directly to the home country plan or remain, frozen or dynamized, overseas.

In any event, a company should endeavour to provide an overall retirement umbrella for such employees to ensure a minimum benefit level and to integrate social security and overseas pension benefits.

EDUCATION OF CHILDREN

Few employers in Europe and North America provide their home country employees with reimbursement of private education costs for their children except where, as in the UK, there may be considerable tax efficiency in doing so. Companies will recognize the problems of returning expatriates who have:

- previously put their children in boarding school in their home country;
- educated their children in the local language of their country of assignment;
- educated their children in the mother tongue of their spouse.

In these cases employers often provide some kind of reimbursement of private education costs, probably on a degressive basis such as:

- reimbursement of 75 per cent of school costs in year one (maximum $6000 per child);
- reimbursement of 50 per cent in year two (maximum $4000 per child);
- reimbursement of 25 per cent in year three (maximum $2000 per child);
- no reimbursement after year three.

After three years, either the child is integrated into the local educational system or the parents have decided to bear the full cost of private education.

TEMPORARY REPATRIATION

In the case of a temporary repatriation, where it is envisaged that the employee will return to an expatriate position within a relatively short period, the problems a company needs to solve are different. The maintenance of an attractive enough compensation package for the returning expatriate and the continuation of high mobility within the context of the home country compensation and benefits policies, tax structure and exchange control regulations needs be addressed, in addition to the issues discussed for permanent repatriation.

It may not be obvious that this kind of 'temporary' assignment in the home country is common. However, to a large degree, it is the rule in major companies with a truly multi-national workforce and activities worldwide. Thus, an Englishman may be brought back to the UK to serve as a district manager, be expatriated again to serve as a division manager, return to London as a regional manager and be re-expatriated once more to become the vice-president of operations in yet another country. Most companies want to be able to use local expertise and knowledge while giving their employees the opportunity to develop to their full potential. This must imply repatriating high potential individuals for relatively short-term assignments.

Especially in the less developed world but also in Europe, an employee repatriated at the company's request will expect to continue a style of life not substantially less favourable than he had as an expatriate. Many individuals join international companies to get out of their home countries and returning home, even for a limited time and with a substantial promotion, is extremely unwelcome. It thus requires a good deal of creativity on the part of the employer to put together a package that not only meets as far as possible the repatriate's needs but also is acceptable to the local employees working in that home country.

The structure of any home country compensation and benefits package has to reflect the market, socio-economic, tax, fiscal and other realities of that particular country. Thus people returning to their home countries should probably always be paid in the currency of that country, should expect to pay income tax, and belong to the social security system of that country. It would be impossible for a company to stipulate a compensation and benefits policy that could apply equally to local employees in a number of different home countries. The same argument applies to the policies for the returning expatriate – what is appropriate for a Nigerian returning from overseas to a management position in Nigeria will be quite different from the case of an Egyptian or a Frenchman returning to their home countries.

MAINTAINING MOBILITY

In essence, a key problem is to maintain the individual's mobility while in his home country and to compensate him for the costs of doing so (eg renting houses rather than buying).

To the extent that companies resolve this problem, there are two major approaches – either providing housing (and possibly paying for utilities) for the individual or giving a housing allowance sufficient to cover the cost of renting accommodation.

Housing provided

There are a number of programmes which provide housing benefits for home country people on a similar basis to expatriates. Thus one major company in such cases provides housing in every home country for temporary repatriates above a certain grading, and ensures that this benefit is tax free for the employee. The cost and method of making this provision will evidently vary from country to country and can involve company purchase and lease to employee, company lease and lease back to employees, reimbursement of actual cost, and so forth. Additional payments to compensate for tax liabilities may also be made in this case although such tax protection in the home country is unusual. This is an extremely expensive area (as it involves paying tax on tax relief) and a company will need carefully to examine the trade off between cost to the employer and employee mobility.

Although the provision of housing for Europeans and North Americans in their home country is uncommon even for temporary repatriates it does represent an effective mobility tool. In the rest of the world a senior manager will expect in his home country exactly the same standard of provision of company housing as the expatriate.

Housing allowance

Unless in some way tax protected, this can represent a tax-inefficient way of paying an employee since he will be taxed normally at marginal tax rates on the allowance. However, it allows a premium above the normal domestic salary to be separated, identified and paid. A typical allowance structure, in this case degressive, is shown in Figure 13.1.

Figure 13.1 *Housing and services allowance, France*

	FF/month	
	Below branch manager	*Branch manager and above*
Single	5000	6000
Married	5500	6600
Married + 1	6000	7200
Married + 2	6500	7800
Married + 3 or more	7000	8200

Paid for four years at:
100 per cent of allowance during first year
75 per cent during second year
50 per cent during third year
25 per cent during fourth year
zero, thereafter

The question of using compensation policies to reinforce mobility is a complex one which may more directly be addressed by stock options, bonuses or other individual arrangements. Normally, the population for whom this kind of mobility is a major issue is small. Individually structured creative packages may be more appropriate than blanket policies.

INCENTIVES

If the temporary repatriate is to be provided with a reasonable financial incentive, this has to be as tax-effective as is possible within company policies and tax law.

The financial incentives that might be considered can be broken down into the following types:

Lump sum bonus payments

Lump sum bonus payments are often made prior to arrival in the home country and after transfer out to a subsequent overseas assignment (in which case they can be tax-protected for the employee – although they are thus unlikely to be tax-deductible for the company – depending on the particular countries involved before, during and after the home country assignment). For example:

pre-transfer bonus (paid overseas prior to repatriation) – 25 per cent of 18 month salary, ie four and a half months salary;
post-transfer bonus (paid overseas after leaving home country) – 25 per cent of salary earned in home country up to three years minus pre-transfer payment.

This is based on a three year assignment in home country and only makes the second payment in the event of the employee re-expatriating. If the employee leaves the company before 18 months' service is completed in the home country a deduction is made from his final settlement.

Additions to salary

These are paid to recognize the difference between expatriate and home country salary levels. This again can be a money figure or a percentage of salary and may have the kind of degressivity shown in the last section.

Clearly, this method of payment, while identifying the individual's addition to salary above the 'normal' level, is the most tax-ineffective method of payment.

A typical example is:

base home country salary $50,000

Year 1 additional premium 30 per cent (limited to the first $40,000 of salary only)
Year 2 additional premium 20 per cent (limited to the first $40,000 of salary only)
Year 3 additional premium 10 per cent (limited to the first $40,000 of salary only)
Year 4 no premium

General increases and merit raises applied to the base salary could effectively mean that the gross salary does not decrease over this period as the premium drops. After three years the integration is complete and relatively painless.

CONCLUSION

Repatriation of employees, particularly those who have spent a long period overseas can present the company with major problems. The change in lifestyle and personal circumstances, the difficulty often encountered in finding a suitable home country position and the general psychological readjustment necessary are sufficiently serious issues in themselves. Most companies find it necessary to assign a senior manager as the counsellor or 'godfather' of each expatriate whose role is crucial in successful re-entry.

While these problems cannot be entirely resolved by good compensation and benefits planning they can be seriously exacerbated by poorly constructed, ill-thought out policies or bad decisions.

14. Administering and controlling the expatriate package

INTRODUCTION

This chapter deals with the administration and control of the expatriate compensation and benefits package. Although there are many similarities to the administration and control of compensation and benefits in a domestic environment, the complexity and cost of the expatriate package demand a considerable amount of management attention.

In many multi-national companies the management of expatriate compensation and benefits is the responsibility of a separate department within the overall personnel function. Even when the expatriate is integrated into the host country structure, he remains, from a compensation and benefits viewpoint, the responsibility of this separate department. This approach has the advantage of developing the necessary personnel expertise in one department, providing a uniform and, one hopes, consistent approach to the way in which the expatriate is treated, and giving the mobile expatriate some stable reference point in the personnel organization. The disadvantages (eg a possible lack of coordination between the domestic and expatriate personnel functions) also need to be considered, particularly when there are frequent exchanges of personnel between the expatriate and domestic employee groups.

CONSISTENCY

Every organization tries to treat its people 'fairly' in relation to the objective criteria it considers important, such as responsibility, performance and seniority. In an expatriate context, in particular, there may be conflict between fairness and simplicity. The 'fairer' the policy, the more complex it needs to be to deal appropriately with individual situations. So, any set of compensation and benefits policies have to have an element of compromise. They have, by definition, to make assumptions about life-style and cost and tend to be generalized imperfect solutions.

A company has a clear choice between attempting to define, in great detail, precisely what policy will apply in all conceivable situations, and sketching in only the basic policy guidelines, thus allowing interpretation by local management in specific circumstances.

One of the major criteria for the successful management of expatriates is consistency. Consistency means that any variation in the interpretation of the package is seen by the employees as fair. For example, a base salary structure needs to be managed in all geographical locations in terms of promotions, merit increases and general adjustments, in exactly the same way. At the same time, the expatriate premium in different places has to be 'fair'. Also, more loosely controlled items such as size of car, quality of housing and club membership, need to be administered consistently. In many ways, it is this last area which creates the greatest dissatisfaction among expatriates, and is quite out of proportion to the relative costs involved. Whenever a company has expatriates in several different geographical locations, and especially when there is frequent mobility and contact between the locations, these issues are of prime concern.

Consistency does not demand uniformity. But it does demand that policies are applied (even more important that they are seen to be applied) in a way that is objective and not seen as personal prejudice or favouritism. At the same time, excessive uniformity can appear to the individuals to produce arbitrary policies.

The larger the number of different overseas locations, the greater the number of expatriates; the wider the range of different local conditions encountered, the greater will be the problems of consistency. These are multiplied even more when some of the overseas locations are experiencing domestic upheaval, eg hyperinflation or social and political changes.

Consistency is best approached by having a clear set of policy guidelines capable of overall application. Local management should be able to interpret these guidelines effectively, which suggests training of the local management, a decentralized decision-making structure and clear guidelines.

DECENTRALIZATION OR CENTRAL CONTROL?

Any organization which recognizes different levels of management has, *de facto*, decentralized certain decision-making responsibilities from the centre. For expatriate compensation and benefits the choice an organization makes is the degree to which local management is able to interpret or make policies. Inevitably, the day to day management of individual expatriates – job responsibility, performance standards, appraisal, discipline and so forth – takes place in a local context and it is often difficult to separate this from the compensation and benefits area. The major benefit of a decentralized organization is to allow the creation of small, responsible units at as low a level as possible to facilitate effective and timely decision making. Decentralized managers need to be able to control their resources (including expatriate employees) in order to exercise responsibility and meet their business goals. Thus, in practical terms, there is strong organizational pressure for local management to have a large say in the compensation and benefits policies of expatriates, whatever formal decentralization is defined.

As a response to the need for consistency and as a way of implementing company policies on salaries, merit increase programmes and long-term benefits for expatriates, many companies try to have a strong degree of centralization in the administration of expatriate compensation and benefits. Such central control can only be exercised over a relatively small part of the total package, it may inhibit necessary evolution of policies and may finally be more apparent than real.

Any decentralization of decision making in expatriate compensation and benefits has to be decided in relation to a company's size, structure and geographical spread. Excessive decentralization makes consistency impossible and thus control of policies is rapidly lost. The criteria are complex and have to be reviewed by each individual company. There is a strong case for such decentralization in a worldwide company, for example, on a geographical region basis or an operating division basis (when the operating divisions are in different industries). Sheer numbers do not in themselves suffice. The number of decentralized units has to be small enough (perhaps not much more than five to eight) to give the centre a reasonable span of management control. The amount of decentralization both qualitatively and quantitatively has to be tailored to the availability of sufficiently able and trained managers within the organization.

In decentralized organizations, regular personnel policy meetings should be held with the aim of maintaining a coherent overall policy. Also essential are frequent visits by members of the central personnel policy-making group, to ensure that company policy is adhered to and maintained effectively and evolves to meet real needs.

LIMITS OF DECENTRALIZATION

The areas of discretion in which local management has authority in the handling of its expatriates need to be defined in terms of what may be done and with what level of employees. The following is a typical example of the personnel decentralization policy of a company which has a number of widespread, relatively independent, geographical regions. The company employs around 1400 expatriates in some 40 countries and was formally highly centralized.

To: Regions
From: Personnel department
Subject: Decentralization of personnel management

This letter restates the responsibilities and authority for personnel management decisions in the decentralized region organization.

EXPATRIATE STAFF

Recruitment

- ○ Proposed trainee engineer hires are submitted by regions to HQ personnel for approval before job offers are made. Nationality, numbers and timing are set out in the HQ personnel recruiting plan.

  Mechanics, electronic technicians and similar operational personnel are recruited as required on region decision.

- ○ Other categories of expatriate personnel are recruited as required by regions in consultation with and with the prior agreement of HQ personnel.

No rehires, hires from competition or clients are entered into without the agreement of HQ personnel.

Documents

- An offer letter is made by the recruiting region. Employment documents signed by the region personnel manager are prepared in the region according to the standard model.

Training

- Internal seminars. Regions will be allotted places on internal seminars run at HQ level and will be responsible for selecting their own candidates. As required, regions will run their own specialist seminars.
- External courses. It is the region's responsibility to select appropriate external management and technical courses and identify candidates. All administration is handled by the region.

Personnel moves

- Intra-region. All intra-region moves, up to and including the moves of people grade 13, are the responsibility of the region. Moves at or above grade 14 are decided in agreement with HQ personnel.
- Inter-region. Moves up to and including grade 11 are implemented and coordinated directly between sending and receiving regions. Moves at grade 12 or above are decided in agreement with HQ personnel. All files of transfers are sent direct to receiving region by sending region.
- To sister companies. All such moves are handled by HQ personnel and not by regions direct.

Terminations

- Terminations of all personnel up to grade 11 are the responsibility of the region. At grade 12 and above, the decision is agreed with HQ personnel. Files of terminees are returned to HQ personnel.

Promotions

- All promotions up to grade 13 are the responsibility of the region. Promotions to grade 14 and above are decided by HQ personnel.

Salaries

- The salary given on promotion or merit increase is the responsibility of the region up to and including grade 13. Salaries at, or above, grade 14 are decided by HQ personnel.
- Salary management is as set out in the accompanying salary policy manual and salary charts.
- Merit increase budgets and guidelines are set by HQ personnel.
- General salary increase policy is decided by HQ personnel.
- Apart from promotions or merit increases given at the appropriate time, other individual salary increases are not given.

Personnel administration

All aspects of expatriate personnel administration, payroll and statistics are decentralized. A comprehensive administrative procedures document sets out all aspects of the personnel administrative system. It is essential that regions comply with this system to ensure uniformity. Any changes to the system can only be made by HQ personnel.

- Pension and group life and accident insurance remains the responsibility of HQ.

- All personal files for personnel in all the regions will be held in the region. HQ will keep mini-files only for personnel up to grade 11 and skeleton files at grade 12 and above.

Policies, compensation and benefits
Expatriate policies remain essentially centralized to ensure consistency. What is decentralized is:

- interpretation of the staff manual
- days-off/field break policy
- rotation system decisions (within agreed pattern).

Any changes to expatriate policies can only be made by HQ personnel. Recommendations for such changes are expected from regions.

Personnel systems
Regions will complete exit interview forms and interview reports in the standard company format.

Policies on performance appraisals remain unchanged.

HQ personnel requires the following routine input, *only* from regions:

- Succession plan form, 1 August, down to division level
- Personnel evaluation, 1 April, 1 October
- Top potential plan, 1 April, 1 October
- Personnel manager's monthly letter
- Exit interviews, when made
- Interview reports, when made, for grade 12 and above only
- Performance appraisals, when made, for grade 12 and above only.

MANUALS

A number of basic written documents are an essential tool in the administration of expatriate compensation and benefits:

- A handbook or manual for employees which sets out clearly their basic terms and conditions of employment. This may be a single booklet or a series of booklets covering the different benefits such as salary, pensions, insurance, and so forth. With the widespread use of word processors, maintaining up to date information and documentation becomes a simple matter to organize.
- A manual for local management which explains how the employees' manual is to be interpreted, what is the intention behind the policies, and provides a compendium of local practices and interpretation.
- A salary policy manual setting out the basic logic and procedures of the salary structure and administration together with the necessary data to enable the system to operate at the local level. This is normally a restricted document given only to senior management and local personnel managers. This document is essential if the overall integrity of the salary structure is to be maintained and if local management is to be able to define salaries, grant merit increases, and so forth.

- Where the local management units are responsible for the expatriate employee payroll and/or generating appropriate personnel statistics, a detailed procedures manual is needed to ensure overall consistency between different units.

The company has to avoid appearing to its expatriates (or any other employees) as an over-centralized, unresponsive bureaucracy. This means:

- local problems and questions of interpretation have got to be resolved quickly. A local manager who has to refer every question raised by an expatriate to HQ half a world away (who may in any event know nothing about the employee or the location) has an immediate prospect of a demotivated subordinate.
- local managers, if they do have discretion, must have at their disposal the procedural tools to arrive at a decision which meets the needs of the particular problems and which at the same time is consistent with overall policy.

COMMUNICATIONS

Communicating a policy, listening to employee reactions and modifying policies in the light of such reactions is an integral part of the work of compensation and benefits. Channels of communication need to exist, be seen to exist and work effectively between the individual expatriate and the compensation and benefits policy makers. The real needs of employees must be properly taken into account when establishing corporate expatriate compensation and benefits plans and the reasons for policies need to be explained to the employees.

It is always a major concern of an organization to ensure that effective two way communication exists between employees and management. For the international company there is no substitute for the compensation and benefits staff travelling widely to overseas locations. This provides the key opportunity to assess conditions, listen to the expatriates' views and explain individually or through briefing groups the reasons for personnel policies.

By whatever means, those responsible for making expatriate compensation and benefit policies need to have clear input from the employees and avoid the danger of relying solely on:

- The input of a field manager which may be selective, and often biased towards what that manager himself feels rather than what his subordinates feel. It may be based on the field manager's memory of what he felt many years ago when he was employed in that particular country or doing a similar job. He has changed, the job has changed and the country has changed. In any event, he is almost by definition something of an exception since he has risen to a management position – a level which most employees do not attain. So, even if nothing else has altered and his memory is perfect, he may still give a

view that has little to do with that of the 'average or worse' employee.
- Corporate personnel philosophy set in general terms which is unlikely to address all the issues of individuals in a particular location, eg many companies have a policy of permanent family assignments rather than rotation to country of origin. In some countries this is an impracticable and foolish policy.

Practical communication problems

In an international context, there are a number of characteristics which differ from the domestic environment so far as communicating compensation and benefits policies is concerned, such as:

- language;
- complexity of what is being communicated;
- geographical dispersion;
- practical difficulties.

Language

Most multi-nationals tend to have one or, at the most, two company languages. Written communications, if in more than one language, need to be in perfect agreement. Often with a single language, such as English, the fact that it is used by managers who have a different mother tongue, can create problems unless the policy document is carefully scrutinized. In one company the phrase 'company furnished housing' was used in a policy manual and whilst the employee expected a house with furniture, the French personnel manager expected to provide the house unfurnished. What is needed is careful attention to linguistic detail, to ensure not only that what is written means what it says but that individuals are able to understand fully what is written, regardless of their original mother tongue.

Complexity of what is being communicated

An expatriate compensation and benefits package tends to be extremely complex. It is certainly more complex than a domestic package. In many cases employees may have decisions to make on investment plans, pension options and so forth, and it is important that they understand fully the issues involved.

This implies an effort to explain in clear terms the policies and the reasons for them. It implies a need for management to understand the policies as they apply to their expatriate subordinates and for a company to cover this area in its formal management development and training programmes. The role of induction training for expatriates is also important, as discussed previously.

Geographical dispersion

The very fact that individual expatriate employees may be widely dispersed in small numbers in any one location, means that many communication tools are hard to apply. Greater reliance may have to be placed on letters to employees from their direct line manager, explaining changes and briefings as well as video films. However geographically dispersed employees may be, they usually find a means of communicating with each other informally and the organization must recognize the existence of this 'grape vine'.

Practical difficulties

Whether it is as simple a problem as the impossibility of telephoning a given country, or of the customs impounding a set of updated staff manuals, or finding that a carefully prepared video tape cannot be played on the equipment available in the overseas locations, a great deal of thought and attention to detail must be given to the practical aspects of international communications. Most international companies have a corporate communications group but few of these groups have the kind of basic data and experience necessary to resolve all these practical problems. A solution demands systematic input from people in the overseas locations and the collection and updating of this information by the centre in an organized way.

PLANNING AND CONTROL OF EXPATRIATE PERSONNEL COSTS

An expatriate often costs as much as ten times the cost of an equivalent local employee. Planning and controlling personnel costs for expatriates is a major concern, not only because of the cost but also because of the complexity of the package and the diversity of factors acting on the various components.

A company needs to plan its expatriate personnel costs at the level of individual locations and also at a corporate level, and be able to monitor the actual situation. This presupposes a planning process and an information collection process. It also requires that personnel costs are identified and correctly allocated to a particular expatriate's location. Thus rules need to be set up to decide, for example, which location pays the cost of transfer, how the cost of vacation and vacation travel is allocated where a transfer happens during a tour of duty, and how accruals for separation payments are to be handled.

Averages (arithmetic means) are needed to establish total costs. When analysing salary structures and distributions, the median (mid point) is used as an indication of the central tendency (in order to eliminate excessive distortion by very high or low data).

One of the difficulties faced by any multi-national company is to decide in which currency it operates its corporate management accounting. If personnel costs are expressed in $US as the company currency, then the impact of the strengthening of the $US in 1981 and 1982 will have been to reduce dramatically the effect of local costs – sufficient in some organizations to give the impression that the cost of employing expatriates had not risen between 1980 and 1981. In the same way, the weakness of the $US in 1979 gave a completely false picture of the increase in the cost of expatriates. Employee costs should be presented both in the company currency at actual exchange rates and also at constant exchange rates, in order that management can identify underlying trends in the cost of the various elements within the total compensation package. The use of modern EDP systems make this process a relatively simple one.

Finally, managers should have a statement which breaks down the cost of their expatriate employees into meaningful categories. The following is a typical example:

Figure 14.1 *Example of a company's expatriate employees cost statement*

Detailed cost statement (consolidated)
All expatriates – cost to date in a given year
$ million

1.	Base salaries	30.1	
	Expatriate premium	6.8	
	Cost of living allowance	7.1	
	Bonus	2.1	
	Total		46.1
2.	Vacation salary	5.2	
	Vacation travel	6.4	
	Total		11.6
3.	Provident fund	2.6	
	Pension plan – company contribution	1.8	
	Tax equalization – net cost	1.9	
	Separation payment accrual	0.7	
	Total		7.0
4.	Medical expenses	1.1	
	Medical travel	0.5	
	Sick pay	1.2	
	Group life and accident	0.9	
	Total		3.7
5.	School fees	1.3	
	Housing – rents	12.1	
	Housing – furniture	1.6	
	Housing – services	3.0	
	Social Security contributions	4.3	
	Hotels and meals	2.8	
	Miscellaneous	1.9	
	Total		27.0
6.	Transfer costs of personnel	8.3	
	Total		8.3
		Total	102.7

PERSONNEL COSTS

The expatriate compensation package illustrated above can be broken down in the following way:

Figure 14.2

Components	*Percentage of total*
Base salary	29.3
Bonus	2.0
Expatriate premium and cost of living compensation	13.5
Pension cost (net of employee contribution)	4.3
Insurance cost	0.9
Housing provision (net of housing deduction)	16.3
Net cost to the company of tax equalization and social security	6.0
Medical costs	2.7
Vacation and vacation travel	11.3
Transfer costs	8.3
Miscellaneous (cars, school fees, etc)	5.4
	100

This is an actual situation – obviously there will be wide variations between companies and between one company and another in the same country.

The different areas of cost can be broken down into a number of component parts: those related directly to base salary; those related partially to base salary; and those which depend entirely on local living conditions. Each part is subject to quite different influences and needs to be looked at separately.

There are two separate elements in the estimation of the evolution of any of these cost areas. What are the forthcoming changes in compensation and benefits policies in the period being studied and how much will they cost? Further, what are the underlying economic factors which will operate regardless of the company policy?

Costs directly related to base salary

Apart from the base salary itself, it is normal for the foreign service premium, the cost of a pension plan, insurance premium and other long-term benefits (eg, separation payments and contract bonuses) to be expressed as a percentage of base salary.

These costs are the easiest to predict no matter what kind of base salary structure is used by the organization. It is easiest where there is a single unified structure for all expatriates, but even with a variety of different base salaries it can be achieved in a straightforward way. The major influences are:

- general salary adjustments;
- merit increase policies; and
- salary distribution of the individuals in a particular location.

General salary adjustments

A company ought to have at its disposal a reasonable estimate of the next year's likely salary increase while recognizing uncertainty in inflation levels and currency fluctuations. It should also have a good idea of the company's situation in the salary market by comparison with its planned position. Major changes in company profitability or the business climate could dramatically affect this estimate but such changes are relatively infrequent. Indeed, there should bc a base salary increase plan for, say, two or three years ahead in order to integrate properly and programme all other compensation changes that might be needed. Inflation properly used is a powerful tool for the salary administrator to rectify problems caused by people whose salaries are too high, implement changes that would otherwise cause a reduction elsewhere in the compensation package and give dynamism to the overall salary structure.

Merit increases

The cost of merit increases is by no means obvious. In any employee group there is a natural process of attrition which tends to result in more highly paid employees leaving and being replaced by younger people, newly promoted or appointed with lower general salaries. So, if the size of the group remains constant, and there is an absence of salary increases, it is conceivable that the average salary could go down. This may seem hard to accept, but a little reflection and study of actual statistics will demonstrate this phenomenon.

Salary distribution

To arrive at an average salary, the planner also needs to know what will happen to the structure of the expatriate population in the location. Will more younger and lower paid people be employed? Will several experienced, highly paid managers be added? The larger the group being considered, the less important the changes in salary distribution will be. In small scale operations, these considerations will have a major impact.

Cost related partially to base salary

Expatriation premiums, moving allowances and hardship allowances are often expressed as a percentage of salary up to a maximum monetary amount. Calculating future cost estimates requires the planner to have a simple model of the salary distribution he expects. Usually, it is sufficient only to know the percentage of the population with salaries above a given level, since most companies do not have more than one ceiling for such benefits.

Cost of living allowances and local living allowances tend to be fixed as a multiple of the part of the salary spent locally and the relative difference between the local cost of living and that in the home location. Spendable income is calculated from basic salary as a diminishing proportion as salary increases. So, an increase of 10 per cent in base salary is not likely to produce an increase of as much as 10 per cent in the cost of living allowance, even if no variation in relative costs exists. The planner also has to estimate the degree to which there will be a divergence in the evolution of overseas costs by comparison with the home location. Relative changes in cost may be balanced by corresponding relative changes in currency exchange rates, but it may be a dangerous assumption to make.

Local costs

A major area of expatriate personnel costs is housing, services, transport and other similar items which depend entirely on the local economic situation and not on the salary of the employee.

In assessing the likely increase in costs, it is generally of little use to take official published price indexes as any kind of guide. Not only do such indexes deal with a broad spectrum of goods and services, rather than the specific areas of concern, but they deal with average local families whose consumption patterns bear no relation to expatriates. In addition, in many developing countries, nobody has any faith in government statistics.

The cost of expatriate housing, for example, can frequently be of the order of $3000 to $5000 per month rent for a reasonable four-bedroomed house. Escalation in rents resulting from clauses in the agreement or a new contract will have a major impact on the cost of expatriates. The impact of sudden increases in demand for housing created by the arrival of a large number of expatriates for a new contract will have a similar effect.

Each location has to monitor the evolution of the cost of each item and make its forecast based on the best information it can obtain. For example:

Housing
- Escalation clauses in contracts
- General level of new rentals

Services
- Extrapolation of previous trends

Cars
- Projected import duty regulations
- If leased, escalation clauses
- General level of new contract

Medical
- Past history and frequency of accidents and illnesses

School fees
- Direct consultation with schools
- General economic indicators

A final area of costs which, in some countries, can be of considerable importance is tax equalization (protection and social security). Whilst social security costs are relatively easy to forecast, once the declared projected income is known, tax equalization costs are very difficult to estimate.

In a typical developing country, the process of tax assessment will be a long and tortuous one. Depending upon the degree of disclosure by the employer, the sophistication of the tax authorities and the amount of 'grossing-up' which is done, taxes claimed can account for 60 per cent to 100 per cent of base salaries. Frequently, appeals are undertaken. The normal practice is for a company to make an estimate of the probable tax liability for each of its expatriates in a given country and to make whatever accounting adjustments are needed once a final settlement is arrived at; this is often several years after the salary has been paid. As most companies use a rather conservative accounting policy, there is a tendency for tax estimates to be overstated in the year in which the salary is paid.

MONITORING ACTUALS AGAINST PLANS

The personnel manager needs to be able to monitor actual costs against these estimates for which he will require data presented in a meaningful form. The data should be presented as either a figure for a particular month, or comparative figures for the past three months (to show a short-term trend), or 'rolling' annual average figures (to show a longer term trend). Obviously the personnel manager needs to work closely with the accountant and EDP specialists to obtain this information.

When a compensation and benefits policy is introduced or modified, an estimate of cost must be made and actual costs must be compared with this estimate. Many multi-national companies insist that any benefit policies, costing more than a certain amount, must be referred to and be approved by the corporate board.

RATIOS

The most effective method of reviewing the costs of a compensation and benefits package is through the use of ratios (cost in comparison with something else, rather than in isolation). Some of the ratios used to compare expatriate costs between different places and over periods of time are as follows:

$$\frac{\text{cost of expatriate employees}}{\text{sales revenue}}$$

ie are expatriate employees generating an acceptable sales revenue? Is this figure increasing as fast as sales and is 'productivity' improving?

$$\frac{\text{cost of expatriate employees}}{\text{operating profit}}$$

ie are the expatriate employees in the areas where the most profit is made?

$$\frac{\text{cost of expatriate employee per month}}{\text{cost of local employee per month}}$$

ie how much more do expatriates cost and which way is the trend going? Clearly, comparing 'like with like' is necessary to obtain the full benefit of this.

$$\frac{\text{total cost of expatriates}}{\text{total cost of local employees}}$$

ie relative importance of expatriate costs within total personnel costs.

In addition, comparison of costs, numbers and ratios should be included with the plan and with previous time periods.

CONCLUSION

In order to ensure a good compromise between consistency, local flexibility, central control, simplicity and fairness, companies should try to adopt some measure of decentralized personnel management. The degree of decentralization depends, of course, on the particular situation. A clear statement of personnel policies, procedures and definitions of the authority of each decentralized level is necessary.

Once the organizational structure of personnel management of expatriates has been decided, great care must be taken with communications and the effective audit of personnel policy application. A loss of control is common in domestic personnel costs. Given the obvious problems of distance and organization in a multi-national company, it is even more crucial to set up an effective system of cost maintenance and cost control.

15. Compensation and benefits for the local workforce in developing countries

INTRODUCTION

In most developing countries a company will be employing not only expatriates in its operations, but will in fact be moving towards employing a substantial proportion of local employees as quickly as possible. This may be because the host countries have insisted on minimizing the use of expatriates in order to improve employment opportunities of their own nationals, or alternatively to minimize the political and cultural instability (often the result of the existence of a large expatriate workforce). In many countries there may be no need for expatriates, as the demand for managerial, professional and technical staff can be met domestically. From the viewpoint of the company the process of expatriation is always expensive; if this need can be met by recruiting from the local labour market then there will clearly be an economic incentive to employ a higher proportion of host country staff. Thus, for a mixture of political and economic reasons, there will be a trend towards 'nationalization' of the multi-national company's workforce in developing countries, even if full financial ownership and management control remain with the parent company and there will always tend to be a residual number of assignments that lend themselves to expatriation. These may be:

- key management positions to retain strategic control;
- specialist jobs requiring knowledge of technology which may be unattainable in the host country;
- specific development projects which can only be accomplished with expatriates on a defined contract basis;
- training assignments; where expatriates are required to transfer skills through on-the-job training, coaching and organizing courses;
- career development; where an international company may require certain employees to pass through a number of expatriate assignments before taking on responsibilities involving general management within a multi-national company.

Such expatriate posts tend to be the exception. Most multi-national companies work hard at recruiting and training local staff. Surveys have indicated that multi-national companies are, in fact, far from being the 'exploiters of cheap labour' they are popularly believed to be. On the whole, foreign companies pay better salaries to their local workforce than their domestic competitors and they also make great efforts to develop the skills and potential of their workforce. For the simple reason of competitiveness, the motivation and management of the host country workforce is certainly of crucial importance.

The expatriate manager, whether American, European or Japanese, will bring to the country where he works his own ideas and theories on work management. The highly participative management styles implemented in Japanese factories are now being established in other countries. From a broader perspective it could be argued that nearly all patterns of work organization in the modern world have been exported, either directly or indirectly by expatriates. Certainly, the ideas of the industrial revolution, originally developed in Britain, were rapidly adopted by other countries and at the beginning of the twentieth century, the systems of mass production and 'scientific' management which were evolved in the USA, were then introduced throughout the world. The introduction by expatriates of work practices to be adopted by local employees is just one side of the coin. At the same time the influences of the local culture are inevitably going to affect the way expatriate management organizes its local workforce. Expatriate managers have to be able to appreciate and understand the attitudes and aspirations of their local employees, and the social and economic context in which they work. This ranges from an awareness of tribal influences in West Africa to the racial problems in South East Asia and from the behaviour of relatively unsophisticated Polynesians to the highly developed *macho* culture present in some South American countries.

It is not possible to review the peculiarities of each local labour situation in detail, but obviously the problems of a company establishing itself in Iraq will be quite different from those encountered by a company setting up in Indonesia. Equally, many of the activities of personnel managers will follow similar guidelines to those used in the home country. This is hardly surprising since the way employees are managed and paid is similar in most countries. Because certain general problems crop up again and again, guidelines for multi-national companies establishing an enterprise in a new country have been established.

PRACTICAL PROBLEMS

Commonly encountered difficulties are those of local language, culture and the peculiarities of national employment legislation.

The problems of a different language are self-evident. The expatriate may find himself faced with incomprehensible manuals, forms and regulations, and then have to rely on translations made by the local employees. The resulting translations may often be incorrect because of linguistic error or deliberate misinformation to serve the particular interest of the translator and his colleagues. For example, in many salary indexing policies the word 'discretionary' (in the local language) is mysteriously translated as 'obligatory'.

A common solution to the language problem is for the company to send its expatriates on a suitable 'crash' course in the local language. While this may be effective for the individual who has some prior knowledge of the language and who simply needs to sharpen up his skills, it would be unsuitable for anyone else. It is generally acknowledged that the learning of a new language by this method is very difficult, especially in later life, and is unlikely to result in the expatriate manager working fluently in the language.

To the good fortune of English mother tongue expatriates, the business language in Anglophone Africa, the Middle East and most of the Far East is English, thus reducing for them the possible communication problems. The English-speaking expatriate in the international industries of oil, aviation, communications and computers, will also probably prosper, or at least survive, without formal language training since the industry's working language is English. Even if the expatriate is able to use his mother tongue, or has a good knowledge of the local language, this does not guarantee any insight into the local culture; this in itself can be a source of endless misunderstanding. The more enlightened company will often, therefore, attempt to brief the expatriate and his family on local conditions and cultural norms before they leave for their assignment. However, such briefings cannot eliminate all the possible misunderstandings. For example:

The promotion case

An expatriate working in a large, locally owned, African transport concern decided to install an open internal vacancy and promotion system. The expatriate hoped this would ensure that only the best managers obtained responsible positions within the company. (Up to this point this had not been the case.) He suggested that all future vacancies should be advertised and that candidates should be interviewed and assessed on their ability to do the job in question. A system of assessment was designed which made allowances for experience, qualifications and work performance. All the local managers liked the proposed selection system and agreed that it should be introduced as quickly as possible.

Some months later he was puzzled by the failure of the system to select managers in terms of their ability. As a result of further investigation it became clear that the system of promotion and selection reflected an elaborate tribal balance that in fact existed in most walks of life. Some ten years earlier, an extremely vicious civil war had been ended only by the creation of a balance between ability and tribal interests, and although this was rarely mentioned to a foreigner, it was a fundamental aspect of the cultural make-up of the country. Without it being explained to the expatriate manager, the 'unbiased' selection scheme had been tailored to meet the requirements of an unwritten rule which ensured that a racial balance existed in the apportionment of the organization's top jobs. This, to the local employees, was far more important than considerations of merit as understood in traditional western business organization terms.

The recruitment interview

Many Asian countries have hierarchical societies emphasizing respect for elders and people in positions of responsibility. An expatriate interviewing local staff for a financial position in one such country found it impossible to make a selection. He told his local colleagues that most candidates had nothing to say to him, appeared very shifty and often seemed on the point of falling asleep during the interview. It was tactfully pointed out that he may have mistaken the candidates' desire to be polite for laziness or ignorance. His colleagues informed him that in the local culture it was polite only to answer back with the minimum of responses and never to look directly at an elder or someone of superior social status. Moreover, actually being physically on a lower level than the manager, was also a sign of great respect; this explained the candidates' desire to be back in their chairs. To the interviewer, the candidates appeared ill prepared, taciturn, shifty and sleepy, whereas they were, in fact, by the standards of their own culture, trying to create a good impression.

There are many other instances of cultural misunderstanding. In Arab countries, for example, the rituals to be observed before discussing business are long and complex. Equally, meetings can sometimes take place in what appears to be a public arena. No expatriate, in an Islamic country, should be surprised by the taking of breaks for prayer. Many eastern cultures equate agreement with politeness – thus a simple answer of 'yes' to a question does not necessarily mean that the listener even understands the question, quite apart from agreeing or disagreeing with the point of view.

Apart from the cultural misunderstandings that can arise in overseas employment, there will be, in many cases, a potential conflict between the philosophy of the company and that of the host country. This can be very important with regard to such issues as individual merit payments, overtime, promotions and job security. The aggressive performance-orientated North American company may find it difficult to introduce its philosophy in a culture where group values and avoidance of loss of face are more important than the rewarding of individual success. Equally, western concepts of productivity may not be greatly applicable in developing countries, where traditional arrangements result in work sharing to ensure a wider distribution of scarce income.

LEGISLATION

Another hurdle for the foreign company will be local labour legislation. Each country has its own set of labour laws and in many cases these can be Byzantine in their complexity and apparent contradictions. If the company is to operate successfully, it will be obliged to conform to local legal requirements on working hours, minimum salaries and compulsory insurance. The problem for foreign companies new to a country is that it is often difficult to distinguish where law differs from custom and practice. A problem can frequently arise where the company puts its trust into the hands of a local legal advisor who is inexperienced in employment law. Like his domestic counterpart, he will tend to interpret the law literally rather than base his advice on how it can be applied in practice. This tendency, together with the understandable inclination to widen the workload, may result in a highly legalistic interpretation of employment relations which may be far removed from normal practice within that country.

LOCAL PERSONNEL MANAGERS

It is seldom likely that the expatriate manager has either the time or the expertise to become intimately acquainted with the details of local labour law. One solution is the hiring of a local personnel manager who, unlike a lawyer, can give advice on local employment. A problem with this solution can be that the local personnel manager may quickly establish himself as the only person who can interpret and explain labour regulations, thus placing him in a highly sensitive position. Where the turnover of expatriate management is fairly rapid, the local personnel manager may become the effective manager of the local staff; obviously this is not always in the company's best interests. This is particularly risky in countries where corruption is common, as the local personnel manager, by controlling employment, can often levy considerable sums of money from other employees and interested parties, without the knowledge of his expatriate manager. Improbable as this may seem to the newly appointed expatriate manager whose experience is entirely domestic, it is a major fact of employment practice in many developing countries.

COLLECTIVE BARGAINING AND INDUSTRIAL RELATIONS

The foreign company must decide at an early stage its policy towards recognition of local trade unions. As a general rule this should be determined only by what is considered normal practice in the host country. There are many cases of multi-nationals who have adhered to their domestic policy of non-recognition even in countries where trade unions have virtual universal recognition enshrined in legal provisions. While this may be considered a worthwhile corporate objective, such a stance is rarely effective in the host country.

In the last ten years various codes of industrial relations conduct for multinationals have been created by, for example, the EEC and the International Labour Organization. Few, if any, effective organizations 'police' the activities of multi-national companies. Trade unions frequently accuse multi-national companies of moving their operations around to destabilize genuine bargaining practice in any one country. For example, moving operations to a country with lower labour costs can always be used as an argument against a high wage demand. This may be feasible in cases where large amounts of plant and equipment are not involved, although it is difficult to envisage in most cases where start-up costs would be high or where the operation has to remain in the country to serve the requirements of the local market. Another trade union accusation is that multi-nationals bring non-union labour across international borders during labour disputes to undermine the strength of the organized labour in a country. There are few examples of this occurring in practice and without behind the scenes government support, would be difficult to organize.

While these considerations are somewhat abstract, they are issues that any personnel manager should be aware of when he comes to develop his overall philosophy for managing a local foreign workforce.

LOCAL PERSONNEL POLICIES

A company employing large numbers of local staff must provide a package which is in accordance with the prevailing conditions in that country. This may seem an obvious statement but a large number of companies disregard this basic tenet with the result that subsequent difficulties are encountered.

There are many reasons why foreign companies often provide pay and benefits which do not accord with local practice, particularly in developing countries. These may include a desire to minimize the difference between expatriates and local managers, ignorance of the local salary market and local political influences.

In many industries a company may employ a pool of international (ie mobile expatriate) staff to retain mobility and flexibility, while at the same time building up a home country workforce in important local markets such as Nigeria and Indonesia. It is natural that employees in similar positions will compare their employment conditions. It may then seem far from clear why an expatriate has a dollar salary, a furnished house and a large number of benefits provided by the company, none of which is given to the home country employee doing exactly the same work. If a racial element is introduced into this equation the work situation may quickly be seen by the locals as a systematic type of exploitation by the foreign company. It may be quite pointless for the company to point out that local pay, judged by the local labour market, is in fact well above average local levels. Political or union pressure may be applied to force increases in wage rates, so that the differential between the expatriate and local employee is compressed. This is a classic example of relative deprivation, where the workforce is already well off by the standards of local comparison but feels aggrieved or cheated by some other expatriate reference group.

The cost implications of such a situation developing are of course very dangerous for the company. It can probably only avoid such dangers by stating its basic philosophy very clearly in terms of separating the expatriate and local compensation and benefits packages. To do this it must have a detailed appreciation of the local employment market.

THE OVERSEAS COUNTRY SALARY AND BENEFITS SURVEY

In some countries local surveys may be numerous and well established; surprisingly so this is the case in a number of developing countries. It may simply be sufficient to subscribe to a survey which covers the correct industrial sector and geographical area. There may also be a sufficient pool of local job advertising to identify very accurately the local market conditions. Failing this, it may be necessary to undertake or commission a survey which shares information with a dozen or so target companies. Normally these will be other foreign employers. Many of the normal salary survey techniques will be used in conducting a survey in the developing world.

Information needed will be in the following areas:

- ○ Market salaries for specified jobs, existence of minimum wages
- ○ Overtime rates and bonus schemes
- ○ Typical salary structure, merit payments
- ○ Sickness, holiday arrangements
- ○ Pension and insurance arrangements
- ○ Any other allowances and benefits normally provided
- ○ Relevant labour laws, hours of work, etc.

The practical difficulties of conducting a salary and benefits survey in the developing countries should not be underestimated. There is no substitute for the direct involvement of a personnel professional (either from the company or an outside consultant) and the need for very careful planning is paramount. The survey must have as its target the real competitor for qualified personnel (typically other foreign employers rather than locally owned companies) and be constructed with the same rigour as for those carried out in the developed world. Great efforts need to be made to ensure objectivity and full disclosure.

The expatriate manager, when in possession of this information, statistics on the local retail price index, and a good understanding of the local tax and social security structure, should be in a position to design a salary and benefits package for his local staff.

SALARY ADMINISTRATION AND JOB EVALUATION

A number of aspects of salary administration and job evaluation present problems for the European or North American expatriate manager in several different developing countries. It is crucial, particularly in the developing world, that he be sensitive to these issues.

Job evaluation

In its domestic operations or for its expatriates, the company may well have developed its own system of job evaluation or have adopted one of the 'proprietary' job evaluation schemes. However, there are inherent dangers of using the same scheme for local staff employed in many different countries. Different cultures stress values concerning jobs which differ from those traditionally found in North America and western Europe. The relative salaries of an engineer and a secretary in Britain and France have already been discussed. Such differences are magnified many times over when examining cultures in developing countries. The most commonly encountered example of this is the high status commonly placed on jobs requiring clerical or administrative skills, to the detriment of jobs involving manual work. Given the weightings used in a typical western job evaluation scheme, this would result in a distorted pattern of relativities by the standards of these countries.

Differentials

The ratio of earnings in developing countries between different hierarchical levels is often quite different from that found in western industrialized countries. Some countries with revolutionary political systems keep salaries very compressed and the manager does not receive more than three or four times the salary of the lowest grade of shop floor worker. In other countries a local administrator will commonly receive ten or even twenty-times the salary of, say, his driver. The salary administration expert could design a job evaluation and salary structure scheme to reflect this on an overall company basis with relative weighting to reflect each country's particular cultural background, but in practice few companies would develop this sort of sophistication. The danger is that a company new to the country might take its salary structure and apply it 'off the shelf', disregarding the relativities commonly encountered in the country.

Job seniority and merit

Merit payments are emotive topics even in industrialized countries. In some cultures they are totally unacceptable in that they are individual rewards given as a result of the subjective judgement of the manager. In these cultures there is usually heavy pressure to design a salary administration programme that compensates everyone for inflation and makes no individual merit payments even if the system is called 'merit approval'. The inflationary factor is also usually considered to apply to the whole salary, rather than applying a ceiling as is common in western countries.

Complexity of allowances and job titles

Local salary systems can develop unnecessary complexity both in the number of job titles and grades, together with the method of salary adjustment. The reasons for this are twofold. First, in many countries job titles are very much a matter of status and the principle of broad job groups will not readily be understood. Second, in many countries inflation rates are extremely high resulting in the need for complicated adjustment mechanism. This type of problem is best illustrated in an example of a company employing 200 staff in Indonesia:

Classification	Seven categories of qualified or trained employees; subdivided into another four categories with 51 separate job titles.
Salary adjustment	Automatic cost of living applied to half the base salary. Base salaries up to Rp 50,000:115 per cent up to Rp 100,000:105 per cent up to Rp 1,000,000:95 per cent of the cost of living increase.

Annual increment	If an employee's performance is outstanding a merit increase in addition to an annual increment may be granted.
Bonus system	A bonus system 50 per cent of which is paid in $US.

Thus, the company has to handle salaries on individual bases, all of which are adjusted three or four times in a year and are then integrated with a bonus scheme involving two currencies. Not only does the administration of such a system require a large workforce, it also becomes almost impossible to monitor or control individual salary levels. The likelihood of working a sensible merit system under such circumstances is very remote as increments become automatic. This structure of course looks far-fetched and the professional personnel manager might wonder how any company could have arrived at such a policy. This package, unfortunately by no means uncommon, was set up over the years by local line managers, with no real personnel input, in a company whose financial and technical results were and are outstandingly good.

This example illustrates how pressure can create a complicated salary structure; the objectives of any manager should be to keep the structure as simple as possible. This implies having a simple grade structure, consisting of usually fewer than ten levels into which jobs can be placed, reflecting acceptable relativities by the standards of the local culture. Pay scales reflecting the intended position in the market place desired by the company should be devised. If a local salary survey has indicated a range, the company may decide to pay in the upper quartile to attract a higher standard of applicant or to avoid criticism of a foreign employer underpaying local staff. Any job which for any reason cannot be fitted into the structure should be treated on a 'red circle' basis, so that it can be integrated into the salary structure at a later date. There should also be a simple method of adjusting for inflation either by the use of a reliable cost of living index and some kind of ceiling, or by having a review date at management discretion. If merit payments are to be introduced into the structure they should reflect management opinion clearly and not be allowed to become a second cost of living adjustment. These are ideal targets and the easiest to implement in a start-up situation. If the manager is taking over a workforce which has already been organized, his task will be that much more difficult.

Finally, a company should resist the temptation to solve its local personnel problems by payment outside the country in hard currency undeclared to the local tax authorities, even though it may be a simple matter to do so, and thus appear to enhance dramatically the tax effectiveness of its compensation package. Developing countries are becoming more sophisticated in detecting such illegal actions, more sensitive to evasion practices and the company puts itself in a highly vulnerable position in relation to its employees if it chooses to act in this way.

Local staff benefits

The simplest solution is to have a salary structure that rewards the employee with a salary and leaves him the maximum degree of flexibility to dispose of the salary in the way he chooses. However, under pressure from tax structures and employee benefits philosophy, many western countries have already moved a long way from this concept, and in many countries the benefit package is at least as important to the employee as his salary. If the expatriate manager adheres to the principle of paying salaries according to local custom he must also apply this principle to benefits. A newly arrived foreign company should not try to lead the way in providing benefits, as this is usually left to the well established domestic organizations – particularly nationalized concerns – in developing countries. Although it may provide generous salary and bonus payments in an attempt to motivate staff, prudence and conservatism are recommended in areas of pensions and insurance until such time as the implications of local common practice are fully understood. A good illustration of this is the manager who installed a pension scheme soon after his arrival. The scheme at the time seemed relatively inexpensive (8 per cent of salaries), but by the time he left, it had become a liability of 30 per cent. His successor was predictably less than pleased with the prospect of renegotiating the scheme to achieve a more acceptable cost structure. In many developing countries the company may take on a wider responsibility for the employee than would normally be the case in many western countries. The primary reason for this is that without a developed social security welfare system the employer is the only person in a position to offer medical and insurance assistance. There are four major areas to review:

- Housing and house purchase
- Medical expenses
- Insurance schemes
- Pensions and severance benefits.

HOUSING AND HOUSE PURCHASE

In many less developed countries where expatriate employment is common, there are two parallel housing markets; a highly expensive expatriate market offering standards of accommodation at western levels and a local housing market. This causes problems if local staff are recruited to fill senior posts, where they feel largely, and understandably, for reasons of status, that they should be given accommodation of the same standard as expatriate staff doing similar jobs. Their salary levels will prohibit them from renting or buying such accommodation and it may be common practice for it to be provided by the company. This is even more important if the company has required them to move locations within their country, thus separating them from their traditional family accommodation. There is no obvious solution for the company which is unwilling to provide expensive housing for its local workforce, since the argument for housing has a certain logic, and it is frequently the practice to provide housing especially for senior staff.

A practical compromise could be for the company to provide some sort of separate housing allowance, linked if possible with a house purchase scheme. In such a scheme the company could either guarantee a bank loan or make a cash advance on a multiple of salary basis, which has the benefit of retaining staff during the duration of the loan as well as reducing to some extent any feelings of jealousy the local staff may harbour.

MEDICAL EXPENSES

In countries where a national health system or medical insurance has not been developed, the company will often be expected to reimburse the cost of medical treatment, particularly for its local senior employees. To some extent this benefit works to the advantage of the company, protecting the health of its key employees. However, such schemes are difficult to control. The benefit is often extended to the immediate family of the employee and can become very expensive, the concept of the family being much wider than in the western world. It is also not uncommon for doctors' and pharmacists' prescription forms to be sold on the local market and then sent to the employer as a regular source of additional income. One control is to impose a clear maximum money ceiling on claims per family per year (although this does tend to ensure that the ceiling is reached by all the employees concerned). Another alternative is regularly to audit the medical claims and undertake a degree of private investigation in doubtful cases, or where possible to insure the plan with a local insurance company.

INSURANCE SCHEMES

A typical situation encountered with multi-nationals is that they tend to insure their expatriate staff very comprehensively but do not fully understand the insurance market for their local employees. Most less developed countries provide only the most rudimentary state cover and the only fully comprehensive insurance cover available is that provided by the private insurance market. It is here that the company must decide the extent of the coverage and the best method of funding.

One approach is to establish a minimum level of accident and/or life insurance cover. A survey of local organizations will quickly establish typical levels defined in terms of multiples of annual salaries. A group policy can then be taken out reflecting these levels.

It is interesting to note that, in some countries, insurance companies will not accept policies offering higher insurance than is normal in the local market. The implication is that such policies can endanger the well being of the insured employees as their lives carry such a high insurance benefit.

The choice of insurance company to be used will usually be dictated by two factors, reliability and price. For the company and the morale of the local employees, the choice of a reputable insurance firm is important. Where a competitive market exists, three or four quotations should be obtained for the

business to give some indication of the average price and level of cover offered.
Multi-national pooling should be used whenever possible.

PENSION AND SEPARATION BENEFITS

Without discussing basic pension concepts in detail, there are a number of long-term benefits issues which are specific to developing countries and might not occur to the expatriate manager:

- a foreign company should carefully survey the particular country concerned and not attempt to apply worldwide benefits philosophies. The stance should be one of conservatism in benefits but generosity with salaries;
- economic factors in developing countries are much harder to forecast than in developed ones, so cost estimates of benefits programmes carry a very high risk;
- seldom is there an effective money or stock market in the country concerned and it is poor practice to fund long-term liabilities in one currency when they are denominated in another. Thus, funding in a developing country presents serious problems;
- retirement ages in many developing countries are low (typically 55 for men) giving less time for benefits to accumulate;
- benefits if defined in terms of a high percentage of salary may be subject to major hyperinflation with a consequent effect on the cost to the company;
- actuarial data is often non-existent. Resulting insurance premiums can therefore be excessive;
- account has to be taken of the frequent requirement for statutory separation indemnities;
- any benefit provided must be integrated with any social security programme and future improvements in any state plan must be taken into account.

For these reasons few multi-national companies allow pension or other long-term benefit decisions to be taken below corporate level.

In many countries, lump sum separation benefits are more usual than private pension plans. Through these plans the company, as a statutory obligation or as a voluntary benefit, undertakes to make a payment to the employee when he leaves. An example of such a scheme (from an African country) is shown below:

African severance plan

Upon resignation, retirement or dismissal, the following lump sum benefit will be paid:

Gratuity based on years of service:

Up to five years of continuous employment:	75 per cent of a base monthly salary per completed year of total service.

From six to 15 years of continuous employment:	100 per cent of a base monthly salary per completed year of total service.
Above 15 years of continuous employment:	150 per cent of a base monthly salary per completed year of total service.

Gratuities are calculated annually and are based on the average base monthly salary during the 12 months prior to departure. Salary includes housing and transport allowances but excludes annual bonus.

The gratuity is not payable in cases of dismissal for acts against the company such as fraud, theft, wilful damage, corruption, etc.

The advantages of such a scheme to the employee is that he receives a cash sum when he leaves, regardless of his age, which he can then spend on a house or a small business as he chooses. Given the life expectancy and the high inflation in many countries, together with the difficulty of administering a formal pension scheme, this is an attractive option for the company. For the expatriate manager designing such a scheme there will always be the problems of pressure to increase the multiples used, together with the possibility of salary manipulation at the end of employment. Another approach is to have a defined contribution plan, the company contributing an amount equal to a percentage of the employee's salary and investing it in an insurance policy or an investment fund.

OTHER ALLOWANCES AND BENEFITS

Other benefits exist, the most obvious among these are vacation policy, paid sick leave schemes and profit sharing. These benefits usually form a part of each country's standard employment practice. In addition there are benefits that may not often be encountered by managers in western countries:

Scholarships

- a company is often expected to provide financial assistance for the education of employees' children. Selection is usually made on the basis of school results by an employee representative committee.

Car purchase

- following house purchase, the car is the largest single investment for local employees. Companies either guarantee bank loans, make internal loans or auction their own vehicles after they are no longer suitable for company use.

Club allowances

- local senior staff in many countries will expect reimbursement for club memberships. These can be extremely important (and expensive) measures of status.

Night guards and servants

- expatriate staff will commonly be allowed to employ such staff in countries where conditions make it appropriate. Local senior staff will frequently request similar privileges.

It should be remembered that benefits once given can seldom be withdrawn, either for legal or industrial relations reasons, regardless of the profitability of the operation or the performance of the individuals concerned. The benefits must be costed, not only in the immediate future, but also in the medium and long-term. An initial low cost commitment can prove to be very expensive over the years, particularly in the areas of long-term benefits and pensions.

LOCAL EMPLOYMENT CHECKLIST

It is frequently the case that an incoming expatriate manager will find himself managing a local workforce, or a number of workforces in different countries, where his predecessors have been responsible for designing the original compensation and benefits packages. He may encounter all or a number of the problems already discussed above and will, therefore, need to understand the local culture and the problems inherent in each particular location. Any redesign, or amendment of the local employment contract, should only be undertaken after the implications of such changes have been considered in relation to industrial relations and political factors.

The following checklist will help to highlight the areas that should be analysed in auditing local staff employment contracts:

A Organization

1. How difficult is the overall working environment – legal, political, social aspects? How well have these difficulties been identified?
2. Are there any specific legal or cultural constraints – hours of work, methods of operation, use of manpower?
3. On what basis are operations organized – by client, product, function, geographical location or a combination of these?
4. Is there any unnecessary duplication of activities or inflexibility between the main operational groups?
5. How are the service functions (finance, administration, personnel) organized? How well do they service operations?
6. Are there any social factors affecting organization (eg one group not prepared to work with others on a racial, tribal, religious basis)?
7. Has any manager or supervisor more people reporting to him than he can reasonably control?
8. Are there cases where the job holder:

   (a) does not know what he has to do
   (b) is not sure whom he reports to
   (c) is being asked to do too much or too little
   (d) is duplicating the work of someone else?

   Do job descriptions exist? Are they up to date?

9. How much authority is delegated to the local administration/personnel/ finance manager? Does the local expatriate manager understand what has been delegated?

B Manpower planning

1. Has a manpower forecast been prepared?
2. Does the manpower plan take account of the nationality mix required, either by head office direction or local legal or practical requirements?
3. Are adequate records kept of labour attrition in terms of numbers leaving by length of service, age, skill?
4. Have the effects of promotions and transfers been assessed?
5. Have any changes in working hours or vacations been taken into account?
6. Is productivity monitored?
7. Are manpower costs being measured by group and by breakdown of costs?
8. Are there adequate plans for local staff:
   (a) recruitment
   (b) training and development
   (c) improvements in productivity
   (d) improvements in retention of staff?

C Recruitment

1. Does the recruitment programme follow on from the manpower plan?
2. Are requests for new jobs:
   (a) fully justified
   (b) accompanied by a job description
   (c) approved by the appropriate line manager?
3. Is recruitment action accompanied by a job specification which lists the following:
   (a) qualifications and training
   (b) experience
   (c) knowledge and skills
   (d) personal qualities
   (e) physical attributes
   (f) special requirements (travelling, night work)?
4. Has the image of the company been analysed in the local market regarding:
   (a) local reputation
   (b) pay, fringe benefits, working conditions
   (c) security of employment
   (d) opportunities for education and training
   (e) career prospects?
5. Are all sources of candidates examined for:
   (a) internal promotion, transfer
   (b) advertising
   (c) recommendations from existing employees?
6. Are there frequent cases of family ties or patronage in recruitment?

7. Are the media chosen to advertise jobs cost effective?
8. Are effective measures taken to screen interview candidates?
9. Does the interview:
   (a) follow a plan
   (b) take place in good surroundings
   (c) have appropriate testing techniques
   (d) have more than one opinion
   (e) take account of local culture?
10. Are the interviewers:
    (a) assessed as to performance
    (b) sure they have a clear view of the job
    (c) free of racial or cultural prejudices?
11. Do the interviewers understand the cultural peculiarities of the environment?
12. Are references and medicals carried out before the offer of employment is finalized?

D Employment

1. Does the new employee receive a contract of employment?
2. Does the contract specify:
   (a) salary level
   (b) bonuses
   (c) fringe benefits
   (d) vacation rights?
3. Has a lawyer been consulted?
4. Is the contract letter supported by a staff manual?
5. Is the staff manual regularly updated?
6. Is there a version both in English and the local language?
7. Does the manual contain explanations regarding grading, pay, discipline, redundancies?
8. Is there an induction course for all new recruits?

E Training

1. Are the training needs of the main groups of staff covered by training schemes?
2. Have training plans and budgets been prepared on an assessment of needs and priorities?
3. Is there a plan for numbers and cost of local staff to be trained?
4. Is there a local training co-ordinator?
5. Are the training courses well documented and in the appropriate language?
6. Are the trainers properly trained? Is adequate attention paid to quality control of the training?
7. Does training meet the requirements of the local authorities?
8. Do a sufficient proportion of local staff progress to senior management positions?

F Remuneration

1. Does the payment system ensure that the local company is:
   (a) competitive
   (b) providing effective motivation
   (c) ensuring reasonable relativities between jobs?
2. Are there an appropriate number of grades in the pay structure to provide adequate differentials but avoid confusion?
3. Is there a job evaluation system?
4. Is there any evidence of serious anomalies within the structure?
5. Are pay levels competitive with local rates? When was the last salary survey undertaken?
6. Is there evidence of high labour turnover because of pay problems?
7. Does the system lend itself towards wage drift?
8. When was the payment system last reviewed?
9. How many different components are there of the pay package? How much of the total earnings is represented by the basic salary?
10. Are adequate benefits provided, in line with the industry and local practice? Do these include:
    ○ housing
    ○ cars
    ○ pension
    ○ profit sharing
    ○ medical scheme
    ○ insurance
    ○ vacation
    ○ sick leave
    ○ special vacation or annual bonuses?
11. How much overtime is paid and how is it controlled?
12. What is the distribution of earnings?

G Management development and appraisal

1. Is the division/district manager committed to developing management staff among local employees?
2. Is there an established system of performance appraisal?
3. Is it used regularly and with all suitable categories of staff?
4. Does a system of 'management by objectives' follow on from the appraisal scheme?
5. Are managers conducting appraisal interviews in the correct circumstances?
6. Are objectives mutually understood and accepted?

H Industrial relations and communications

1. What is the track record regarding industrial disputes in the country?
2. Can causes of industrial disputes be identified:
   ○ pay system
   ○ fluctuation of earnings

- ○ working conditions
- ○ safety record
- ○ supervisory style
- ○ bad communications
- ○ cultural difficulties?

3. Has a trade union been recognized? If so, what are its representational and negotiating rights?
4. Is there a procedural agreement which specifies union facilities, dispute procedure, disciplinary procedure, grievance procedure, redundancy agreement?
5. Does the manager have a systematic plan for employee communication?
6. Does the manager undertake regular briefing or operations improvement meetings?
7. What does the notice board look like?
8. Is there any evidence that language or cultural difficulties are inhibiting communication?

I Records and information systems

1. Are local pay records kept manually or by computer?
2. Can salary sheets be easily broken down to establish constituent parts of the total?
3. Is there evidence of frequent payment errors?
4. Are personal files kept on every employee?
5. What condition are they in?
6. Are these files regularly updated?
7. Is there a quick reference index system?
8. Are personnel records kept in a secure location?

CONCLUSION

No one book, let alone one chapter of a book, could discuss the variation in employment throughout the world. However, the personnel manager of a multinational company will need to develop a systematic approach in organizing the personnel management of locally employed staff in developing countries. Over a period of time, the numbers and importance of local staff tend to grow as the expatriate element diminishes. Given that every country will offer its own specific communication problem and cultural difficulties, there are some basic rules which should be followed. The expatriate company should try hard to recruit a competent professional local personnel manager who has the determination to develop a long-term career with the organization worldwide and who can therefore develop primary loyalty to the company. Despite frequent pressure, the local workforce should be managed so far as is possible in relation to the local market, and not with regard to relativities with the expatriate workforce. The company will have to pay more allowances and provide some benefits which are not 'normal' in the country's home base. Finally, where the manager is faced with a well established employment situation, he should, within the bounds of political possibility, attempt to ensure it is run on sound personnel management principles. A manager who ignores this, or who delegates excessively to a local administrator, can find himself rapidly facing massive cost escalation and innumerable anomalies.

16. Sources of information

Every personnel manager appreciates the importance of information for the designing and maintainance of appropriate compensation and benefit programmes. In the home country managers usually have access to a number of publications designed to keep them up to date concerning changes in employment legislation, current salary agreements and a multitude of other topics concerning the management of human resources.

Unfortunately access to information on a multi-national basis is more difficult to obtain and no 'standard' work on the subject exists which gives up to date information on a country by country basis. This chapter is a guide to the sources of information which the authors' have found particularly useful. It is not an exhaustive list, concentrating on information available in the United Kingdom, the USA and France and organizations based in these countries.

Even with suitable published information available there is no substitute for going to the location and making a personal judgement. The problem with the use of general information is that it does not deal with the particular industry in question and includes figures for the capital city of the country concerned, not the provincial town 500 miles away which is to be the operation's base. Perhaps it is best to obtain as much information as possible from published sources and then, if necessary, to commission a firm of qualified consultants to undertake a full survey. Armed with this data, the personnel manager will then be in a position to visit the location and make relevant decisions. The company that runs its international operations from a department centred at the head office (having only a world map on the wall and a stream of official statistics at its disposal) will not be in touch with the real situation in its expatriate locations.

LIVING AND WORKING OVERSEAS

There are a number of good guides to overseas locations. Some concentrate on general introductions, others give advice specifically directed at visiting businessmen, but there are also useful sources of information for resident expatriates. There are specialist publications for relocation, language and taxation problems and several good general guides aimed at briefing expatriates prior to moving abroad for the first time. There are also several periodicals produced specifically for expatriates.

Useful publications and courses

Accepting a Job Abroad – A Practical Guide
M Tideswell, British Institute of Management, Management House, Parker Street, London WC2
A review for the prospective expatriate.

Barclays Bank International PLC
54 Lombard Street, London EC3P 3AH
Publishes business profiles for many countries.

British Overseas Trade Board
1 Victoria Street, London SW1H 0ET
Publishes 'Hints to Businessmen' for every overseas country giving details of climate, laws, business etiquette, and so forth.

A Businessman's Guide to Language Courses
British Institute of Management, Management House, Parker Street, London WC2
A guide to intensive language courses available in the UK.

Business Traveller
60-61 Fleet Street, London EC4Y 1LA
Aimed at the home based businessman but also useful for the travelling expatriate.

Centre for International Briefing
Farnham Castle, Farnham, Surrey GU9 0AG
Organizes residential foreign service briefing sessions for most countries, aimed at helping expatriates and their families to minimize culture shock.

Directory of International Schools
European Council of International Schools (ECIS), 18 Lavant Street, Petersfield, Hampshire 6U32 3EW
A directory of necessary information for English speaking expatriate families.

The Expatriate
The Centre of Legal and Business Information, 85 Portland Road, London W11 4CN
Examines topics of interest to expatriates. (A monthly journal on subscription.)

Guide Financier des Francais de l'Etranger
Ministère de l'Economie, 93 rue de Rivoli, 75001 Paris, France
Tax and exchange control advice for French expatriates.

Moving Abroad Kit
Pickfords Removals Ltd, Enfield, Middlesex EN1 3YB
This is one of many moving guides from the large UK removals company.

Price Waterhouse Country Guide
Price Waterhouse, 1251 Avenue of the Americas, New York, NY 10020, USA
On a country by country basis details of tax, social security and business conditions in a wide range of countries (one book per country).

Resident Abroad
Financial Times Business Publishing Ltd, Greystoke Place, Fetter Lane, London EC4A 1ND
A monthly magazine for UK expatriates covering financial matters, plus reviews of major overseas centres and information on UK living costs, house prices and exchange rates.

The Taxation of Foreign Earnings and Pensions
UK Inland Revenue
A guide for the UK expatriate. A similar guide is also produced by the IRS in the USA.

Working Abroad: The Daily Telegraph Guide to Working and Living Overseas
Golzen, Godfrey, Kogan Page, 120 Pentonville Road, London N1 9JN
(Also available from Daily Telegraph Publications Dept, 135 Fleet Street, London EC4P 4BS)
A general guide to expatriate living followed by reviews of specific countries.

Impact of the new 1981 US tax laws on Americans Abroad
Price Waterhouse, 1251 Avenue of the Americas, New York, NY 10020, USA
Self explanatory contents.

COST OF LIVING INFORMATION

A number of specialist bodies issue cost of living information together with judgements on hardship in overseas locations. These range from government sponsored reports and international agency surveys to consultancies offering information to individual clients.

Associates for International Research Inc (AIRINC)
1100 Massachusetts Avenue, Cambridge, Mass 02139, USA
Similar to the ORC and the Conference Board in producing regular statistical data for clients working in an international environment.

Cindex
54 Avenue de Versailles, 75016 Paris, France
A group sponsored by French employers which produces salary surveys and information concerning French expatriates.

Confederation of British Industry (CBI)
21 Tothill Street, London SW1A 9PL
Publishes guides to living costs in Western Europe, the Middle East and Asia.

The Conference Board
845 Third Avenue, New York, NY 10022, USA
An independent research organization with 400 associates. Research in many areas of international activity with publications on updates cost and other statistical information.

Conseil National du Patronat Francais (CNPF)
31 Avenue Pierre le de Serbie, 75016 Paris, France
A French managerial organization which undertakes studies on the French expatriate workforce.

Cost of Living
Organization Resource Counselors (ORC), 1211 Avenue of the Americas, New York, NY 10022, USA
Publishes cost of living tables for most cities, updated quarterly.

Cost of Living Survey
Employment Conditions Abroad Ltd, Devonshire House, 13 Devonshire Street, London W1N 1FS
An annual survey of cost of living in approximately 140 countries. Measures the difference in day to day costs for expatriate staff between the home base and the foreign country. (Home bases include UK, Netherlands, Sweden, West Germany, Australia. Other locations covered at specific request.)

HAY (France)
13 rue Alphonse de Neuville, 75017 Paris, France
Prepares expatriate studies for French subscribers.

Indexes of Living Costs Abroad
US Department of State, Washington DC, USA
US government statistics on overseas prices established for defining allowances for government employees (available from US embassies).

Key Cities Program Report
International Compensation Inc, Boston, Massachusetts, USA
Cost of living differentials in 35 different countries – information on tax services and tax equalization programmes.

Main Economic Indicators
OECD Economic Statistics Division, 2 rue André Pascal, 75775 Paris, Cedex 16, France
Monthly issue of statistics on all member countries gives details of prices, wages and salaries, and many other economic indicators.

INTERNATIONAL SALARY SURVEYS

Two distinct types of survey services exist. These are:

○ surveys which look at general salary levels on a country by country or

regional basis;
- ○ commissioned studies by consultancies.

ECA Employment Reports
Employment Conditions Abroad Ltd, Devonshire House,
13 Devonshire Street, London W1N 1FS
Reports are produced for about 75 countries and contain information on:

- ○ expatriate remuneration;
- ○ local staff remuneration;
- ○ cost of living information;
- ○ personal taxation;
- ○ background information for expatriates.

(Reports are available for member companies.)

Executive Compensation Service – International Studies
Management Centre Europe, Avenue des Arts 4, B1040 Brussels, Belgium
The European Branch of American Management Association publish three major surveys annually. These are:

- ○ Top Management Remuneration Europe (job definition and salary information);
- ○ The European Benefits Report (international benefits planning);
- ○ Office and Administrative Personnel Remuneration Europe (for financial, administration and EDP Personnel).

IDS International Report
Income Data Services, 140 Great Portland Street, London W1N 51A
A similar service to the *European Industrial Relations Review.*

International Transfers USA – Europe – Middle East
MICA International SA, 437 Avenue Louise, B91050 Brussels, Belgium
in collaboration with Management Centre Europe.
An annual survey of rates of exchange, working conditions, cost of living comparisons and spendable income in each country. Centres covered include:

USA	*Europe*		*Middle East*
Houston	Athens	Lisbon	Abu Dhabi
New York	Brussels	London	Al Khobar
Washington	Copenhagen	Madrid	Bahrain
	Dublin	Oslo	Dubai
	Frankfurt	Paris	Jeddah
	Geneva	Rome	Riyadh
	The Hague	Stockholm	Cairo
	Helsinki	Vienna	

Particularly useful for users of the balance sheet approach and gives details of transfers between countries.

Consulting organizations

The major consultancies and chartered accountants with consultancies all undertake specialized surveys for their clients. The large multi-national insurance companies, brokers and actuaries also provide a wealth of information on international pension and insurance matters.

European Industrial Relations Review
Industrial Relations Services, IRS, 67 Maygrove Road, London NW6 2E3
This publication reviews salary settlements and makes benefit comparisons for European organizations. Published monthly.

EMPLOYMENT COMPENSATION AND BENEFITS OVERSEAS

The main problem with this information is separating genuinely useful information for expatriate employment from the mass of detail on a country by country basis.

Benefits International
Pension Publications Ltd, 30 Queen Anne's Gate, London SW1H 9AW
Exclusively concerned with occupational pension schemes around the world.

ECA Information Quarterly
Employment Conditions Abroad Ltd
Reviews recent developments in international personnel operations.

Guide Pratique pour les Francais à l'Etranger
Chambres Syndicales des Sociétés de Commerce International,
31 Avenue Pierre, Premier de Serbie, Paris, France
A guide to French nationals considering working overseas.

IBIS International Benefits Information Service
Charles D Spencer and Associates Inc, 222 W Adams Street, Chicago, Illinois 60606, USA
IBIS has an extensive information service and also sponsors conferences and seminars. For example:

- IBIS Briefing Service – published monthly with news of international employee benefits;
- IBIS Reference Manuals – detailed information on eight countries (Australia, Belgium, Canada, France, Germany, Japan, Netherlands, UK);
- IBIS Meetings – annual conferences held in various European cities and other regional seminars.

Concentrates on social security and long-term benefit plans but also discusses compensation policy.

Memento des Francais de l'Etranger
Union des Francais de l'Etranger, 146 Boulevard Haussman, 75008 Paris, France
Publishes advice on aspects of tax, social security and pensions for French expatriates.

NFTC Memorandum and Bulletin
National Foreign Trade Council Inc, 100 East 42nd Street, New York, NY 10017, USA
Regular updates for subscriber of a variety of subjects which include index of living costs abroad and foreign post differentials.

Social Security Programs throughout the World
US Department of Health Education and Welfare, Washington DC, 20402, USA
An exhaustive publication revised periodically, giving details of social security in every country in the world.

Survey of Personnel Practices and Compensation for Expatriate Employees
ORC Inc, 1211 Avenue of the Americas, New York, NY 10022, USA
An annual survey of some 300 companies reviewing all aspects of personnel practice. Very useful as an overview.

GUIDES TO THE EMPLOYMENT OF EXPATRIATES

Essentially the sort of material covered in this book and complementary to it.

Administering Expatriate Pay
Organization Resources Counselors Inc, 78 Buckingham Gate, London SW1
Regular seminars on explaining the fundamentals of the balance sheet approach and the interrelationship between change in rates of exchange and expatriate pay differentials.

Compensation Review
American Management Association (subscription service), Box 319, Saranac Lake, NY 12983, USA
A quarterly publication which from time to time deals with expatriate compensation problems.

Innovations in International Compensation
Organization Resources Counselors Inc, 1211 Avenue of the Americas, New York, NY 10036, USA
This monthly publication, first produced in 1974, regularly reviews problems encountered in the management of expatriates. Topics include:

- taxation;
- legislation;
- benefits;

- ○ base pay and allowances for US expatriates;
- ○ third country nationals and locals.

International Compensation Briefing
Management Centre Europe, Avenue des Arts 4, B1040 Brussels, Belgium
Regular courses pertaining to expatriate compensation and benefits.

The Management of Expatriates
Lewis, Brian, editor, Institute of Personnel Management, IPM House, Camp Road, Wimbledon, London SW19 4UW
Essays by Len Peach, Brian Ellis and others on aspects of expatriate management. (Still in preparation at the time of writing.)

So Smith is for Export: A Series of Essays on the Employment of Expatriates
Wardon, John N, Employment Conditions Abroad Ltd
First published in 1977, this collection of essays covers many aspects of expatriate employment.

Index

INDEX OF ADVERTISERS

ACTION SCIENCE

HOT AND COLD

Neil Ardley

Series consultant: Professor Eric Laithwaite

Franklin Watts

London New York Toronto Sydney

The author
Neil Ardley gained a degree in science and worked as a research chemist and patent agent before entering publishing. He is now a full-time writer and is the author of more than fifty information books on science, natural history and music.

The consultant
Eric Laithwaite is Professor of Heavy Electrical Engineering at Imperial College, London. A well-known television personality and broadcaster, he is best known for his inventions on linear motors.

First published in Great Britain
1983 by Franklin Watts Ltd
12a Golden Square
London W1R 4BA

First published in the USA by
Franklin Watts Inc.
387 Park Avenue South
New York
N.Y. 10016

Printed in Belgium

UK edition:
ISBN 0 86313 023 2
US edition:
ISBN 0–531–04614–1
Library of Congress Catalog
Card No: 82–62990

Designed by
David Jefferis

Illustrated by
Janos Marffy
Hayward Art Group
Eagle Artists

Contents

Equipment

In addition to a few everyday items, you will need the following equipment to carry out the activities in this book.

- Candles
- Clothes pin
- Denatured alcohol
- Electric bar heater
- Flour
- Health salts, or sodium bicarbonate and vinegar
- Heavy cream
- Ice cubes
- Ink
- Large glass bowl or aquarium
- Liquid detergent
- Long metal file
- Margarine
- Matches
- Medicine dropper
- Metal strainer
- Metal tube or metal foil
- Milk
- Plasticine or modeling clay
- Salt
- Sweetened condensed milk
- Table lamp
- Thermometer
- Vanilla extract
- Wire

Introduction

Heat is a form of energy that we need all the time. Heat keeps us warm, and we put heat to use in engines and stoves. We make heat by burning fuel. We also get heat from the Sun. Removing heat produces cold, and we make use of cold in refrigerators and freezers.

By doing the activities in this book, you'll find out how to make heat and why things burn, and see the effects that heat has on objects. You'll discover how to produce cold and explore the strange way in which ice behaves. Among the activities are some easy tricks that you can play with heat, as well as projects like making an expansion indicator and instant ice cream.

One word of warning: several of these activities involve using matches and candles. Be very careful not to burn yourself or to set fire to things. Blow out all matches and candles as soon as you have finished with them.

This symbol is used throughout the book. It shows you where to find the scientific explanation for the results of the experiment.

Making heat

Change the energy in your muscles into heat.

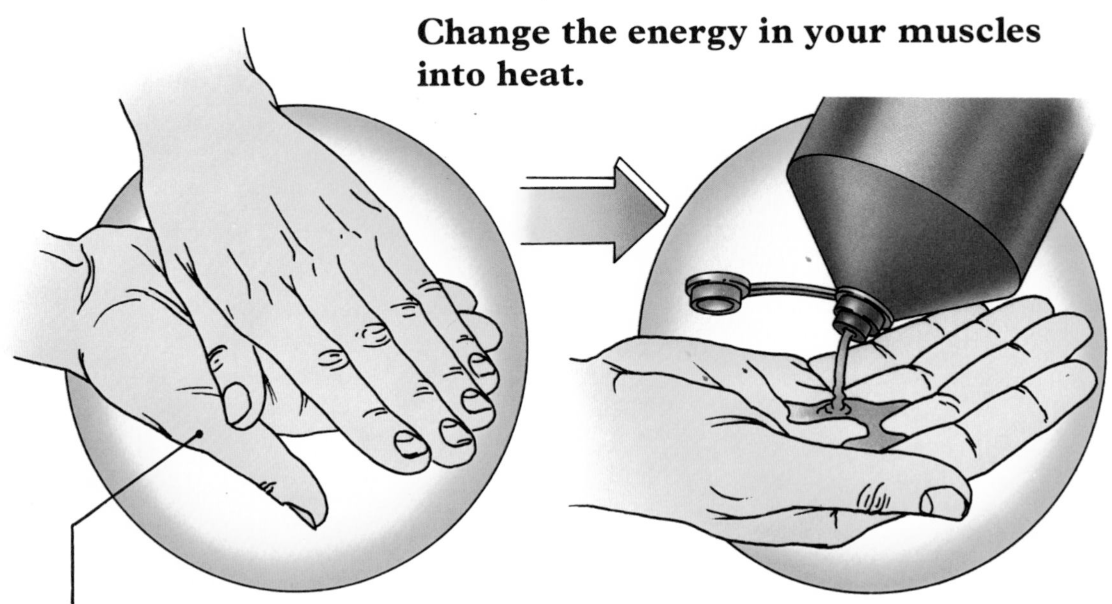

Make sure your hands are dry.

△ Rubbing to make heat in this way is called friction. It happens because the skin on your hands is slightly rough. Rubbing harder needs more effort and produces more friction, turning more of your muscle energy into heat. Liquid detergent or soap makes your skin smooth and there is very little friction, so slippery hands do not get hot.

Heat is energy

Rub your hands together lightly. Feel that your hands are beginning to get warm. Rub them more strongly and your hands get really hot. Try this again, but spread a little liquid detergent or soap on your hands. Add a few drops of water to make them slippery. Now your hands stay cool.

Heat is a form of energy and it is always made from another form of energy. You change some of the energy in your arm muscles into heat if you rub your hands together when they are dry, but not if they are slippery.

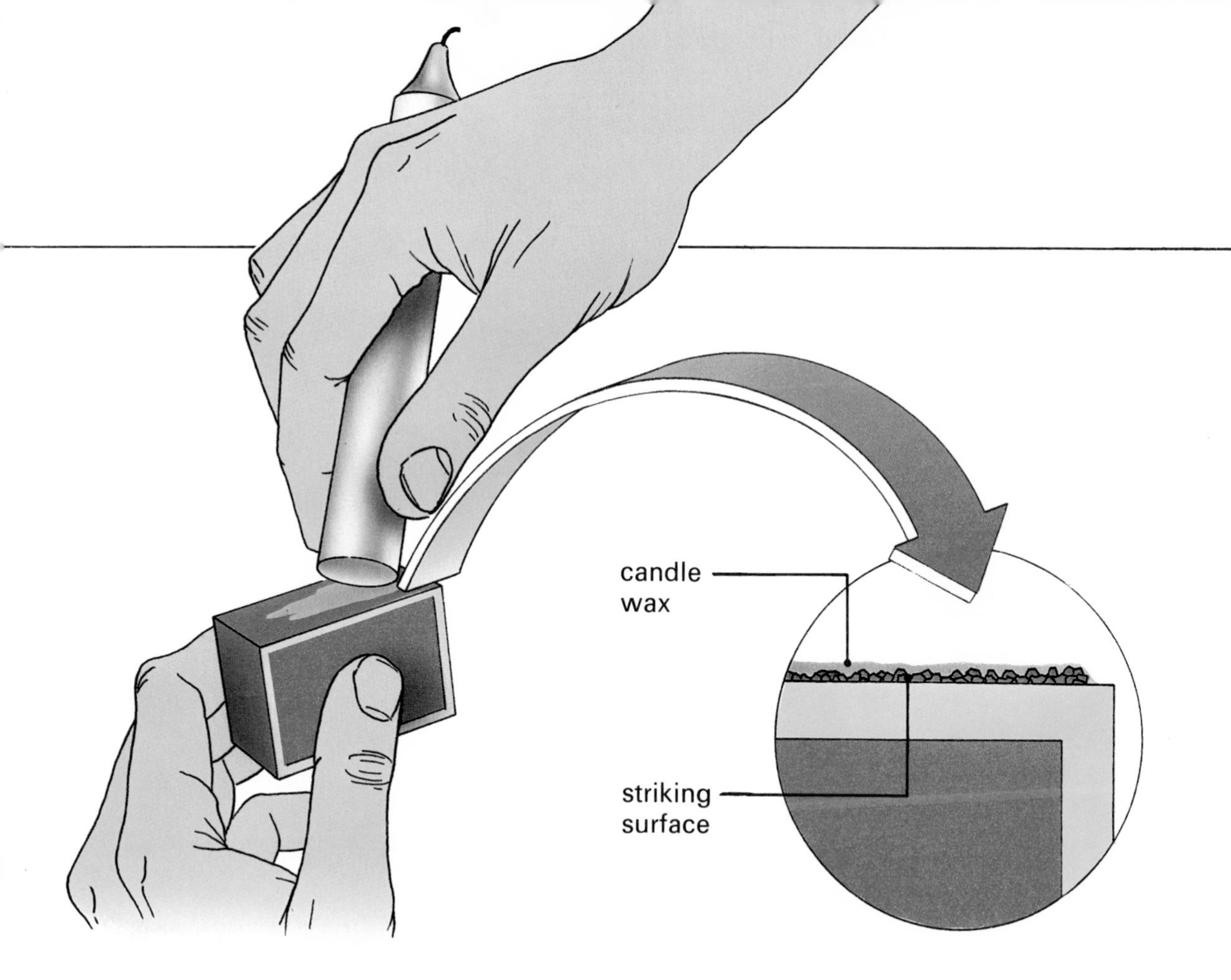

Useless matches

You can play this trick on a friend. Take a matchbox and rub a white candle over the striking side. Push the candle wax into the rough surface with a finger so that it is invisible but very smooth. Now the matches will not light!

A match normally lights because friction with the striking surface produces enough heat to make it catch fire. The candle wax makes the surface so smooth that there is not enough friction to give sufficient heat to light the match.

△ Lubricating oils work in the same way as the candle wax. They make surfaces very smooth so that they move easily and do not produce much friction. We put oil into car engines to stop friction from making lots of heat and harming the engine.

Why things burn

A fire needs oxygen in order to burn.

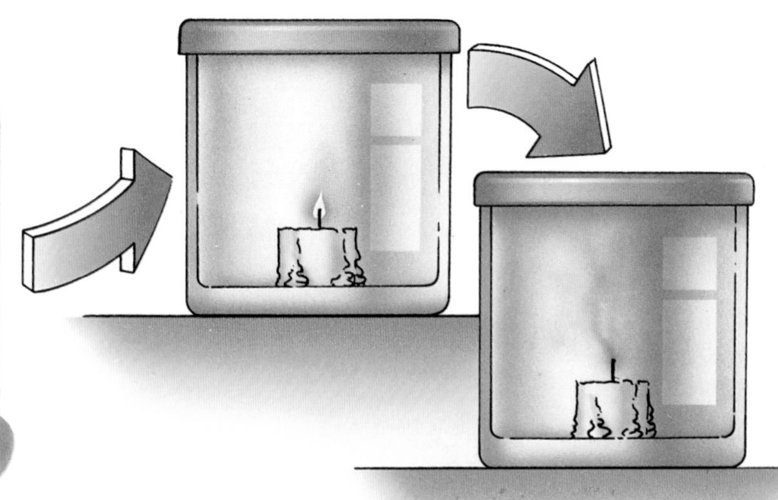

▽ Fire extinguishers work by smothering a fire to stop the oxygen in the air from getting to it.

The disappearing flame

Take a large glass jar with a metal lid. Place a short candle in the jar and light it. Gently lower the lid on the jar and watch the flame. It gets smaller and soon goes out.

When anything burns, it uses up an invisible gas in the air called oxygen. When the lid is placed on the jar, the candle soon uses up the oxygen in the jar. As no more oxygen can get into the jar, the candle flame dies.

Invisible flame killer

Take two small glasses. Place a teaspoon of health salts in one and add a little water. Strike a match. See that it burns well in the empty glass. But as soon as you lower the match into the other glass, the flame goes out.

As the health salts fizz, they produce an invisible gas called carbon dioxide. The air in the empty glass contains oxygen, so the match burns in it. But carbon dioxide fills the other glass so that the match cannot burn. It goes out.

▽ If you do not have any health salts which fizz in water, use a teaspoon of sodium bicarbonate and a little vinegar instead. Carbon dioxide is heavier than air, so it pushes all the air out of the glass.

Warning—this experiment needs care. An adult must supervise it.

Fire and flames

Why is heat needed to make fire?

Two flames from one

Take a metal tube about $\frac{1}{4}$ in across and several inches long. Hold it in a clothes pin and put one end into a candle flame. Smoke comes from the other end. Light it with a match—it catches fire!

Unless they are already hot enough, things need to be heated to make them take oxygen from the air and catch fire. When you light a candle, the heat of the match first melts the wax. Then it gives off a hot, smoky vapor that catches fire. The hot vapor travels up the tube and will catch fire when lit. The candle flame continues to make enough heat to produce more vapor and keep the flames burning.

△ You can make a tube by wrapping metal foil tightly around a pencil, taping the foil in place and then removing the pencil.

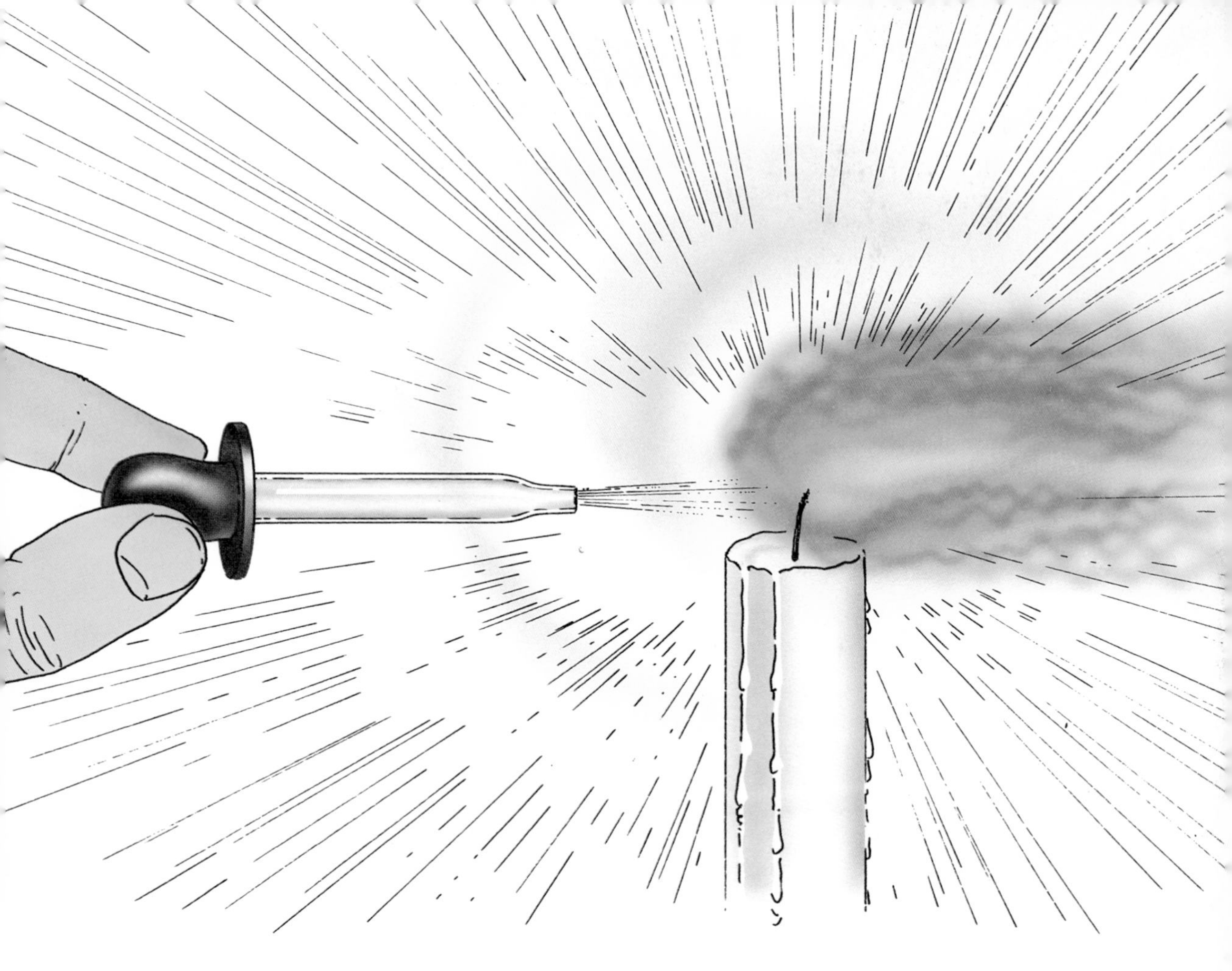

Flour flame

Take a glass tube with a nozzle and a rubber bulb, such as a medicine dropper. Squeeze the bulb and then let go to suck some flour into the tube. Puff the flour into a candle flame. It catches fire with a quick burst of flame.

✸ The flour is made of very small particles like dust. Each one is surrounded by lots of air, so it does not need to get very hot in order to take oxygen and catch fire. The flour lights quickly and easily in the candle flame and very soon burns out.

▽ Use fine white flour for this experiment.

Expand or contract

See how heat changes the size of things.

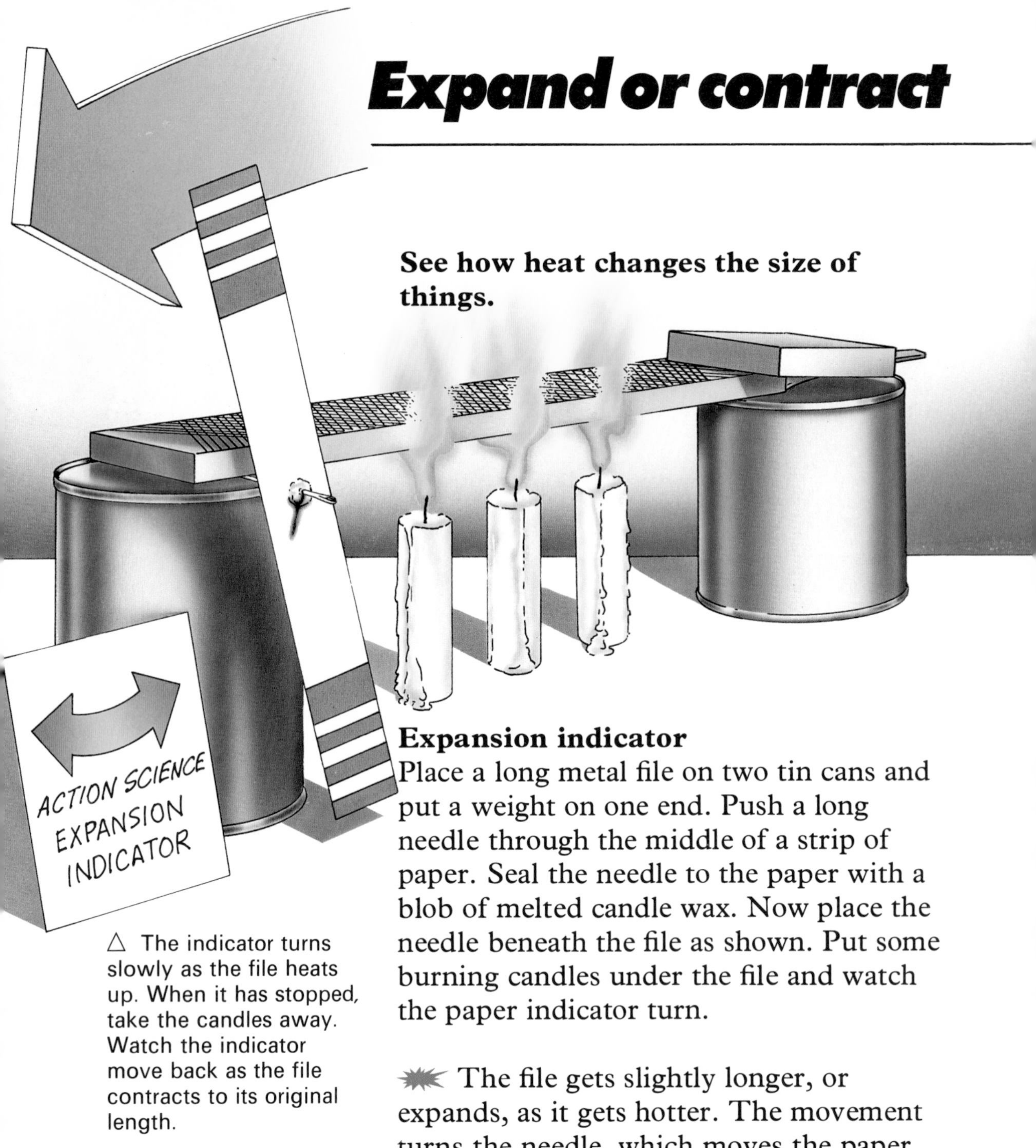

△ The indicator turns slowly as the file heats up. When it has stopped, take the candles away. Watch the indicator move back as the file contracts to its original length.

Expansion indicator

Place a long metal file on two tin cans and put a weight on one end. Push a long needle through the middle of a strip of paper. Seal the needle to the paper with a blob of melted candle wax. Now place the needle beneath the file as shown. Put some burning candles under the file and watch the paper indicator turn.

The file gets slightly longer, or expands, as it gets hotter. The movement turns the needle, which moves the paper indicator. Structures like bridges are built to allow them to expand in hot weather.

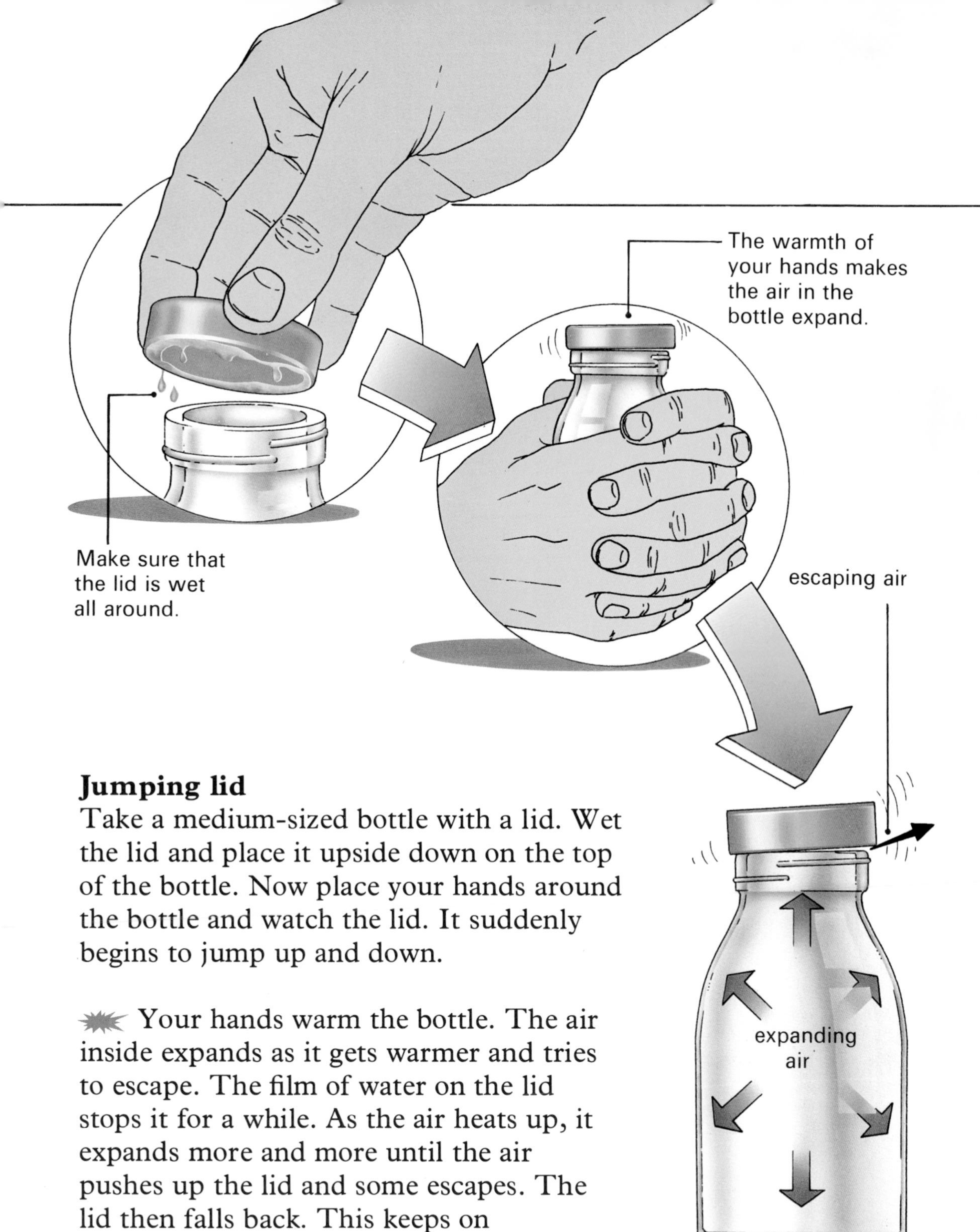

Jumping lid

Take a medium-sized bottle with a lid. Wet the lid and place it upside down on the top of the bottle. Now place your hands around the bottle and watch the lid. It suddenly begins to jump up and down.

Your hands warm the bottle. The air inside expands as it gets warmer and tries to escape. The film of water on the lid stops it for a while. As the air heats up, it expands more and more until the air pushes up the lid and some escapes. The lid then falls back. This keeps on happening as the air continues to expand.

Hotter or colder?

Seal the lid with plasticine and fit it tightly to the bottle.

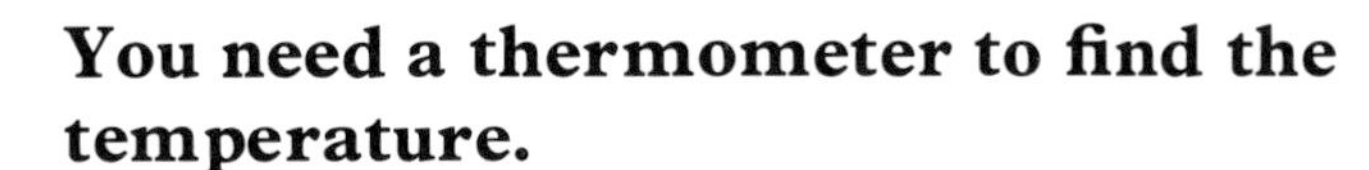

You need a thermometer to find the temperature.

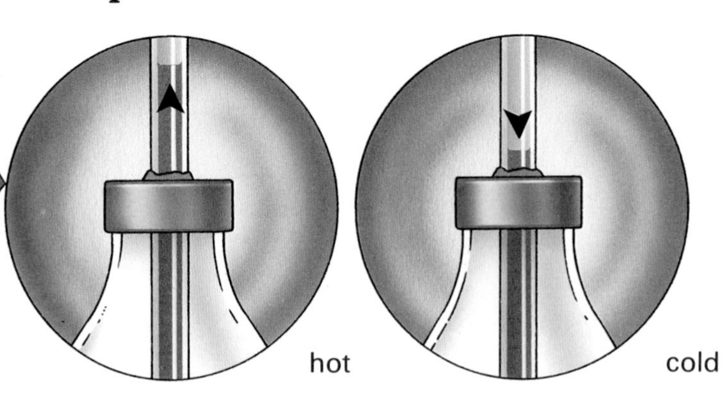

Make a simple thermometer
Half fill a clear bottle with water, colored with a little ink. Make a hole in the lid and push a clear plastic tube through it. Blow gently into the tube so that water comes to rest about halfway up the tube. Place the bottle in a sink and pour hot water over it. The colored water rises in the tube. Repeat with cold water and the level falls.

The level indicates the temperature of the water poured over the bottle. The hot or cold water causes the air inside to expand or contract, making the colored water rise or fall in the tube. In a real thermometer, a liquid expands or contracts in the same way.

Test the temperature

Fill two glasses with cold water. Place some ice cubes in one and leave it for a few minutes. Put a finger in the ice water for a minute, and then put this finger and the finger next to it in the cold water. To one finger this water feels warm, while to the other it feels cold!

You cannot judge the temperature of something just by feeling it. You need to use a thermometer.

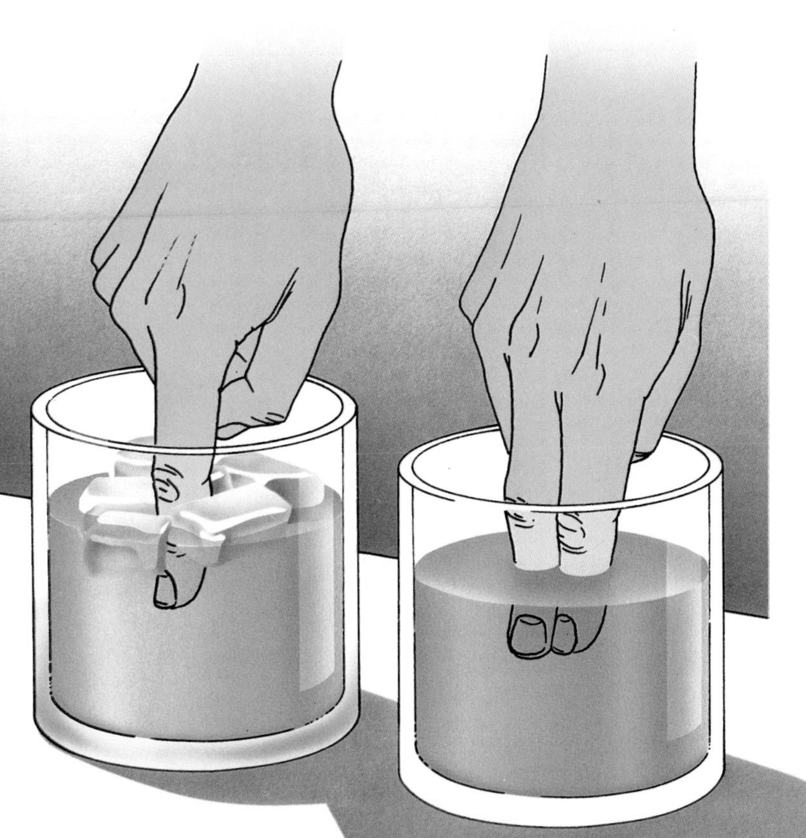

△ Something can feel either hot or cold depending on whether your skin is cool or warm. When swimming, the water often feels cold when you first get in but soon seems to warm up. In fact, your skin gets cooler in the water, so the water feels warmer.

Heat on the move

How does heat get into things?

△ These five objects are a plastic straw, a steel hair grip, a glass dropper, a twist of aluminum foil, and a wooden stick. The best conductor is aluminum; then come steel, glass, plastic and wood. The last two are such bad conductors that they may stop heat getting to the margarine and may not fall off. Poor conductors of heat are called insulators.

Find the best heat conductor
Take several thin objects of about the same length, and stick each one to a piece of wood with a dab of margarine. Place the wood across a bowl, and pour some very hot water into the bowl until it touches the bottom of the objects. The objects soon begin to fall into the water one by one.

Heat spreads up through the objects by conduction and melts the margarine. The best conductor of heat falls first.

Heat strainer

Light a candle and lower a metal strainer upside down into the flame. Notice that the flame does not go through the strainer. Instead, smoke rises above it. Gently lower the strainer down to the candle and the flame will go out.

The steel wires in the mesh of the strainer conduct heat well. The heat of the flame flows into the strainer, cooling the burning vapor in the flame. The vapor becomes too cool to burn as it passes through the wire mesh, and rises as smoke.

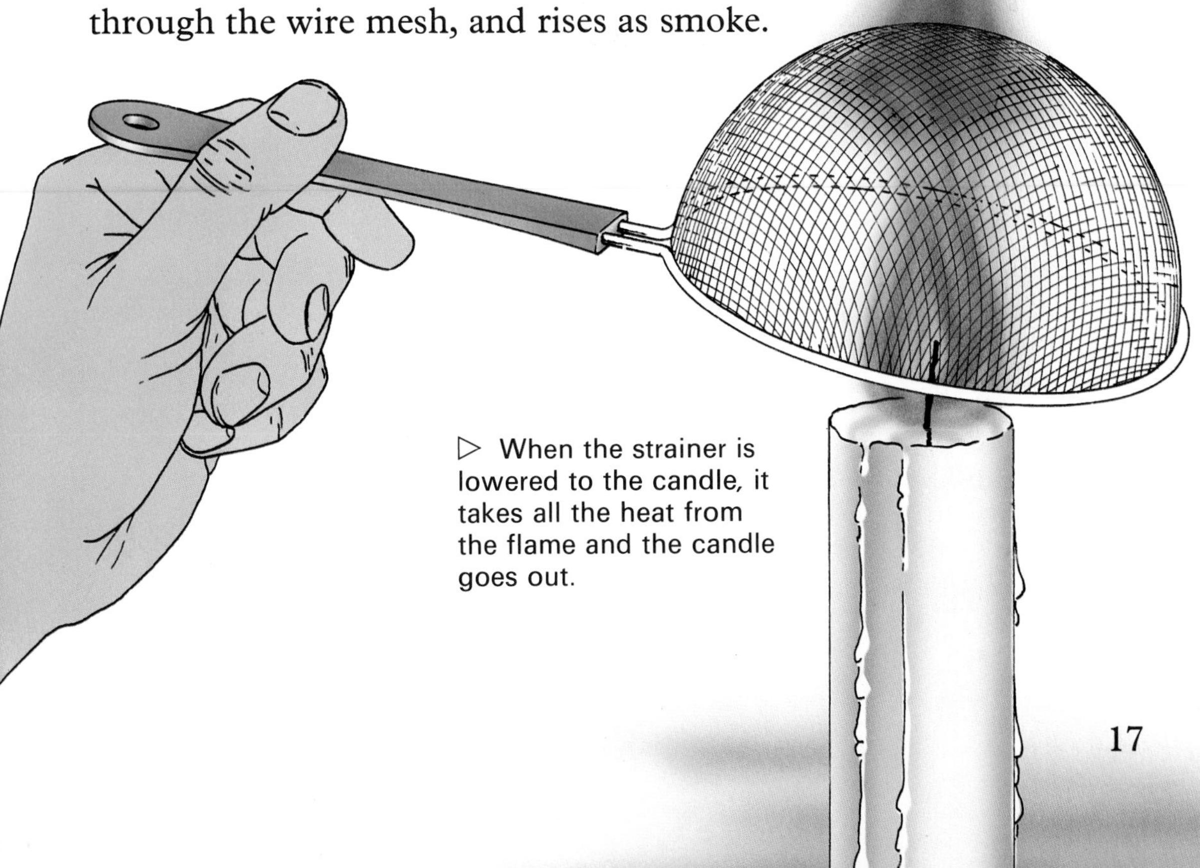

▷ When the strainer is lowered to the candle, it takes all the heat from the flame and the candle goes out.

Heat rays

Heat can also travel in rays, just like light rays.

Take care not to cut your fingers on any jagged edges.

Black hot tin can

Take two empty tin cans and remove the tops and labels. Place some black paper around one and make sure that the other is clean and shiny. Put some cold water in each can. Place the cans near an electric bar heater and cover them. Touch the cans: only the black can gets warm. Measure the water inside with a thermometer. The water in the black can gets hotter.

Heat rays from the fire warm both cans. The black can gets hotter because the dark side takes in the rays. The shiny side of the silver can reflects the heat rays like a mirror, so this can does not get as hot.

△ Heat rays travel with the light rays from the fire to the cans.

Penetrating heat

Take the home-made thermometer described on page 14 and put a table lamp close to it. Switch on the lamp and watch the level rise in the tube.

Heat rays from the hot bulb in the lamp pass through the clear sides of the bottle just as the light rays do. But once inside, the heat rays do not leave. They begin to warm up the air inside, and the increase in temperature causes the water level in the tube to rise.

△ A greenhouse keeps warm during the day because the Sun's heat rays go through the glass walls. Once inside, the rays remain there.

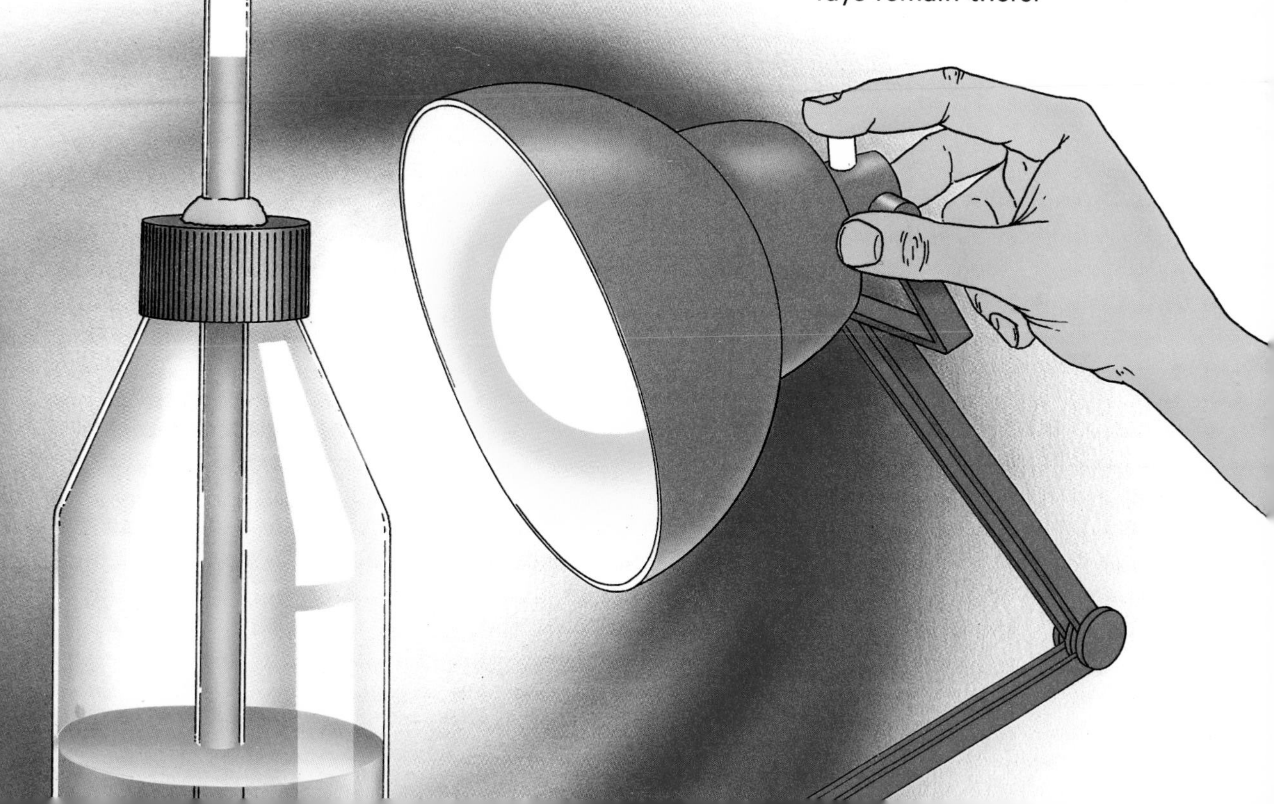

Rising heat

Heat can also move by rising to a higher level.

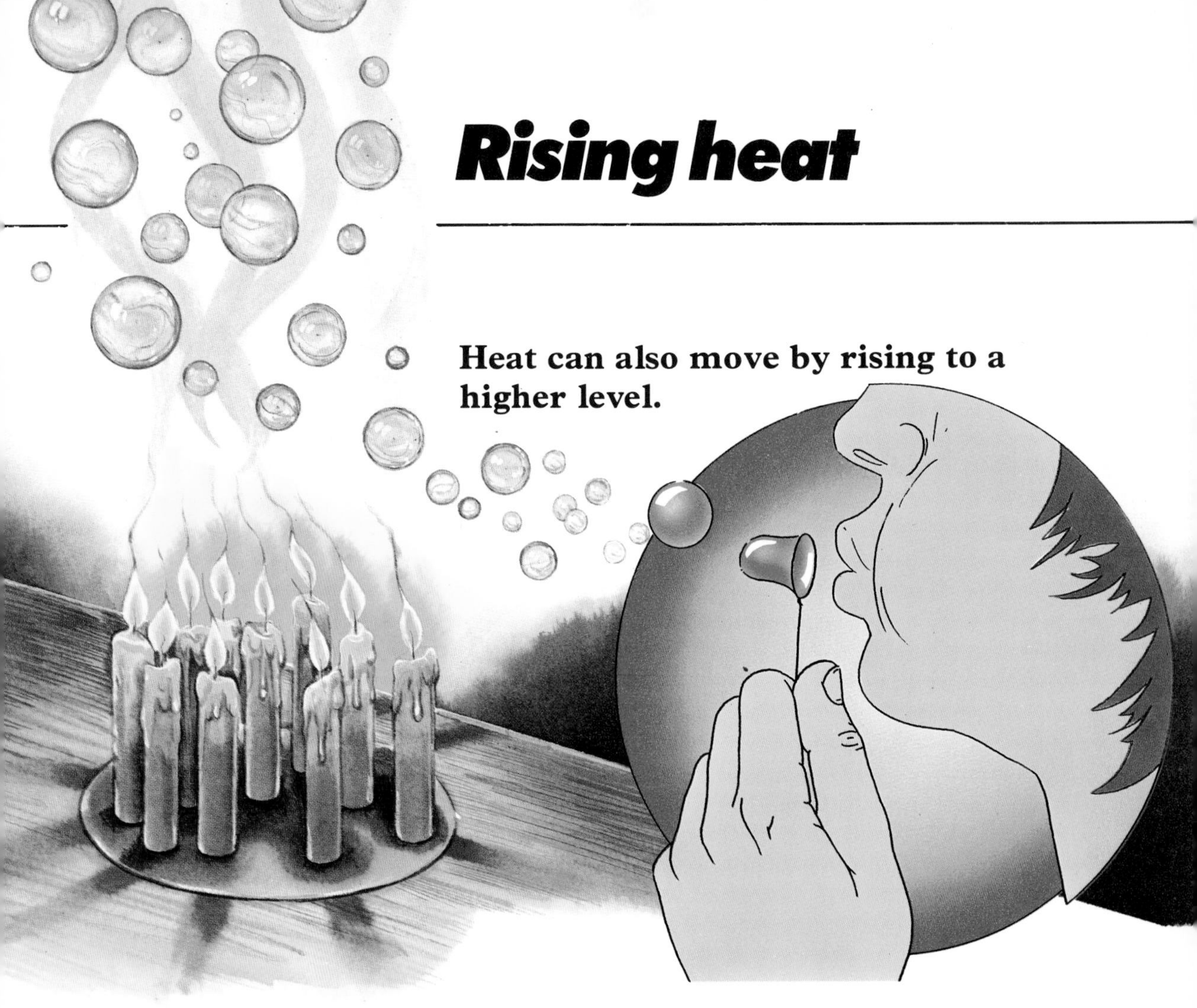

△ Make some bubbles by bending a piece of wire into a loop about half an inch across. Dip the loop into some liquid detergent, and blow gently through it to send a stream of bubbles over the candles. Hot-air balloons work in a similar way, but carry their own supply of heat.

Bubble balloons

Take several candles and place them in a circle on a tray. Blow bubbles over the candle flames. The bubbles suddenly zoom up into the air like tiny balloons.

The air heated by the candles is lighter than the cooler air around it. It floats upward, carrying the bubbles with it. This kind of heat movement is called convection. Warm air rises from heaters and spreads through a room by convection.

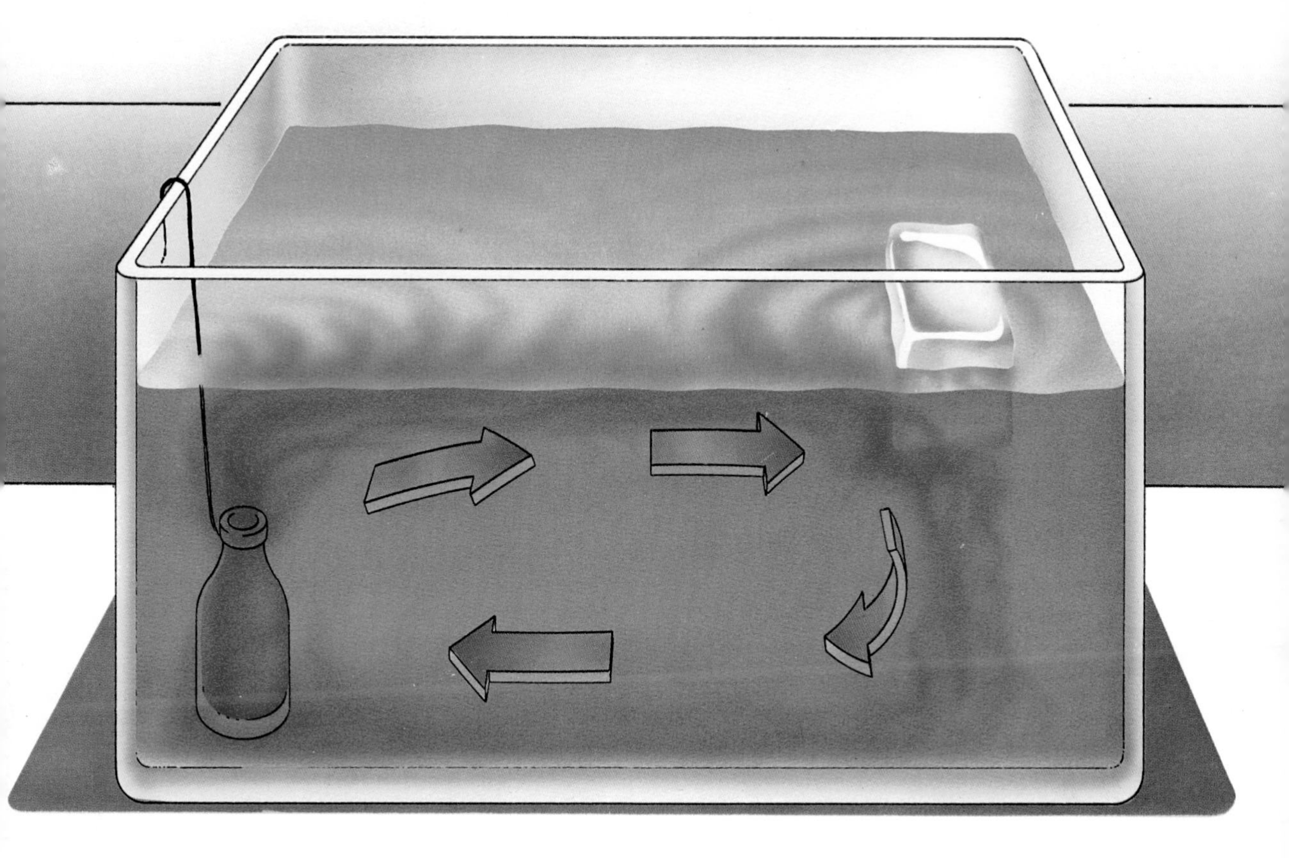

Underwater chimney

Fill a large glass bowl or aquarium with cold water. Float an ice cube at one end. Next fill a small glass bottle with hot water, colored with ink. Lower the bottle into the water opposite the ice cube. The colored water rises from the bottle like smoke from a chimney, then sinks beneath the ice cube.

Convection causes the hot colored water to rise. It then cools as it reaches the ice cube, becomes heavier than the surrounding water, and sinks.

△ Use a piece of stiff wire to lower the bottle and keep it in place underwater. Notice that a slow current of moving water is set up in the bowl or aquarium. This is a convection current. Currents like these spread heat through the air as well as through water. Winds are convection currents set up in the atmosphere by the Sun's heat.

Keeping heat in — or out

Stop heat moving to keep things hot or cold.

△ Outside the bowl, heat leaves the water by conduction through the table and by convection currents in the air. In the bowl, the cover, corks and the still air trapped inside stop the heat moving. Try using ice instead of hot water. The ice in the bowl stays cold because heat cannot now get in. A vacuum flask keeps things hot or cold in the same way.

Store some heat

Pour some hot water into two tumblers as shown. Rest one tumbler in a bowl on pieces of cork and cover it with a piece of card. Then cover the bowl. After a few minutes, test the temperature of the water with a thermometer. The water in the tumbler inside the bowl is still hot, but the water in the other tumbler has cooled.

Inside the bowl, heat cannot leave the tumbler quickly. It stays in the water, keeping it hot.

Warning—this experiment needs care. An adult must supervise it.

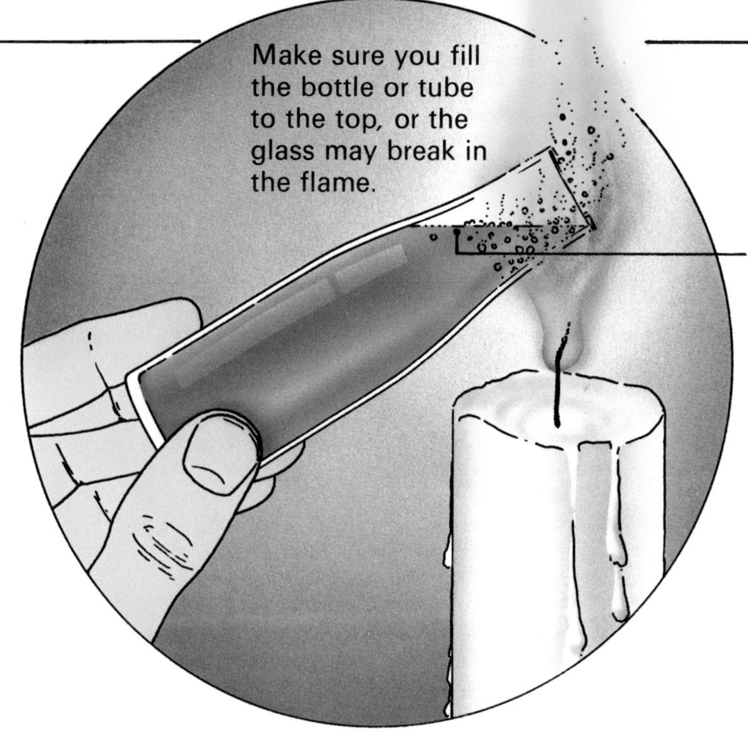

Hold the bottle or tube steady and be patient. It takes a little time for the water to start boiling.

▽ A diver with a wet suit keeps warm under-water because a layer of water between the suit and the skin stops heat from leaving the diver's body.

Too hot to handle?

Take a small glass bottle or a test-tube at least 3 in long. Fill it with water and hold it by the bottom end. Place the top end in a candle flame. The water there soon begins to boil, but you can still hold the bottle or the tube! Take care not to spill the boiling water on your hands.

Convection makes heat rise in water. Water is also a bad conductor, so heat does not flow very far down the bottle or tube. The water at the bottom stays cold, even though the water only a few inches away at the top is boiling.

Producing cold

How do things lose heat and get cold?

Instant ice cream

Crush some ice by placing ice cubes in a plastic bag and striking them with a hammer. Make the ice-cream mix shown and put some in a plastic carton. Place the crushed ice in a bowl and stir in about a third as much salt. Put the carton in the ice and cover the bowl. The ice cream will be ready in about 15 minutes.

The salt takes heat from the ice, making it get even colder and freezing the ice-cream mix in the carton. It also lowers the freezing point, making the ice melt. This is why salt is used to melt ice and snow in winter.

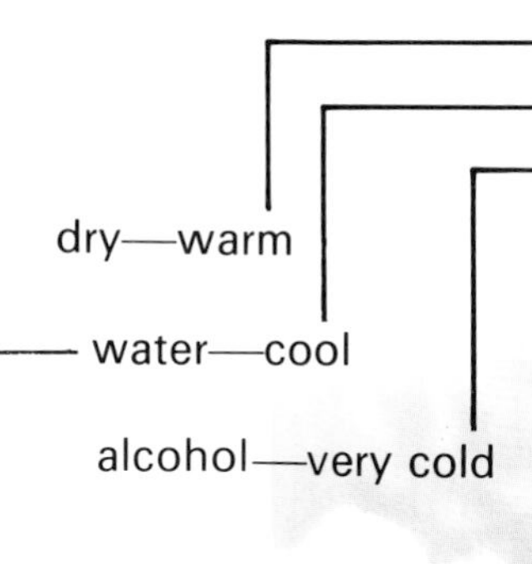

Which way does the wind blow?
Lick a finger to wet it and hold it up in the air. If a wind is blowing, one side begins to feel cool. This side is the direction of the wind. Try using denatured alcohol to wet another finger. This finger feels much colder. If there is no wind, do this experiment by blowing on your fingers.

As the wind dries your finger, it turns the water on your skin into water vapor. This takes heat from your skin, so your finger feels cool. Alcohol turns to vapor more easily than water, so it takes more heat and makes the finger feel very cold.

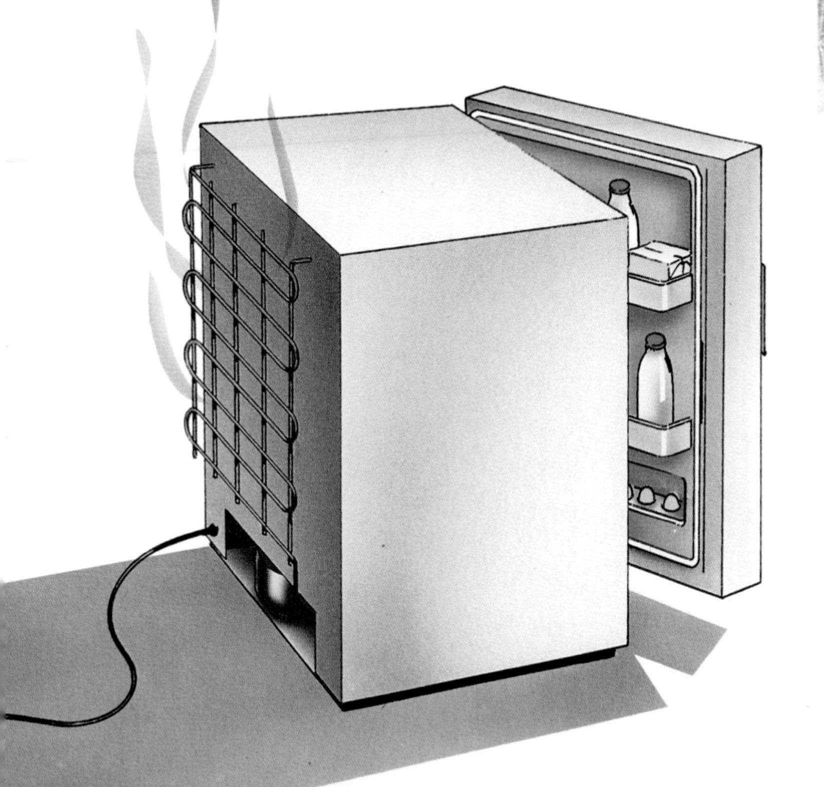

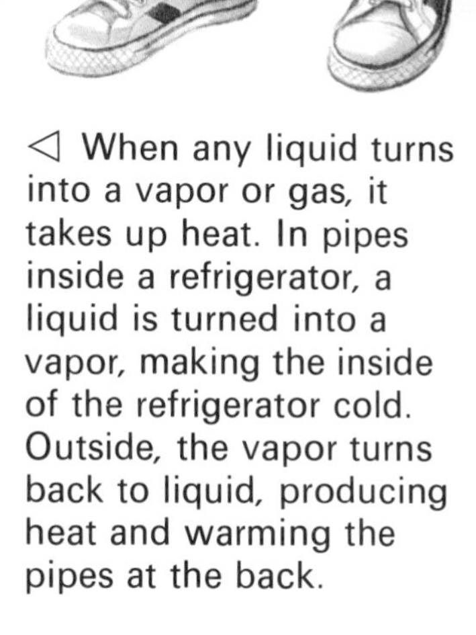

◁ When any liquid turns into a vapor or gas, it takes up heat. In pipes inside a refrigerator, a liquid is turned into a vapor, making the inside of the refrigerator cold. Outside, the vapor turns back to liquid, producing heat and warming the pipes at the back.

Freezing fun

Make ice melt and instantly freeze again.

△ The wire should be as thin as possible but strong enough to support the weight of the two bottles. Electrical wire or copper wire are suitable.

Put pressure on ice

Fill two large bottles with water and firmly fix a piece of strong wire around both tops. Make a column of tins slightly higher than the bottles and place an ice cube on top. Fit the wire over the ice cube and suspend the bottles as shown. The wire slowly moves down through the ice without slicing it in two!

The bottles are so heavy that the wire puts very strong pressure on the ice. This lowers the temperature at which water freezes. The ice melts just under the wire, and the wire sinks. But the water produced immediately freezes again because the freezing point returns to normal.

The ice and fork trick

This is how to pick up an ice cube with a fork. First make the ice as cold as possible in a freezer. Warm the prongs of a fork in a candle flame, plunge them into the ice cube, wait 30 seconds and pick up the cube.

The warm prongs melt some ice, but the cube is so cold that the water quickly freezes again, sealing the fork in the ice cube.

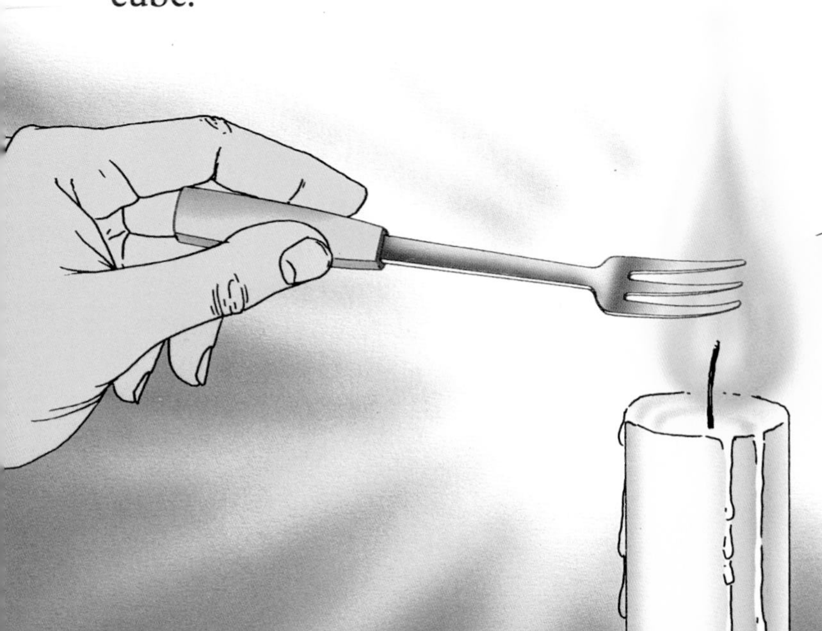

Ice afloat

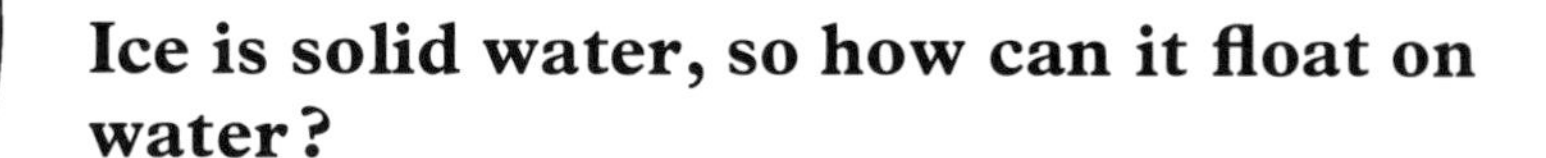

Ice is solid water, so how can it float on water?

Expanding ice

Take a small glass bottle with a narrow neck and a cork to fit it. Fill the bottle to the brim with water, and *lightly* push in the cork. Now place the bottle in the freezer or the freezing compartment of a refrigerator. Leave it until all the water has frozen. See how the ice sticks out of the top of the bottle, pushing out the cork!

This experiment shows that ice expands when it forms. As water freezes into ice, it gets bigger in size, making ice less dense than water. Ice therefore floats on water. This is why icebergs float in the oceans near the North and South Poles.

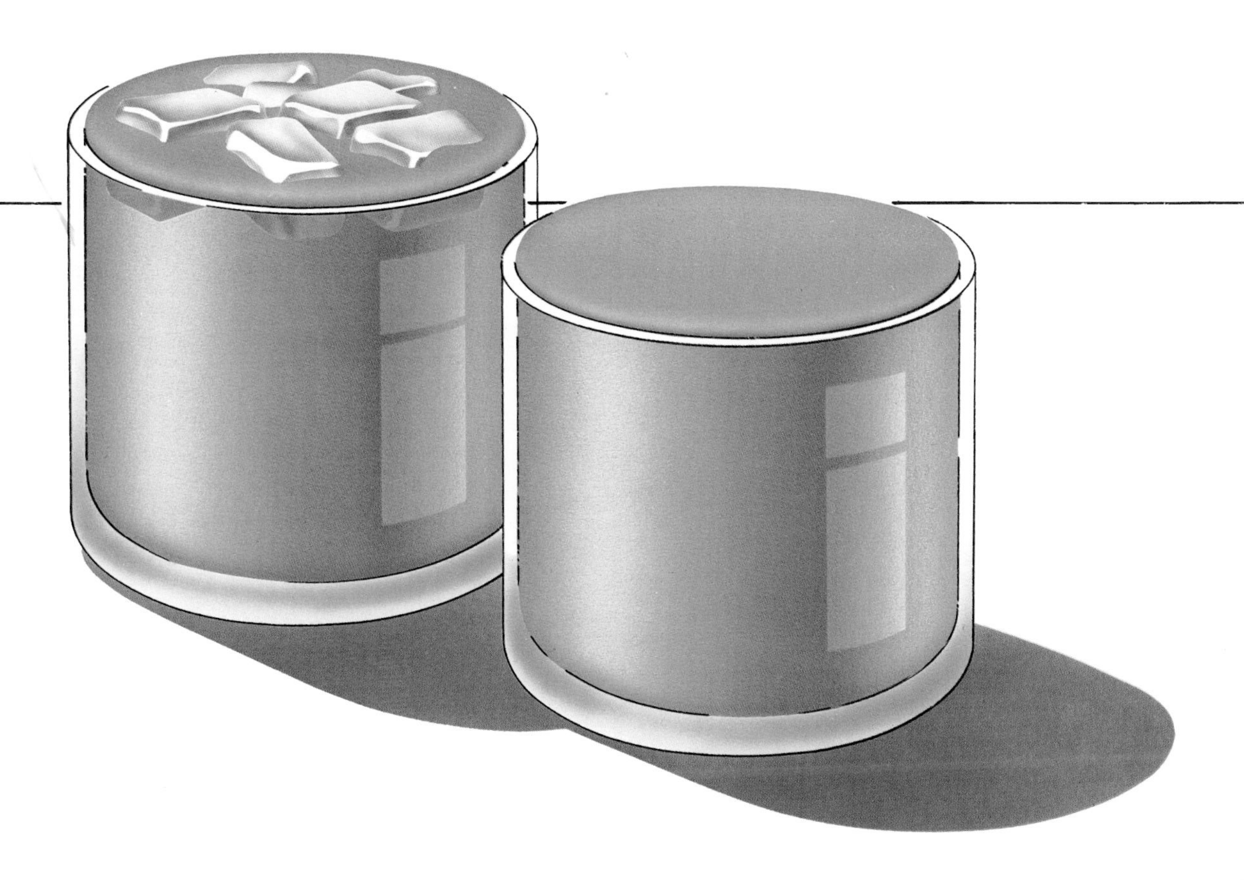

Miniature icebergs

Place some ice cubes in a glass and fill the glass to the top with warm water. Now ask yourself or some friends if the water will overflow when the ice cubes melt. Wait and see what happens. You will find that the water level remains exactly the same.

As each ice cube melts, it gets smaller. The amount of water it forms is exactly the same as the amount of ice that was below the surface. The level of water in the glass therefore does not change. This means that even if *all* the icebergs in the sea were suddenly to melt, there would be no rise in sea level at all.

▽ An iceberg has about nine times as much ice below the water as above it.

Glossary

△ Clothes keep us warm in winter because the materials are good insulators and stop heat escaping from the skin.

In wool, the air trapped among the fibers prevents heat getting through.

Boiling
When a liquid boils, it turns to a gas. Water boils at a temperature of 212°F (100°C). Everything melts and then boils if it is heated enough, even rocks and metals like steel.

Conduction
When heat moves through a solid object or into a liquid or a gas, it moves by conduction. This happens because the hot part warms the part next to it and so on.

Contraction
Liquids, gases and solid objects get smaller when they get colder. This shrinking is called contraction. It is much more noticeable in liquids and gases.

Convection
If a source of heat is placed in a liquid or gas, it makes the liquid or gas around it rise. This movement is called convection. It happens because a liquid or gas gets lighter as it gets warmer.

Expansion
Liquids, gases and solid objects get bigger when they get hotter. This increase in size is called expansion. Liquids and gases expand more on heating than solid objects.

Freezing point
The temperature at which a liquid freezes and becomes a solid is its freezing point. It is the same as the temperature at which the same solid melts to a liquid.

Insulator
An insulator is anything that lets very little heat pass through it. Plastics, cloth and wood are good insulators.

Temperature
The temperature of something tells you how hot or how cold it is.
It is measured in degrees centigrade (°C) or fahrenheit (°F). Water freezes at 32°F and boils at 212°F. If you are well, your body temperature is about 98·4°F.

Thermometer
A thermometer measures the temperature of something. The liquid inside expands (moves up the tube) or contracts (moves down the tube) until it reaches the same temperature as the object being measured.

Vapor
A vapor is a kind of gas that is produced by a liquid. The vapor is usually invisible and normally lies above the liquid. Hot liquids give more vapor than cold liquids.

▷ Many thermometers have two temperature scales—centigrade, or celsius, (C) and fahrenheit (F). This thermometer is reading 21°C, or 70°F. Water freezes to ice at 0°C or 32°F. In winter, centigrade temperatures may therefore often go below zero to minus figures. It has to be very cold in winter before the fahrenheit thermometer goes below zero.

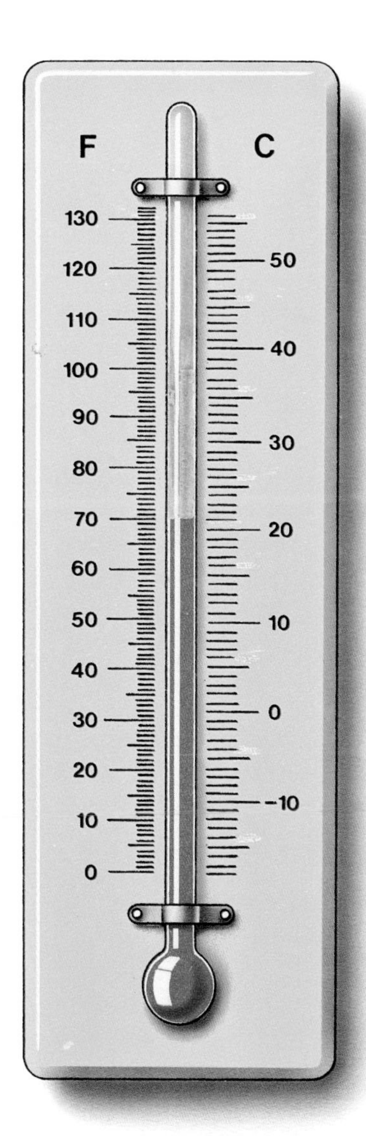

Index

PRINTED IN BELGIUM BY proost INTERNATIONAL BOOK PRODUCTION